Baroque Architecture

Christian Norberg-Schulz

Baroque Architecture

Electa/Rizzoli
NEW YORK

Photographs: Pepi Merisio and Bruno Balestrini
Drawings: Studio Enzo di Grazia
Layout: Arturo Anzani

Library of Congress Cataloging in Publication Data
Norberg-Schulz, Christian.
    Baroque architecture.

    Bibliography: p.
    Includes index.
    1. Architecture, Baroque. I. Title.
NA590.N6   1986   724'.19   85-30011
ISBN 0-8478-0693-6 (U.S.: pbk.)

© Copyright 1979 by
Electa Editrice, Milano

Paperback edition first published
in the United States of America in 1986
by Rizzoli International Publications, Inc.
597 Fifth Avenue, New York, NY 10017

This volume is the redesigned paperback
of the original Italian edition published in 1971
by Electa Editrice, Milan,
and the English translation published in 1972
by Harry N. Abrams, Inc., New York

Printed in Italy

TABLE OF CONTENTS

In the present book we have treated in detail only certain aspects of the complex totality of Baroque architecture. A full iconographical interpretation has not been possible within its limited number of pages. The method employed concentrates attention on the analysis of spatial structures, understanding space as one of man's basic existential dimensions. In this way the general intentions as well as the regional varieties of Baroque architecture are illuminated, and its roots in Cinquecento architecture are explained. The book covers a period which comprises the last two or three decades of the sixteenth century and most of the seventeenth. As buildings and building types cannot be properly understood in isolation from a more comprehensive context, the urban dimension is included in the exposition. In Baroque architecture, in fact, the single elements are highly determined by the "system" of which they form part.

The author wants to thank those who have offered him inspiration and help through their writings or in direct discussion, in particular Prof. Hans Sedlmayr, Prof. Paolo Portoghesi, Prof. Werner Hager, Prof. Rudolf Wittkower, Prof. Staale Sinding-Larsen, Prof. Giulio Carlo Argan and Prof. Ferdinand Schuster. He also wants to thank Dr. Carlo Pirovano who has been in charge of the production of the volume, as well as all those who have collected biographical and bibliographical information. Special thanks are due to Mrs. Marcia Berg for correcting and typing the manuscript.

Ch. N. - S.

Chapter One
THE BAROQUE AGE

The Baroque and Its Buildings

The seventeenth century was characterized by a diversity unknown before. The unified and hierarchically ordered *cosmos* of the Middle Ages had disintegrated during the Renaissance, and a new element of choice had been introduced into the life of man. "In the religious system of the Middle Ages as it crystallized in scholasticism, every phase of reality was assigned its unique place; and with its place goes a complete determination of its value, which is based on the greater or lesser distance which separates it from the First Cause. There is no room here for doubt and in all thinking there is the consciousness of being sheltered by this inviolable order which it is not the business of thought to create but only to accept."[1] With the rise of Humanism, however, the question of man's free will came to the fore, and in Florence it received a social and political foundation. In his funeral oration for Nanni Strozzi (1428), Leonardo Bruni said: "Equal liberty exists for all—the hope of gaining high office and of rising is the same for all." Even a hundred years before this, the Florentines had gone as far as to appoint their magistrates by lot. The absolute system of the Middle Ages was thus replaced by an active political life, which found a new basis in the *studia humanitatis*.

The idea of the ordered universe, however, was not relinquished by the Renaissance. Rather it obtained a new interpretation based on geometry and musical harmony, whereby a new scale of values was introduced, assigning everything a place according to its degree of "perfection."[2] Within this framework man had his freedom of choice, as expressed in the famous paraphrase on the Creation by Pico della Mirandola: "He therefore took man as a creature of indeterminate nature and, assigning him a place in the middle of the world, addressed him thus: 'Neither a fixed abode nor a form that is thine alone nor any function peculiar to thyself have we given thee, Adam, to the end that according to thy longing and according to thy judgement thou mayest have and possess what abode, what form, and what functions thou thyself shalt desire... Thou shalt have the power to degenerate into the lower forms of life, which are brutish. Thou shalt have the power, out of thy soul's judgement, to be reborn into the higher forms, which are divine.'"[3]

But the Renaissance idea of freedom within a harmonious and meaningful universe did not last long. Erasmus and Luther represent doubt in the freedom and "dignity of man," and Copernicus (1545) removed the earth from the center of the universe.[4] The political foundation of Florentine civilization broke down, and the division of the Church ratified the disintegration of the unified and absolute world. During the sixteenth century the new diversity was experienced as a frightening split giving man a sense of doubt and alienation. The general attitude found its artistic manifestation in the phenomena which are usually brought together under the label of "Mannerism." In the tragic world of Michelangelo, it comes forth with singular intensity:

"Rend Thou the veil, my Lord! Break down that wall / whose thickness delays the light / of Thy sun, which the world sees not."

Towards the end of the sixteenth century, the attitude changed. The case of Descartes is particularly illuminating. Having found that everything can be doubted, he concludes that his own doubt being a *thought* represents the only certainty! "Examining attentively what I was, and seeing that I could pretend that I had no body and that there was no world or place that I was in, but that I could not for all that, pretend that I did not exist, and that on the contrary, from the very fact that I thought of doubting the truth of other things, it followed very evidently and very certainly that I existed..."[5] On the basis of this certainty he goes on constructing a comprehensive system of "facts." "The great originality of Descartes, and that which enables him to avoid the conclusions of Montaigne and the Sceptics is that, instead of considering the objects of doubt, he detaches the act of doubting from anything external to itself and in that way cuts the ground from beneath the feet of scepticism."[6]

The general spirit of the seventeenth century, however, rarely possessed this originality. Rather man sought security by a choice between the current alternatives of the period. The new state of affairs was accepted none the less, and the old unified world was gone forever. But this does not mean that the conflicts were over, since the disintegration of the old world actually culminated with the Thirty Years' War, which paralyzed a great part of Central Europe during the first half of the seventeenth century. But nobody any longer believed in a re-establishment of the old order, and man again started to look ahead. The new world of the seventeenth century, therefore, may be called "pluralistic," in so far as it offered man a *choice* between different alternatives, be they religious, philosophical, economic or political. All the alternatives were characterized by the aim we have found in Descartes' thinking: to arrive at a complete and secure *system* based on *a priori* axioms or dogmas. Man wanted absolute security, and he could find it in the tradition of the restored Roman Church, in one of the schools of Reformation which were all based on the belief in the absolute truth of the Biblical word, in the great philosophical systems of Descartes, Hobbes, Spinoza or Leibniz, or in the absolute monarchy "by divine right." The attitude was most natural; in fact, it represented different but analogous attempts at establishing a substitute for the lost *cosmos*.

In spite of the new pluralism, we may therefore consider the seventeenth century a unified epoch, the Baroque Age. In doing this we neither evoke a mystic "spirit of the age," nor refer to mere "stylistic similarities." Rather we have in mind the basic human *attitude* which prevails in spite of the differences of choice, the *esprit de système*, to use the term of D'Alembert.[7] Through the freedom of choice, man immensely widened the possibilities for structuring his own life, at least in theory; in reality the choice was limited by his immediate situation. In other words, all the alternatives were not available everywhere, but were confined to particular geogra-

phical areas, whose general distribution was settled after the Thirty Years'
War.[8] The seventeenth century, therefore, experienced certain migrations
of human groups, such as the expulsion of the Huguenots from France
(1685). Although they were connected with particular "areas," the systems were in a certain sense "open." Not being single units, their *propagation* was essential, and a dynamic, centrifugal character became general.
Propagation, however, only becomes meaningful and effective in relation
to a *center*, which represents the basic axioms and properties of the system.
The religious, scientific, economic and political centers were foci of radiating forces, which, seen from the center itself, had no spatial limits.

The systems of the seventeenth century, thus, had an open and dynamic
character. Departing from a fixed point, they could be infinitely extended. This new relation to the infinite first appears in the writings of
Giordano Bruno who says: "Infinite space has infinite potentiality, and in
this infinite potentiality may be praised an infinite act of existence." He
then goes on to imagine a plurality of worlds: "Thus there are innumerable
suns, with countless planets likewise circling about these suns..."[9] In this
infinite world, *movement* and *force* are of prime importance. Related ideas
are found in the philosophy of Leibniz a hundred years later; also in the
simpler and more rational world of Descartes we find the idea that spatial
extension is the basic property of all things and that their differences are
based on different movements. Geometry, therefore, is the appropriate
tool for understanding the world. Whereas the geometrically ordered universe of the Renaissance was closed and static, Baroque thought makes it
open and dynamic.

We thus understand that the two seemingly contradictory aspects of the
Baroque phenomenon, systematism and dynamism, form a meaningful totality. The need for belonging to an absolute and integrated but open and
dynamic system was the basic attitude of the Baroque Age.

This attitude was nourished by the characteristic achievements of the
period: exploratory travels (opening up an ever larger and more complex
world), colonization (extending the social and cultural borders of European pluralism), and scientific research (substituting empirical study
and research for the traditional idea of harmony and degrees of perfection).[10] This general *expansion* had as a necessary correlate a growing
specialization of human activities; every discipline, every activity was
forced to define its own field. In our context it is important to point out
the split of that unity of art and science which had formed the basis for the
uomo universale of the Renaissance. The artist no longer dared to be a phi-
losopher or scientist, and as a consequence artistic theory lost much of its
impetus during the seventeenth century. In fact, if we want to understand
the intentions of Baroque architects, we must infer them from the
treatises of the previous or following centuries.[11] Rather than pursue the
ideal of "universal man," the Baroque Age therefore assigned the individual a fixed place within the social hierarchy. To a certain extent, he

could choose his preferred system, but hardly his own place within it. Socially the Baroque Age was still closed.

Virtually no other epoch has to the same extent aimed at making its form of life visible or manifest. *Persuasion* was the basic means used by all the systems to make their alternatives operant. Science and philosophy certainly ought to demonstrate rather than persuade, but even Descartes uses a "common" language and he begins his Discourse with an account of his own life to strike a note of sympathy in his reader. In fact, "the ultimate aim of Descartes was to persuade men that, in their task of reconstructing the world, a method, his method, was alone effective. That is to say that his method was essentially an instrument for action."[12] Leaving in principle what can be demonstrated to science, religion became more dependent on persuasion than ever before. This was already realized by St. Ignatius Loyola, and motivated his "Spiritual Exercises" which were first written in plain Spanish and which aim at an imitation of Christ by means of imagination and empathy. Later the Roman Church came to give particular importance to the visual images as a means of persuasion. "And the Bishops shall carefully teach this: that, by means of the Stories of the Mysteries of our Redemption, portrayed by paintings or other representations, the people are instructed and confirmed in the habit of remembering, and continually revolving in mind the articles of faith..."[13] But even the Protestant churches practiced persuasion by means of sermons in the common language and sacred music.[14] The absolute monarchies, finally, used great festivals and fêtes to make the glory of the system visible.

Persuasion has *participation* as its goal. The Baroque world, in fact, may be characterized as a great theater where everybody was assigned a particular role. Such a participation, however, presupposes *imagination*, a faculty which is educated by means of art. Art, therefore, was of central importance in the Baroque Age. Its images were a means of communication more direct than logical demonstration, and furthermore, accessible to the illiterate. The art of the Baroque, therefore, concentrates on vivid images of situations, real and surreal, rather than on "history" and absolute form. Descartes says: "The charm of fables awakens the mind." The general aim was to instigate a way of life in conformity with the system. Art thereby became official and was institutionalized in the *academies*.[15] At the same time, however, the character of Baroque art brought forth a "phenomenization" of experience, which made man more conscious of his own existence. Baroque participation, which should have secured the system, in the end therefore led to its disintegration.

The Baroque Building Tasks

To describe the basic human attitude and the form of life of the Baroque Age, we have used terms such as "system," "centralization," "extension" and "movement." All these terms may just as well be used for a description of Baroque architecture. If we take a look at a map of Paris and environs from 1740 we find that the whole landscape has been transformed into a network of centralized systems which, ideally, have an infinite extension. Most of them stem from the seventeenth century. In a still larger context, Paris formed the center of an analogous system, comprising the whole of France. And if we use a magnifying glass on the same map, we recognize that the single elements, the buildings, are organized on similar patterns. In fact, there is hardly any historical epoch which more evidently manifests a correspondence between the form of life and the architectural environment. This correspondence is easy to understand when we remember that the world was considered to have a geometrically ordered extension as its basic property. This extension is always referred to as a "center of meaning," that is, a place embodying the basic "dogmas" of the form of life. In relation to this focus, man's existence became meaningful, spatially expressed through a system of possible movements, or "paths," which converge on the center.

Renaissance architecture also gave great importance to centralized patterns of organization, in buildings as well as in plans for "ideal cities." Renaissance centralization, however, has a static and enclosed character. The systems never extend beyond clearly defined limits, and the elements remain isolated in the landscape. They also have a pronounced individuality. The elements of Baroque systems, however, interact and subordinate themselves to a dominant focus. During the sixteenth century the static harmony of Renaissance space was broken, and a strong interest in movement and contrast came to the fore, as well as a new relationship between interior and exterior space.[16]

Although many of the formal structures which are basic to Baroque architecture were developed during the sixteenth century, Mannerist architecture did not arrive at any true typology.[17] The century was characterized rather by an incessant experimentation, reflecting the general human doubt and insecurity of the period.

Towards the end of the sixteenth century, however, a pronounced wish for systematization became evident. It started in Rome, as a manifestation of the accomplished restoration of the Catholic Church. Its basis was thus religious, and the aim was to express the role of Rome as the dominant focus of the Catholic world. It is therefore most natural that the "turning-point" was marked by a work on the *urbanistic* level. In 1585 Pope Sixtus V introduced a grandiose plan for the urban transformation of Rome.[18]
The basic ideas of the plan must have been developed already before Felice Peretti, Cardinal Montalto, rose to the Papal Chair in 1585 as Sixtus V. In fact, he put his chief architect, Domenico Fontana, to work at once, and in 1586 the first great new street, Via Felice (today Via Sistina), was completed. The principal aim of the plan was to connect the main religious foci of the city by means of wide, straight streets. Fontana writes: "Our lord, now wishing to ease the way for those who, prompted by devotion or vows, are accustomed to visit frequently the most holy places of the City of

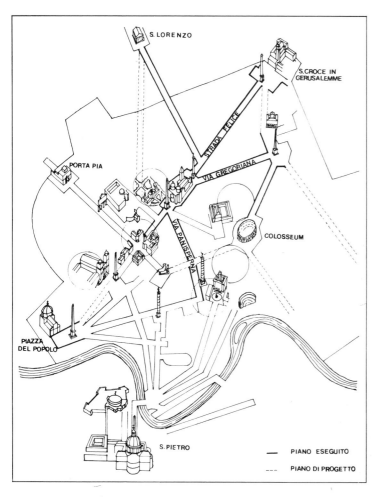

Rome, and in particular the seven churches so celebrated for their great indulgences and relics, opened many most commodious and straight streets in many places. Thus one can by foot, by horse, or in carriage, start from whatever place in Rome one may wish, and continue virtually in a straight line to the most famous devotions."[19] Sixtus V also integrated in his plan the fragments of regular Renaissance planning carried out by his predecessors, in particular the trident of Piazza del Popolo, where three streets branch out to connect the main city-gate with different urban districts.[20] The new streets planned by Sixtus V also structured the large, abandoned areas between the medieval town and the Aurelian wall. In general, the plan gave a new coherence to the city. The isolated "nodes" of the past were united to form a network, whereby the role of the individual element as part of the general religious system was expressed.

The City

The plan of Sixtus V made Rome the prototype of the basic unit of Baroque architecture: *the capital city*. This is most natural, considering Rome's role as the center of one of the great systems of the epoch and also its glorious past as the *caput mundi* of the ancient world. The development of the capital city is thus the first concrete answer to the need for a "visible" embodiment of the structure of the Baroque world. The quotation from Domenico Fontana shows that the plan employed also served as a means of persuasion; it made a "systematic" visit of the holy places imperative and easy. The whole area of the city was thereby imbued with ideological value; it became a real *città santa*.

Whereas the cities of the Middle Ages and the Renaissance were relatively static and enclosed worlds, the new capital city became the center of forces extending far beyond its borders. It became a point of reference for a whole world, in a more concrete sense than, say, Jerusalem or Rome itself had been before. While the building types of Baroque architecture represent the further development of existing models, the capital city is basically an original conception which influences the whole system to which it belongs. Already in the seventeenth century, it was recognized that the capital reduced the secondary centers to mere satellites having no real life of their own.

During the sixteenth century, we find for the first time that the network of urban streets tends to become integrated with the "territorial" roads outside. Such an integration, however, could rarely be carried through in accordance with the ideal intention. First, most cities still needed a wide belt of fortifications separating them from the surrounding countryside, and second, the existing inner structure hardly allowed for the development of a consequent Baroque plan. What we usually find are fragments of a Baroque system, which, however, give a clear indication of the general intention. This is also the case in the main capital cities, such as Rome and Paris. The shortcomings resulting from the adaptation of the

4. Basic types of Baroque churches.
Elongated central plan and
centralized longitudinal plan.

new ideas to an existing urban situation led Louis XIV to build a new city outside the old capital. Versailles, in fact, is more than a palace; the hunting lodge of Louis XIII became the center of a complete "ideal city" which seems to have an infinite extension.

The dynamic and "open" character of the capital city is also expressed in its inner structure. The wide and straight streets allowed for an intensified movement of people and vehicles, in accordance with the new need for "participation." They also made the Baroque desire for systematization manifest. Already in 1574, Pope Gregory XIII gave new rules for the erection of buildings in Rome, thereby preparing for the great plan of his successor. The rules stipulated that the houses should be joined together and that the open spaces between buildings should be closed by blank walls.[21] Evidently the aim was to *unify* the cityscape, forming coherent urban spaces defined by continuous building surfaces. In his Discourse, Descartes writes: "...often there is less perfection in works composed of several separate pieces and made by different masters, than in those at which only one person has worked... So it is that these old cities, originally only villages, have become through the passage of time great towns, and are usually so badly proportioned in comparison with those orderly towns which an engineer designs at will on some plan, although the buildings, taken separately, often display as much art as those of the planned towns or even more..."[22]

In the Baroque city, therefore, the single building loses its plastic individuality and becomes part of a superior system. This means that the *space* between the buildings acquires a new importance as the real constitutive element of the urban totality. The plan of Sixtus V, in fact, is a plan of spaces rather than a distribution of buildings. The Baroque plan organizes extensions in relation to foci, among which *one* is usually dominant. As these foci represent a termination to the horizontal movement, they should be defined by means of a *vertical* axis. Sixtus V and Domenico Fontana were conscious of this basic spatial problem, and used Egyptian obelisks found among the Roman ruins to mark the nodes of their system.[23] In other cases buildings were used for the same purpose; the tall domes of the churches were particularly suited for terminating the horizontal extension of the city, so that the symbolism of the Church became an organic part of the urban system. Although these monumental buildings may have a strong plastic value, they are never isolated from the whole. Even the freestanding volumes of Late Baroque residences acquire meaning as foci of a comprehensive system. The Baroque façade is thus just as much a function of the urban space in front as of the building to which it belongs. In general, we may say that the Baroque city converges on (or radiates from) monumental buildings which represent the basic values of the system. "The monument constitutes a focal point of the very greatest prestige within the framework of a city and is generally placed in the center of a vast area, planned so as to enhance the monument's aesthetic values..."[24]

Argan justly recognizes St. Peter's as the prototype of such monuments.[25]

The foci of the urban totality may also be defined in purely spatial terms, that is as *piazze* or squares. The square, of course, has a long tradition as the real core of the city, but while its function usually was of a public and civic nature, the Baroque Age made it become part of the general ideological system. This is particularly evident in the French *place royale*, where the space is symmetrically centered upon a statue of the sovereign. The prototype was created by Henry IV in the Place Dauphine (1605). The greatest of all "ideological" squares, however, is the Piazza S. Pietro in Rome where Bernini by means of colonnades accompanying the oval space on both sides wanted to symbolize the "open and embracing arms" of the Church. Because of its particular meaning and its particular shape, the piazza thus forms a complement to the dome of the church behind it, whose symbolic vault is transformed into a functional container covered by the natural dome of the sky.[26] The creation of monumental squares became imperative to all Baroque cities, usually in relation to the main buildings of the system.

The structure of the Baroque city consists thus of foci (monumental buildings and squares) which are interconnected by straight and regular streets. The buildings are integrated with the pattern of movements defined by the streets, so that a new interaction between inside and outside is achieved. An analogous interaction is also established between the city and its surroundings. Between the main streets, districts were formed which were given a certain uniformity so as not to interfere with the main properties of the system.

In fact, the buildings of a district had to submit to a *program* which established the general character of the design. When the Rue Dauphine in Paris was created at the beginning of the seventeenth century, the inhabitants were ordered to "make the fronts of their houses all in the same manner..."[27] The Baroque environment, therefore, is ordered in terms of hierarchic centralization. The city as a whole is the focus of a territorial network. Within the city, we find a more condensed network which is focused on monumental buildings, which in turn are geometrically organized into still more condensed systems, until the very center is reached: in Versailles, the bed of the sovereign! The main monumental buildings of Baroque architecture, of course, were the church and the palace, manifesting thereby the two primary powers of the epoch. Let us first consider the traditionally most important of the two, the church.

The Church

The role of the church as an urban focus was clearly recognized during the fifteenth and sixteenth centuries. Thus Alberti says: "In the whole compass of the Art of Building, there is nothing in which we ought to employ more Thought, Care and Diligence than in the laying out and adorning of a Temple; because, not to mention that a Temple well built and handsomely

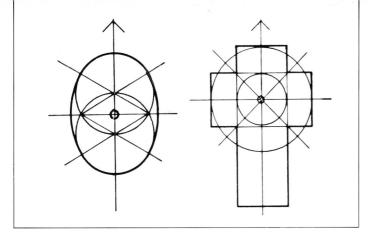

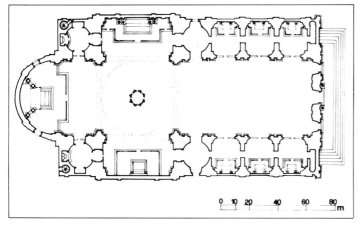

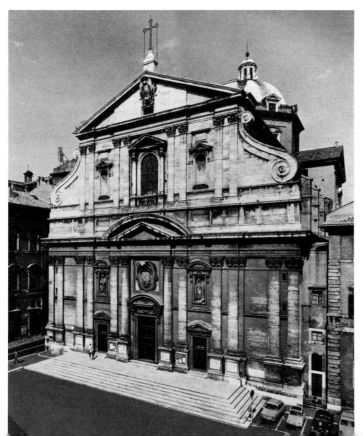

adorned is the greatest and noblest Ornament a City can have; it is more-over the Habitation of the Gods..."[28] And Palladio adds: "...if in the city there be hills, the highest part of them is to be chosen; but in case there be no elevated places, the floor of the temple is to be raised, as much as is convenient, above the rest of the city."[29] During the same period, we find that the theorists recommend a centralized plan for the church, as the circle and the regular polygons are the "perfect" forms.[30] But the centralized plan was not well suited to meet liturgical demands, though at the same time it signified a departure from the general tradition of the Church which had sanctioned the basilica.[31] Criticism of the "ideal" centralized plan, therefore, was raised already during the fifteenth century, and even Alberti designed his most important church, S. Andrea in Mantua, on a Latin cross plan, although a strong inclination towards centralization is evident.[32] In general, centralized plans were accepted in smaller buildings (chapels), and when a particular function or dedication made it a natural solution.[33]

During the sixteenth century, we encounter the first attempts at an integration of the central and longitudinal schemes, a problem most naturally solved by means of the oval, which appears in projects by Peruzzi and Serlio.[34]

After the conclusion of the Council of Trent (1563), a more pronounced negative attitude towards the centralized plan became general, although the Council had carried through liturgical reforms which made it functionally acceptable. The reason was obviously a wish to strengthen tradition and to abolish the "pagan" forms of the Renaissance. Thus St. Charles Borromeo writes: "A church should, in accordance with tradition, be of *cross plan*; round plans were used for the temples of pagan idols and seldom for Christian churches."[35] When these words were published, the Church of Il Gesù in Rome had already been built.[36] In Il Gesù, Vignola satisfied the new ideal of a congregational church which allowed a great number of people to participate in liturgical functions. The plan shows a longitudinal disposition with a pronounced spatial integration. The façade by Della Porta emphasizes the main axis and appears as a great gateway. The building thereby becomes part of the space outside; it participates as an active element in the urban environment. The dome is no longer the symbol of an abstract cosmic harmony, rather its vertical axis forms an expressive and persuasive contrast to the horizontal movement. Il Gesù thereby gives a new active interpretation to the two traditional motifs: the path of redemption and the heavenly dome.

The solution corresponded well to the needs of the Jesuits, and many scholars have maintained that the Order used it as a general model. Later research has demonstrated that this is not the case, since the churches of the Counter-Reformatory movement are based on a much more complex typology and show many local variants.[37] Il Gesù, however, contains many of the basic intentions of Baroque church building, and therefore requires due attention. First, it demonstrates a leaning towards pronounced integration of the longitudinal and centralized schemes, and second, the desire to make the church become part of a larger whole, that is, urban space. The articulation of the façade as well as the interior must be interpreted as a function of these general aims. Today Il Gesù has a richly decorated Baroque interior. As planned by Vignola it was simpler, but it still corresponded to the general wish for persuasive splendour expressed by St. Charles Borromeo.[38]

The development of Baroque church architecture is based on the main types and principles outlined above. The larger churches are usually derived from the traditional basilical scheme, while the smaller ones and the chapels show centralized solutions. It is essential to recognize, however, that the disposition of the large longitudinal churches as a rule consists of a strong center, marked by a dome or an incorporated rotunda, while the smaller churches usually contain a longitudinal axis. Both types are thus adapted to the new need for participation in an extended spatial system. Regardless of its size and particular function, any church is a focus or a "place" where the basic dogmas are demonstrated. Baroque centralization, therefore, differs from Renaissance centralization both in content and form. The two basic types of Baroque sacred architecture may be called: *the centralized longitudinal church* and *the elongated centralized church*. We must repeat that the choice between the two alternatives depended upon the building task in question. By introducing this distinction, it became possible to order very complex and varied material in a meaningful way.

In Baroque churches, *space* gains a new constitutive importance. In contrast to a construction of plastic "members," the building is made up of interacting spatial elements which are modelled according to the outer and inner "forces" which form the particular building. One may, of course, also talk about space in connection with Renaissance architecture, but as a uniform continuum which is subdivided by the geometrically disposed architectural members. Baroque space, on the contrary, cannot be understood in this way, as it contains strong differences of quality related to properties such as movement, openness, enclosure, etc. Argan says: "The great innovation was the idea that space does not surround architecture but is created by it..."[39]

The critical spatial problems are the transitions between different realms, such as outside and inside, or between the spatial elements of a complex architectural organism. In the church, the problems are particularly evident and may lead to strong and consequent solutions, as the building task is relatively simple and does not include many separate or qualitatively different spaces.[40] We therefore find that Baroque architecture obtains its first strong *momentum* in the sacred buildings of the fully developed Roman Baroque, that is the works of Bernini, Borromini and Pietro da Cortona. The ultimate conclusions are drawn later in the sev-

enteenth century by Guarino Guarini, who extends his activity to a great part of the Catholic world.

The Palace

Two building types dominate seventeenth-century secular architecture, the city-palace (*palazzo*, *hôtel*) and the country-house (*villa*, *château*). We also find interesting transitions between the two types (*villa suburbana*). Three basic environments are thereby related to each other: the private world of the dwelling, the public world of the city and the natural world of the garden and the landscape. The city-palace gives man his "place" in a social context, the villa relates him to nature, and in the transitory cases, all three elements are brought together. It should be pointed out that the city-palace and the villa did not provide different people with dwellings; they represented two aspects of the same form of life.

The origin of this distinction may be traced back to the fifteenth century.[41] In Renaissance Tuscany, we find, besides the older city-palace, the villa[42] and transitory solutions such as city-palaces with a garden.[43] Alberti gives due attention to all the basic types. "The Country House and Town House for the Rich differ in this Circumstance; that they use their Country House chiefly for a Habitation in Summer, and their Town House as a convenient place of shelter in the Winter. In their Country House therefore they enjoy the Pleasures of Light, Air, spacious Walks and fine Prospects; in Town, there are but few Pleasures, but those of Luxury and Night."[44] But he also sees the value of joining the two ways of life more closely: "There is another sort of private House, in which the Dignity of the Town-House, and the Delights and Pleasures of the Country-House, are both required... And these are the Pleasure-Houses just without the Town... Such a suburban villa would afford the pleasure of being never tired either with the Town or Country."[45]

Serlio repeats the Albertian typology and presents a series of plans for "dwellings to be built in town" and "dwellings to be built out of town" or "country-dwellings." The latter should be made "in spacious areas far from the piazze among the greenery."[46] It is interesting to note that he shows twenty-four projects for country-houses and only one city-palace, which indicates that the latter was considered a fixed type with less possibilities of variation.

Palladio adopts a similar point of departure in his second book and talks about "houses within and out of the City." The villa is a place where "the body will the more easily preserve its strength and health; and, finally, where the mind, fatigued by the agitations of the city, will be greatly restored and comforted..."[47]

The development of the city-palace and the villa is related to the significant change in political, economical and social structure which we have referred to above, and which we have found behind the rise of the capital city. In this context it meant a loss of importance of the feudal seat, the

I. Versailles, perspective view.

II. Rome, Fountain of the Four
Rivers, detail.

7. Giacomo da Vignola, Il Gesù,
interior.

castle, and the need for a substitute within the city, that is, a city-palace. This development is basically similar, whether the palace was the seat of a new type of "capitalist" (Florence), a "prince" of the Church (Rome) or an aristocratic member of a centralized court (Paris). The need for a complementary country-house is stated by Alberti and his followers in the quotations above. The two types of building, however, from the very beginning tended towards a synthesis, as the idea of the villa suburbana indicates. In the seventeenth century, the problem found its solution in garden palaces such as the Palazzo Barberini in Rome and the Palais du Luxembourg in Paris, which became the models of the great European residences from Versailles to Schlaun's Schloss in Münster (1767).

Basically the city-palace was a *family* seat. It represented a "house" in the double meaning of the word. Through its size and articulation, it defined the position of the family in a wider civic context, and gave the city as a whole a new and larger scale, contrasting with the tight texture of the medieval town.[48] Several smaller dwellings were often brought together in one palace, thereby integrating the less well-to-do in the same general pattern. With the rise of a new bourgeois society in the eighteenth and the nineteenth centuries, however, this discrepancy between content and form was increased to such an extent that the palace lost its meaning.

The character of the palace was basically that of a private place. It was an enclosed world, hiding its inner structure behind massive walls. "Private," however, does not mean individual and subjective, qualities that were rather expressed in the villa. Alberti again points out the difference: "Between a House in Town and a House in the Country, there is [the]... Difference... that the Ornaments, for that in Town ought to be much more grave than those for a House in the Country, where all the gayest and most licentious Embellishments are allowable. There is another Difference between them, which is that in Town you are obliged to moderate yourselves in several Respects according to the Privileges of your Neighbor; whereas you have much more liberty in the Country."[49] This basic distinction was still valid in sixteenth- and seventeenth-century Rome and even in imperial Vienna at the beginning of the eighteenth century.[50] We thus find the heavy and austere Roman city-palace being developed during the Cinquecento, at the same time as varied and playful villas were being built in the suburbs and the Roman region. No wonder then that the same architect employed seemingly different "styles" in his city-palaces and his villas.

The wish for a synthesis, however, which became manifest during the seventeenth century, also led to certain changes in the basic types. We will analyze this problem in detail later. The city-palace tended to become less closed and to interact in more varied ways with its surroundings, whereas the villa became typified, as illustrated by the French châteaux and the later *Garten-paläste* of Central Europe. This development was related to the growing centralization of absolutist power, which interfered with the private character of the city-palace as well as with the individualistic expression of the villa. The palace of the sovereign obviously could not be limited by subtle interplay between building and civic environment which we find in the palaces of the Renaissance. It was recognized rather as a focus of forces which freely extended out in infinite space. It thereby associated some of the traditional properties of the villa, and a synthesis was most natural.

Articulation

The spatial character of a building is expressed by the relationship between inside and outside, and the definition of this relationship is not merely derived from the spatial properties of the two realms, but from the articulation of their point of contact, that is, the wall.[51] In the buildings of Renaissance and Baroque architecture, all elements have a characterizing function, either because of their spatial properties or because of their conventional meaning. The classical *orders* are of particular importance in this connection. Up to the end of the eighteenth century, in fact, architecture had a Vitruvian basis. The character of a given building was defined by employing classical elements which had a generally understood meaning. As late as 1716, Leonard Christoph Sturm wrote: "The orders are the alphabet of architecture: just as one can make up an infinite number of words and conversations with 24 letters, so, by combining the orders, one can arrive at the most diverse form of architectural decoration according to six kinds of orders..."[52] The French theorist Daviler calls the orders "caractères expressifs" (1691),[53] and still in 1923 Le Corbusier wrote: "All great works of art are based on one or other of the great standards of the heart... We shall be able to talk "Doric" when man, in nobility of aim and complete sacrifice of all that is accidental in Art, has reached the higher levels of mind: austerity... There was a breath of tenderness and Ionic was born."[54]

We thus understand that the orders may be considered as concretizations of basic human characters. In fact, Vitruvius recognizes the masculine character of Doric and the feminine of Corinthian, whereas the Ionic represents the mean. The building task, therefore, will determine a choice among the orders. "To Minerva, Mars and Hercules, Doric temples will be built; for to these gods, because of their might, buildings ought to be erected without embellishments. Temples designed in the Corinthian style will seem to have details suited to Venus, Flora, Proserpine, Fountains, Nymphs; for too these goddesses, on account of their gentleness, works constructed with slighter proportions and adorned with flowers, foliage, spirals and volutes will seem to gain in a just decor. To Juno, Diana and Father Bacchus, and the other gods who are of the same likeness, if Ionic temples are erected, account will be taken of their middle quality because the determinate character of their temples will avoid the severe manner of the Doric and the softer manner of the Corinthian;"[55] Forssman has

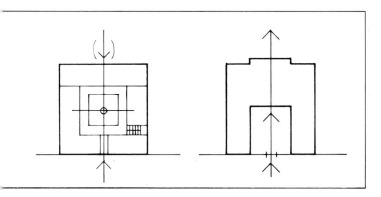

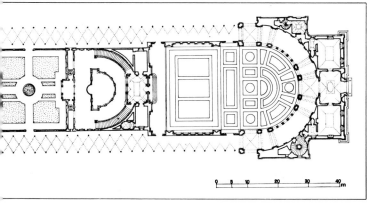

shown that the classical characters were transferred to the buildings of Renaissance and Baroque architecture, the sacred as well as the profane.[56] Serlio says: "The ancients dedicated these Doric temples to Jove, Mars, Hercules, and to others among the mighty, but after the incarnation of Our Saviour, we Christians were obliged to follow other orders: but having to build a church in honour of Jesus Christ Our Redeemer, St. Paul, St. Peter, St. George, or similar saints... such saints as we have had, whose courage and strength led them to expose their lives for the faith of Christ, it is fitting to adopt this Doric manner..."[57] It was generally assumed that the three classical orders were capable of expressing all basic characters, as they comprise two extremes and a mean. The Tuscan and Composite orders were added as a further differentiation. A particular role, however, was assigned to *rustication*. Rather than being an order, expressing a human content, rustication was considered to represent nature itself, as something unformed and raw existing as a dialectical opposite to the works of man. Serlio thus calls rustication "opera di natura," while the orders are "opera di mano."[58]

The character of a building, however, was not only determined by a choice between the orders but also by the way they were employed. In Renaissance architecture the Vitruvian principle of superposition was introduced, whereby the "lighter" orders rested on the more "heavy," and the whole system on a rusticated basement. In certain works of the Mannerist period a fundamental doubt in this humanist expression arises. Peruzzi, for instance, in his Palazzo Massimo (1532-36) lets the order carry a tall rusticated wall. He, so to speak, puts the world "upside down." In Baroque architecture, we again find the orders placed over a rusticated basement, but in general superposition is replaced by a giant order which integrates the whole wall and gives the building *one* dominant character. Adding furthermore the possibilities of plastic modelling, varying proportions and ever new combinations of the traditional elements, "classical" architecture offered a very flexible and expressive language indeed. And still we encounter many attempts at breaking away from its canons. The tendency is natural in Mannerist architecture and the new inventions of Michelangelo were of great importance for later developments. During the seventeenth century, Borromini continued these researches, and the character of his works was characterized as "chimeric" by the more classically minded Bernini.[59] During the period of the Enlightenment, finally, the belief in the dogmas of Vitruvian architecture withered.

Conclusion

In this general introductory chapter, we have attempted to outline the basic properties of the form of life of the Baroque Age and its spatial counterpart, architecture. All forms of life have spatial consequences. In fact, any human activity has spatial aspects, because it implies movements and relations to places. Heidegger says: "The single world always reveals the spatiality of the space that is proper to it."[60] From childhood on, man constructs a spatial image of his environment, which we may call his "existential space."[61] Certain basic properties of this existential space necessarily have to be public, in order to allow for social participation and integration. The structure of existential space may be analyzed in terms of "places," "paths" and "domains." The places are the foci of man's activities, the paths describe his possibilities of taking possession of the environment, and the domains are qualitatively defined areas which are more or less well known. All these elements appear on different environmental levels. *Landscape* is the most comprehensive level we generally have to consider, and it is determined by man's interaction with his natural environment. It contains the *urban* level, which is mainly determined by social interaction. Finally we should consider the level of the *house*, which basically is a private space within the urban context. On all levels, the relation between "inside" and "outside" is of prime importance, that is, the relation between a place and its environment. We may define architectural space as a concretization of existential space.[62]

Baroque architecture presents, as we have seen, a clear system of places, paths and domains, organized to form a hierarchy focused on a dominant center. The building types of past periods are transformed to fit within this general scheme. The traditionally enclosed city is thus opened up whenever possible, the church is organized relative to an axis which integrates it with the urban environment, and the palace becomes a center of radiating movements, rather than a massive fortress. The landscape, finally, during the seventeenth and eighteenth centuries in many parts of Europe was saturated with Baroque elements, either as extended paths of profane gardens, or sacred "objects" such as road crucifixes, chapels and sanctuaries. Although authoritarian, the Baroque world was dynamic and open, and contained elements which have been of basic importance to our present world. Before we discuss the actuality of Baroque, however, we have to consider in further detail the structure and development of the basic components of Baroque architecture. We will start with the public environment, namely the city, and afterwards treat its main foci, the church and the palace.

11. Philibert de l'Orme, Château d'Anet, frontispiece (Paris, École des Beaux-Arts).

Introduction

The history of the Baroque city is the history of the diffusion of the general intentions and principles outlined above.[1] It started in Rome, and during the seventeenth century the great program initiated by Sixtus V was continued. As a general system was already adopted, the new contributions mainly consisted in the creation of great monumental foci. The second capital city of Europe, Paris, gained a completely new urban structure during the seventeenth century. In Paris the point of departure did not lie in the wish to link already existing foci, such as the great Roman basilicas, and a new structure could be developed in a more systematic way. In London, some attempts at systematization were carried out during the first half of the century, but were hampered by the Civil War. After the great fire in 1666, a real Baroque integration was planned. Madrid acquired a new Plaza Mayor in 1617, but it does not form part of a more extensive Baroque system, which is rare in the Iberian peninsula.

One of the most interesting urban developments of the seventeenth century, however, is found in a smaller city, Turin, the capital of Piedmont (Savoy) which had reached a certain importance as an independent duchy. In Turin the Roman and French experiences were unified to form a singular urban synthesis, which was facilitated by the regular plan of old Turin having a Roman *castrum* as its origin. In Central Europe, urban development was hampered by the Thirty Years' War and in Austria by the Turkish invasion. The more interesting city plans of these regions therefore belong to the eighteenth century. Many smaller cities were rebuilt or founded during the seventeenth century, particularly in France. Charleville (1608) and Richelieu (1635-40) are well-known examples, although their plans do not contain the new principles we find in Versailles (1671). The many new towns in Scandinavia were based on conventional Renaissance models and the same holds true for the cities rebuilt after the earthquake in Sicily in 1693. The latter, however, have a townscape of pronounced Late Baroque character. We cannot in this context treat the whole range of examples in detail, but wish to concentrate on the three main cases: Rome, Paris and Turin.

Rome

We have already given an account of the general intentions behind the plan of Pope Sixtus V. The resulting network is not centered on one principal focus, but connects a multitude of foci, buildings as well as piazze. A few planned connections were not carried out, such as the street between S. Giovanni in Laterano and S. Paolo fuori le Mura. Particularly important in the system is the trident leading into the city from the Porta del Popolo, and the starlike disposition around S. Maria Maggiore.[2] The main roads were marked by obelisks which not only introduce a vertical accent, but serve as "axes" for the change of direction of the streets. Sixtus V also incorporated the Roman columns of Trajan and Marcus Aurelius in his scheme, topping them with statues of St. Peter and St. Paul. Giedion justly points out how some of these obelisks and columns have induced the development of squares during the following centuries.[3] The water supply in Rome had been rather insufficient since the fall of the Empire, so that Sixtus built a new aqueduct which brought water to twenty-seven public fountains (1589). The building of the fountains that contributed so much to the character of Baroque Rome was thus initiated.[4] Perhaps the most original of all the ideas of Sixtus V was to transform the Colosseum into a wool-spinning factory. His early death stopped the project.

Most of the plans of Sixtus V were carried out by Domenico Fontana. He is generally considered a dry and unimaginative architect, but we should not forget that he obviously had some quite new and fertile ideas about the handling of space. In fact, his dryness may be understood as an aspect of his desire for systematization, a desire which his followers were to carry on with more artistic imagination.[5] In general, the network of streets he executed for Sixtus V appears rather hard and schematic in relation to the topography and urban texture. Thus Fontana writes: "Now at a truly incredible cost, and in conformity with the spirit of so great a prince, Sixtus has extended these streets from one end of the city to the other, without concern for either the hills or the valleys which they crossed; but causing the former to be levelled and the latter filled, has reduced them to most gentle plains..."[6] In fact, the topographic ideal of the Baroque Age was the flat land, allowing for infinite extension.

The plan of Sixtus V and Fontana, however, did not represent a fundamental innovation. It stemmed from the general interest in *movement* typical of Mannerist architecture. In many cases this interest signified a more active contact between a building (or a group of buildings) and its environment. As a particularly interesting example, we may mention Giacomo della Porta's transformation of Michelangelo's project for the Capitoline Hill.[7] Michelangelo had planned an enclosed space full of tensions. Dupérac's prints show that all the buildings were intended to have the same type of wall treatment, thereby forming a continuous boundary around three sides of the square. As the fourth side was narrower, giving the square a trapezoid shape, an effect of contraction resulted. In contrast to this movement, Michelangelo inscribed an oval floor-space which seems to expand outwards from the centrally placed statue of the emperor Marcus Aurelius,[8] because of its convex section and a radiating, starlike pattern in the pavement. This oval probably represents the *caput mundi*, thereby making the Capitol the first intended focus of Counter-Reformatory Rome.[9] After Michelangelo's death in 1564, Della Porta made significant changes in the design. First of all, he modified the façade of the Palazzo dei Senatori, making it appear lighter and more distant and visually separated from the two lateral palaces. The central axis of the Palazzo dei Conservatori was given importance by means of a large window, so that the uniform enclosure of the space became still smaller. Finally he turned the statues on the balustrade to face the city rather than the entrance ramp. All in all, Della Porta transformed the enclosed space of Michelangelo into a Baroque composition based on a longitudinal axis which joins the square to the city below.[10] The final solution in several respects resembles the "U"-shaped palaces (hôtels) of the seventeenth century where a *cour d'honneur* forms a transition between outer and inner space. Still earlier, Michelangelo himself had planned to create a connecting axis between the Palazzo Farnese and the Farnesina on the other side of the Tiber (1549),[11] manifesting a developing desire to break up the static, self-sufficient units of the Renaissance city.

We have already mentioned the *Piazza del Popolo* as a particularly important pre-existent element which was incorporated in the plan of Baroque Rome. The Piazza del Popolo actually represents the prototype of one of the basic motifs of the Baroque cities—the radiating streets, which either concentrate upon or lead away from a significant place.[12] In the case of the Piazza del Popolo, the focus is the main entry of the Holy City. For centuries Via Flaminia led visitors towards Rome along the narrow strip of land between the Parioli-Pincio hills and the Tiber. The city-gate is placed where the hills and the river separate to allow for the extended surface of the city. Until the time of Sixtus V, the Piazza del Popolo was simply the starting point of the three streets, but the obelisk put up in 1589 made it become a true urban node, and about the middle of the seventeenth century it was transformed into a Baroque piazza. On March 15th, 1662, the foundations for Carlo Rainaldi's twin churches were laid. The two churches are symmetrically placed on the two building sites formed between the three radiating streets, and thus appear as a monumental entrance to the city with its principal street, the Corso, as the main gate.[13] The visitor who enters the city has the domed churches before him, and thereby "gets introduced to the treasures hidden in the famous city," as Titi wrote in his guidebook of 1686. The inviting trident has been transformed into an instrument of Baroque persuasion.

The churches of Rainaldi represent an interesting case of city-building and therefore deserve a more detailed discussion.[14] The radiating streets of the Piazza del Popolo invited the development of a monumental symmetry dear to the Baroque Age, and what could be more appropriate to the Holy City than the erection of two churches. But a seemingly insuperable difficulty had to be conquered: the two building sites had different widths. Even if Rainaldi had straightened out the house-fronts on either side, the land between the Via di Ripetta and the Corso remained wider than that bordering the Via del Babuino. In other words, the two churches would have received domes with a different diameter and would have appeared dissimilar rather than symmetrical. Rainaldi solved the problem in an ingenious way. By making the church on the narrow lot oval, he pushed its diameter back until it became equal to the diameter of its twin. Seen from the city-gate the churches appear similar, in spite of their actual differ-

ence. We thus understand that *architectural* equivalence does not necessarily mean *physical* similarity. The churches of Rainaldi also create a successful transition between the block of houses behind and the piazza, as they have deep porticoes protruding into the urban space in front. The columns of the porticoes continue along the lateral walls of the churches which are joined without interruption to the block-fronts behind. The porticoes thus are not volumes "added" to the churches, but form an organic part of the whole.[15] The churches therefore appear as a monumental front to the mass of houses behind, and in fact, to the whole city. At the same time, the porticoes together with the three streets form a rhythmic succession of openings which define the boundary of the piazza. Rainaldi thus achieved a convincing synthesis of space definition and movement in depth. A few years before the planning of the twin churches, Bernini rebuilt the city-gate to mark the arrival of Queen Christina of Sweden (1655). Bernini executed the crowning terminal of the central bay.[16]

Today the Piazza del Popolo appears fundamentally different. In 1816 Giuseppe Valadier started a transformation which introduced a transverse axis defined by large exedrae on both sides.[17] The idea was to connect the square with the slope of the Pincio on one side and the Tiber on the other. Valadier also marked the four corners of the new space thus formed with similar palaces. His changes reduce the effect of the Baroque trident; rather than forming a node between Via Flaminia and the three radiating roads, the piazza has become a large and somewhat unresolved organism. In fact, nothing could be more harmful to the *urban* structure than introducing a "green" transverse axis the moment one is led into the city. The idea is obviously derived from Bernini's Piazza S. Pietro where it has quite a different meaning. The well-known *veduta* by Piranesi (c. 1750) depicts how the Piazza del Popolo was experienced before the intervention of Valadier—as an active interplay of mass and space, with movement in depth as the dominant quality, and the obelisk acting as a necessary point of reference for the whole *ensemble*.

Among the Baroque squares of Rome, *Piazza Navona* plays a particular role. Its main shape was established in advance; it was in fact determined by the Stadium of Emperor Domitian which was used for the first time in A.D. 86. During the Middle Ages houses were built on the Roman ruins but the space remained free and became the stage for popular games. Pope Sixtus IV (1471-84) made the square a market-place for the nearby Renaissance district. But in spite of its complex history, Piazza Navona forms a part of Baroque Rome. Pope Innocent X (1644-50), whose palace faced the square, transformed it into a characteristic focus of the period, and because of its singular spatial qualities, it managed to dominate its environment, although it is not integrated in any Baroque system of streets. During the seventeenth century, in fact, Piazza Navona became the *Salotto dell'Urbe*, the very center of civic life. Today the square still acts as a magnet, which more than any other urban space in Rome attracts the visitor.[18]

14. *Giovanni Battista Piranesi, Rome, Piazza del Popolo (engraving).*

15. *Carlo Rainaldi, Rome, Piazza del Popolo, plan, Cod. Vat. Lat. 13442 (Rome, Biblioteca Apostolica Vaticana).*

16. *Rome, Piazza del Popolo, diagram of the trident.*

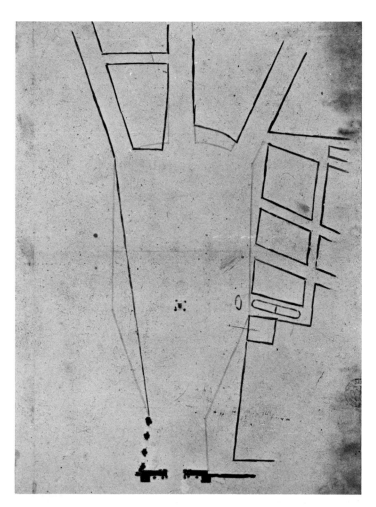

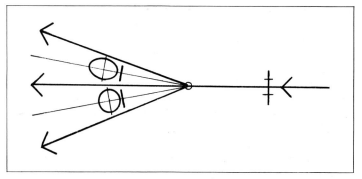

17. *Giovanni Battista Piranesi,
Rome, Piazza Navona (engraving).*
18. *Francesco Borromini, Rome,
Piazza Navona, S. Agnese in
Agone, drawing of prospectus.*

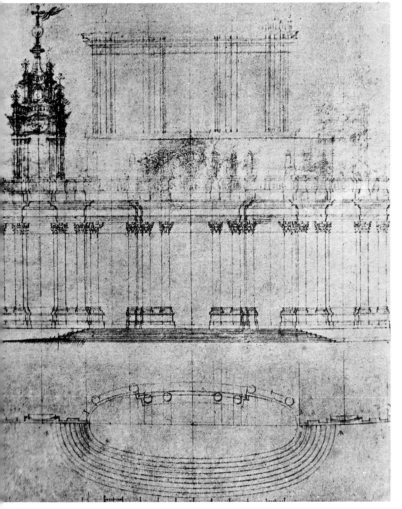

What then are the architectural qualities which give Piazza Navona this importance? The space is long and relatively narrow, and may be characterized as an enlarged street. It therefore has a direction which makes us experience it as a continuation of the surrounding streets. At the same time, however, it is limited in such a way that it becomes a "place" rather than a thoroughfare. This limitation results from the fact that a *continuous* wall runs all around the space. The buildings have the same general scale and appear as surfaces rather than masses. The streets leading into the square are thus quite narrow and irregularly placed. Wide, symmetrically disposed streets would easily have broken down the character of enclosure. The continuity is enhanced by a common scale of colors, and by the employment of related architectural details. The simpler houses as well as the elaborate façade of S. Agnese are articulated by means of the same classical elements; they are different "statements" within the same "language." The church serves as a main focus. If we imagine it were not there, the totality would lose much of its value, not so much because the church dominates, but because it makes the other buildings appear as simpler variations on the same basic themes, so that they obtain a meaning they would not have alone.

The bordering wall of Piazza Navona thus has a Baroque hierarchical structure. The façade of S. Agnese forms an organic part of this wall, and helps the square become an "interior." The basic quality of Piazza Navona, in fact, lies in its being a *space* in the Baroque sense of the term. Rather than having an abstract, geometrical quality, it lives in continuous interaction with its boundary, which is particularly evident in the concave façade of S. Agnese.[19]

Borromini here achieved two things: first, the church and the piazza become engaged in an active relationship, so that the outer space seems to penetrate into the volume of the building; second, the convex dome above is brought into contact with the square. The dome of S. Agnese is the *only* large mass taking part in the totality, and the concave façade by Borromini brings this out with full plastic force. An active space-mass relationship typical of Baroque architecture is thus created. The three fountains also play an important role in the composition. They divide the space into four varied zones with human dimensions, at the same time as they populate the space and exclude the possibility of experiencing *horror vacui*. Bernini's large Fountain of the Four Rivers (1648-51) constitutes the real focus of the piazza.[20] Its obelisk marks a vertical axis which limits and centralizes the horizontal movement of the space, at the same time as its allegorical figures introduce a new dimension of content, symbolizing the power of the Church which extends to all four parts of the world, here represented by the Danube, Plate, Ganges and Nile rivers. The fountain is also one of the most convincing answers to the Baroque desire for a synthesis of the two traditional opposites: *opera di natura* and *opera di mano*. The ingenious use of water furthermore adds to its persuasive impact on the be-

III. Rome, S. Maria della Pace,
upward view.

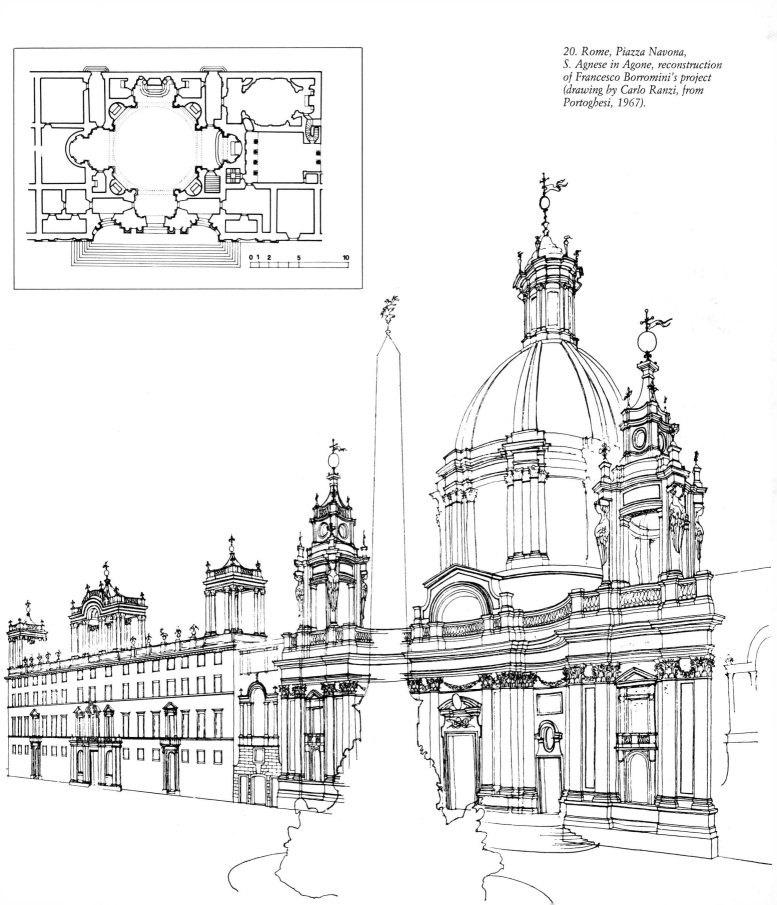

20. Rome, Piazza Navona,
*S. Agnese in Agone, reconstruction
of Francesco Borromini's project
(drawing by Carlo Ranzi, from
Portoghesi, 1967).*

0 1 2   5   10

21. Rome, Piazza Navona,
S. Agnese in Agone, façade.

22. Gianlorenzo Bernini, Rome,
Piazza Navona, Fountain of the
Four Rivers, detail.

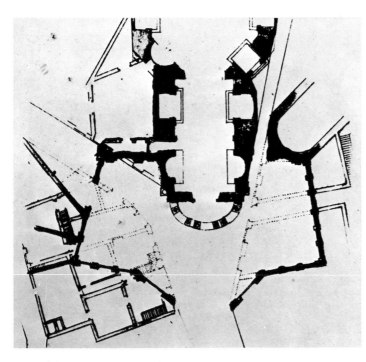

23. *Pietro da Cortona, Rome,
S. Maria della Pace, project (from
P. Portoghesi, Roma Barocca).*
24. *Pietro da Cortona, Rome,
S. Maria della Pace.*

holder, which finds its consummation in the inviting façade and crowning dome of S. Agnese, built by Bernini's great rival. The general effect is somewhat weakened by the two *campanili* which were built much higher than planned by Borromini.

In general, Piazza Navona represents the typical space of Roman Baroque architecture, a space that is eminently dynamic, vital and varied. It makes us understand to some degree how a city planned by Bernini and Borromini would have appeared: pulsating, expressive and rich in human content. The hard and schematic movements of Domenico Fontana are left far behind, just as the rational systems of French city-planning reflect a fundamentally different interpretation of the Baroque desire for integration and unity.

Close to Piazza Navona we find another square which is its direct opposite in regard to size. In fact, the piazza of *S. Maria della Pace* is a tiny space. But it is one of the rare examples of an urban space that has been planned and executed by one architect, and, more important, it is one of the most exciting achievements of Baroque architecture. The distinguishing quality of this masterpiece by Pietro da Cortona is the active interplay of mass and space. We have already pointed out similar qualities in connection with the Piazza del Popolo and Piazza Navona, but here this basic Baroque problem is presented in condensed and intensified form. In 1656 the Roman population suffered severely from the plague, and at the same time there was the threat of a French invasion. Pope Alexander VII thus decided to rebuild the church of S. Maria della Pace as an "invocation for mercy and peace."[21] The commission was given to Pietro da Cortona, who had to improve the access to the old church which was situated at the bifurcation of two narrow streets. The only possible solution was the creation of a small piazza. A preserved drawing by Cortona shows the demolition necessary to execute the plan, and also how he intentionally gave the piazza a delimitation which causes the church to protrude far into the space. This solution gives the visitor the feeling of being within the church as soon as he enters the piazza; the deep portico is in the middle of the space, at the same time as it also forms an organic part of the church behind. The integration of the church and the square is furthermore strengthened by the wall treatment. The houses, which form a continuous surface around the piazza, have two stories and a low attic. The cornice and parapet of this attic are carried on behind the lateral wings of the church, turning inwards along a concave curve. We may speak of an *interpenetration* of elements belonging to the piazza and the church respectively, while the projecting movement of the church is reinforced at the same time. This interpenetration is strengthened by the fact that the curved walls which "belong" to the *houses* are articulated by pilasters that form a continuation of the members of the upper story of the *church*. A simpler continuity all around the piazza is found on the ground-floor. The church is thus defined both as an independent projecting volume, and as part of a

25. *Gianlorenzo Bernini, Rome,*
Piazza S. Pietro, plan.
26. *Rome, Piazza S. Pietro,*
diagram of the final solution.

27. *Gianlorenzo Bernini, Rome,*
Piazza S. Pietro, project for a third
"arm" (engraving by Falda).

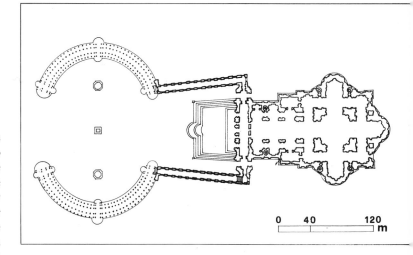

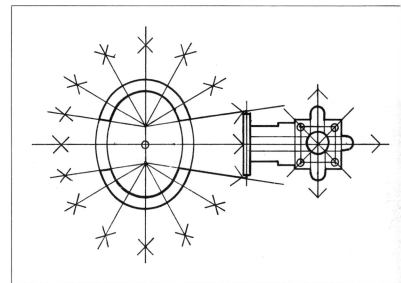

continuous wall around the square. The solution is related to Borromini's façade for S. Agnese, but whereas Borromini bent the façade inwards to make the dome active, Pietro da Cortona had to give plastic value to the nave of the existing church. The result is the most inviting of all Baroque church entrances. The persuasive effect is strengthened by the masterly handling of the plastic details, as well as light and shadow.[22] The upper story protrudes convexly to receive the strong sunlight. It indicates the volume of the church behind, but not as a separate realm; a vertical split in the middle and a strong double pediment transform the whole into a large gateway. Cortona thus gave a "High Baroque" interpretation to the theme of Il Gesù. The solution was repeated in a simplified form in Bernini's S. Andrea al Quirinale (1658), where the projecting porch is also present. Pietro da Cortona actually planned a similar but much more monumental setting for Il Gesù during the pontificate of Alexander VII.[23] A symmetrical access is created by means of lateral projecting porticoes behind which a piazza appears. The church itself has been separated from the Jesuit house on its right side by the breaking through of a new street, so that it acquires the significance of a real Baroque "focus."

We began by talking about S. Maria della Pace as an *urban* event, and ended up analyzing particular *architectural* properties. This goes to show how Roman Baroque architecture is characterized by a continuous interaction between the two levels. The urban spaces prepare for the churches, which on the other hand give meaning to their environment. Both form part of the same public realm. S. Maria della Pace also demonstrates how Baroque space is no general and isotropic quality given *a priori*. In fact, it changes continuously according to the situation; in other words, space is phenomenized.

The series of Baroque squares in Rome is crowned by Bernini's Piazza S. Pietro. The history of the square is long and complex and need not be retold in this context. What interests us here is the final solution that was carried through under the pontificate of Alexander VII (1655-67).[24] In the summer of 1656, Bernini made a first project showing a trapezoid piazza with the sides converging on the present Piazza Rusticucci. This barely satisfactory idea was soon dropped and Bernini turned to a circular plan. After some studies on the site, he settled for the final *oval* solution, presented to the Pope on 17 March 1657.[25] The main oval space, the *piazza obliqua*, is linked to the church by a smaller trapezoid square, the *piazza retta*, whose sides diverge at the church. The shape of the main piazza was determined by several functional demands, such as full visibility of the façade of St. Peter's, comfortable access to the Vatican Palace, and a covered "ambulatory" for processions. But first of all it has a symbolic basis as expressed in Bernini's own words: "...for since the church of St. Peter's is the mother of nearly all the others, it had to have colonnades, which would show it as if stretching out its arms maternally to receive Catholics, so as to confirm them in their faith, heretics, to reunite them to the Church, and

27

61

31. Carlo Maderno, Rome,
St. Peter's, detail of façade.

32. Rome, Piazza S. Pietro, detail
of colonnade.

infidels, to enlighten them in the true faith."[26] The space thus becomes a kind of immensely enlarged *atrium*, a character which would have been strengthened by the monumental entrance planned by Bernini to be built between the two "arms." This *terzo braccio* was never executed, owing to the death of Alexander VII in 1667.[27]

Virtually no other square has been analyzed more often than Piazza S. Pietro, especially to demonstrate how Bernini's solution counteracts the excessive length of Maderno's façade. As the originally planned campanili were never built, the façade received rather undecided and dull proportions. In Bernini's solution, the opening between the piazza obliqua and the piazza retta is more narrow than the façade, but it is spontaneously perceived as being equal (the piazza retta, thus, is experienced as being rectangular), hence the façade appears shorter than it is and correspondingly taller.[28] This effect is strengthened by the treatment of the lateral walls of the piazza retta which decrease in height as they approach the church. The height of the church façade is thus "measured" in relation to smaller pilasters than the similar ones at the beginning of the piazza retta. The transverse oval of the piazza obliqua, finally, brings the church relatively closer to the beholder. Bernini's final design for the front, with campanili separated from the main façade, would have completed the ingenious solution.

The real importance of Bernini's plan, however, does not lie in these "tricks" of perspective. What makes the Piazza S. Pietro one of the greatest squares ever conceived are its general spatial properties. The piazza obliqua may be characterized as *simultaneously closed and open*. The space is clearly defined, but the oval shape creates an expansion along the transverse axis. Rather than being a static, finished form, an interaction with the world beyond is created, which is also expressed by the "transparent" colonnade. Originally, gardens were seen through the columns, making the piazza appear as part of an open, extended environment. The space really becomes "the meeting-place of all mankind," at the same time as its message radiates to the entire world.[29] The trapezoid piazza retta also forms part of this general pattern. The obelisk has an important function as the node where all the directions are unified and connected with the longitudinal axis which leads to the church. An ideal synthesis of concentration and longitudinal direction on a goal is thereby created. The theme is repeated inside the church, where the movement finds its final motivation in the vertical axis of the heavenly dome. Argan says: "...the cupola rises and reveals itself above the colonnades, just as its original symbolic meaning is clearly revealed in the allegorical purpose of Bernini's piazza... the enclosed shape of the round cupola is implicit, both in a plastic and symbolic sense, and visually too, in the open, elliptical curve of the colonnades, whose allegorical purpose, as declared in one of Bernini's designs, is to constitute the arms of an imaginary body, of which the cupola is the head: the universal embrace of the Church is thus a prologue to the supreme revelation..."[30]

VI. Paris, Place Vendôme.

VII. Turin, Piazza S. Carlo.

VIII. Turin, Via Po.

33. Giovanni Antonio de Rossi, Rome, Palazzo Altieri (engraving by Specchi).

34. Martino Longhi the Elder, Carlo Rainaldi, Rome, Palazzo Borghese, plan.

Piazza S. Pietro is thus a supreme example of space composition, worthy of its function as the principal focus of the Catholic world. It shows how a system of "places," which is related to its environment in a particular way, is capable of symbolizing a content that embraces the deepest problems of human existence. At the same time, Bernini has succeeded in concretizing the essence of the Baroque Age with a singular simplicity, although his work never ceases to challenge the beholder. Better than any other example, Piazza S. Pietro shows that the basis of Baroque art is found in general principles rather than in exuberant detail. The *magnum opus* of Bernini, in fact, is composed of one single element: the classical column.

We have discussed Baroque Rome by analyzing its most important urban elements. In fact, Baroque Rome does not form a systematic totality of a geometrical kind. The seven basilicas, taken as the main point of departure for the plan of Sixtus V, are placed in relation to historical events, rather than topographical or urban reasons. Some of them are outside the city wall, some within. Baroque Rome therefore reflects the adaptation of singular circumstances rather than an ideal plan, and its "system" lies in the creation of a general character, rather than a concrete ordered image. This is particularly well illustrated by some minor adaptations, where the Baroque desire for spatial continuity and interaction has been realized in spite of very special conditions.

The extended and complex organism of the Palazzo Borghese underwent a final remodelling by Carlo Rainaldi in 1671.[31] Rainaldi joined all the rooms from the old façade to the Ripetta wing to form a long *enfilade* by putting the doors on a straight line. The vista thereby created, however, was the blank wall of the adjoining house. As this house also belonged to the Borghese, Rainaldi opened an oblique passage through the building to extend the view to the Tiber. A fountain was placed in the opening to make the effect still more convincing. In fact, it gave the impression that the fountain lay across the river. Another example, illustrating a very different kind of adaptation, is furnished by the Palazzo Altieri (1650-60).[32] The long wall of this palace partly runs along the side of Il Gesù, and partly faces the piazza in front of the church. Adapting to this difference in situation, Giovanni Antonio de Rossi designed that part of the wall which faces the piazza as a symmetrical *risalto*, complete in itself. In order not to allow the whole organism to fall asunder, he had to create a strong asymmetry in the remaining section, so that a symmetrical wing was needed to bring about a total equilibrium. De Rossi solved the problem by means of a "pseudo-*risalto*" at the right end, and above all, by erecting a long asymmetrical *belvedere* on top of the roof.

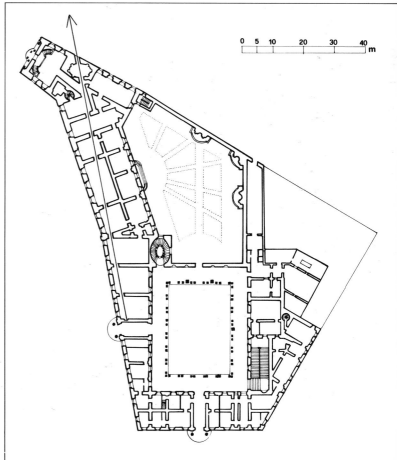

Roman Baroque architecture thus abounds in unexpected and original inventions. Rome is therefore the most varied of all Baroque cities. Rather than enforcing a dominating system, the Baroque Age made a great contribution to its eternal, but evolving structure.[33] The patrons and the masters of the High Baroque must have been aware of this, as they did not really develop the intentions of Sixtus V, but concentrated rather on the significant case.

Paris

The urban development of Paris during the seventeenth century took a course very different from that of Rome. Instead of starting with a system, Paris experienced a series of monumental movements, which slowly came together to form a coherent, systematic structure. This development was actually carried on during the eighteenth and nineteenth centuries. We should, however, add that the desire for a system was present in more or less concrete form from the very beginning. But there are also similarities between the two cities: in both cases a "Baroque" form of life needed to be concretized, and in both cases the basic means was the creation of meaningful "foci." What Sixtus V did to Rome, Henry IV did to Paris. The period of time is virtually the same, with some delay because of the French civil war. After his entry into Paris in 1594, Henry IV restored and strengthened the monarchy, and by liberal concessions, won general recognition of his authority. During the last years of his life, Henry wanted to transform his capital city into a worthy expression of the new system. After having won his kingdom, and after having secured the succession, he wanted to give his achievement eternal form. "People say that I am mean, but I do three things that have no connection with avarice, for I make war, I make love, and I build."

Whereas Sixtus V could take as his point of departure urban foci already in existence (i.e. the seven basilicas), Henry had to start afresh. He thus created a new urban element, the place royale. The place royale is an urban space centered on, and developed around, a statue of the sovereign. The absolute ruler is thus the real focus. The prototype, obviously, is the Capitoline Square of Michelangelo, where the first monarch of divine right is placed in the center of a space which symbolizes the center of the world.[34] The place royale as intended by Henry IV, however, is in an important respect different from the prototype, being surrounded by *dwellings* rather than serving purely monumental (civic) purposes. It therefore concretizes the new relationship between the sovereign and his people, at the same time as it may be used to express a certain bourgeois pride. The place royale was of decisive importance for the urban development of the following centuries, not only in France.

The first of Henry's projects, the *Place Dauphine*, is of particular interest because of its relationship to the city as a whole. In front of the Ile de la Cité, there were two small islands. Henry III had already started the construction of a new bridge across the river at this point (1578). It was to have been lined by houses on both sides, following the traditional model. The construction of the *Pont Neuf*, however, was stopped by the civil war, and only finished in 1606. Henry IV eliminated the houses and allowed the bridge to become part of a more comprehensive urban scheme. Be-

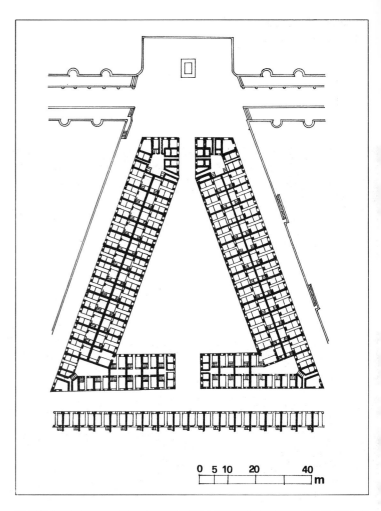

0 5 10 20 40 m

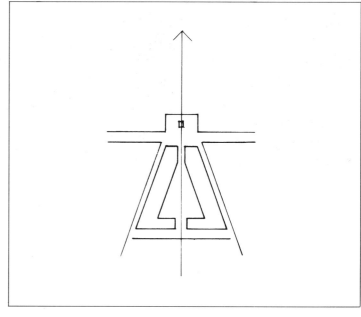

38. *Paris, Place des Vosges, detail of a palace.*

39. *Paris, Place des Vosges (engraving by Perelle).*
40. *Jules Hardouin-Mansart, Paris, Place des Victoires (contemporary engraving).*

tween the bridge and the old Ile de la Cité, he developed a new square of triangular form, the Place Dauphine. Where the axis of this square crosses the bridge, an equestrian statue of the sovereign was put up.[35] The bridge was connected on both sides with straight streets leading to the church of St. Eustache on the northern side, and Porte St. Germain to the south. Paris thus received its first urban axis. This transverse path crosses the man axis of the scheme, which is the Seine itself, at a right angle. The Place Dauphine, in fact, makes the axis of the river architecturally manifest, and was the first of a series of projects which gave the Seine an importance that surpasses that of the rivers of all other capital cities.[36] The *place* consisted of two long buildings with wings attached to form a triangle.[37] Streets run along the outside, so that together with the main axis, a trident centered on the statue is formed. The buildings contain a uniform series of relatively small apartments with shops on the ground-floor. The articulation shows a rather uncertain emphasis on surface and volume (defined by tall, steep roofs), rather than an Italian use of masses and plastic members. There is no monument in the square itself; the statue of Henry IV was located so as to act as a center for the whole city as well.

About the same time as the Place Dauphine was planned, Henry IV started another, more typical place royale, the present *Place des Vosges*.[38] This square is located in the Marais district and was intended as a *promemoir* for the inhabitants. It is surrounded by houses of a general character similar to those of the Place Dauphine, with apartments for the well-to-do. Everybody had to adhere to a common plan, and the continuity of the wall defining the space was emphasized by arcades. The single units, however, are indicated by divisions in the roofs and by tall chimneys. A certain axial effect is created by the taller Pavillons du Roi et de la Reine, which also serve as the main access. The whole square is centered on an equestrian statue of Louis XIII, put up in 1639. The articulation of the fronts shows a "Gothic" interplay of vertical and horizontal lines, rather than a classical structure. The ground-floor pilasters thus do not carry any entablature, but merely a thin string-course. The general effect, however, is not that of a skeleton; in fact, the walls appear as a decorated surface. The place royale was imitated in many European cities, especially in London.[39]

Further east, between the Bastille and the Temple, Henry IV planned another great urban development (1610).[40] His *Place de France* is the first true starlike composition in Baroque urban design, showing eight streets radiating from a base-line, with a new city-gate serving as the center. The eight streets should have carried the names of the main French provinces, thereby making the scheme a spatial expression of the new national system. Whereas the city-gates to date had taken their names from particular "geographical" circumstances, the *Porte de France* was a purely symbolic name, in accordance with the role of Paris as capital city. The execution of the project was started but could not be carried through because of the death of the King. The Place de France was not intended as a place royale.

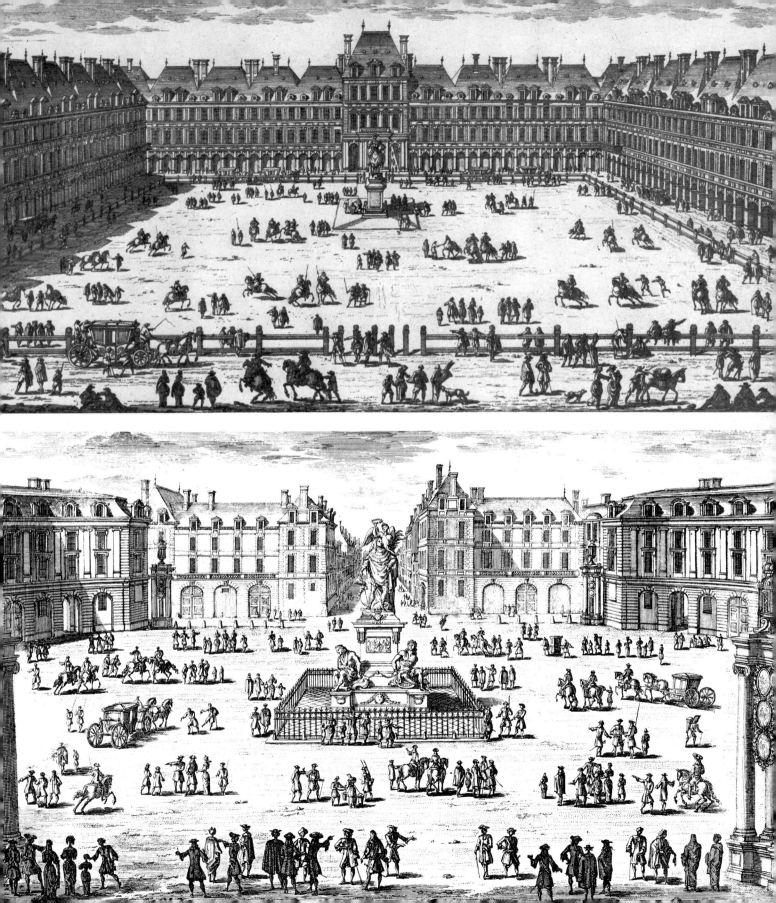

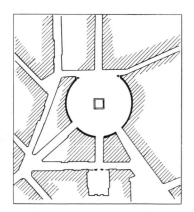

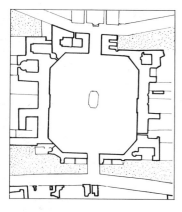

Rather it indicated the direction towards an integrated urban structure, and, in fact, a hundred years later the whole region of Paris was covered by its starlike pattern.

During the reign of Louis XIII (1610-43), new urban foci were not created. The activity was rather concentrated on the development of regular city *districts*. One of the first was the Rue Dauphine, built as a continuation of the Pont Neuf. Here the inhabitants were ordered to "make the fronts of their houses all in the same manner, for it would be a fine ornament to have at the end of the bridge this street forming one long façade."[41] More important was the complete construction of the Ile St. Louis on the basis of a systematic orthogonal layout.[42] Building continued for several decades and Louis Le Vau, who lived on the island, took an active part. The district of Richelieu was developed after 1633 outside the old city walls, to the north of the Louvre and the Tuileries. Like the Ile St. Louis, it was planned around two main streets crossing each other at right angles. More important than the achievements in city planning was the general architectural development during the reign of Louis XIII. In fact, a more "correct" and creative classical language was taken into use by Salomon de Brosse and François Mansart,[43] who laid the foundation for the great French classicism of the following period.

During the long reign of Louis XIV (1643-1715), Paris underwent several changes which were to have a decisive influence on the further development of the city. Two more royal squares were created, and the gardens of the Tuileries were taken as the point of departure for a great spatial extension towards the west. Most important, however, was the abolishment of the fortifications completed under Louis XIII, which were substituted by an almost complete ring of *boulevards*,[44] so that Paris became a spatially open city. Let us first consider the new squares.

Between 1682 and 1687, the district to the north of the Louvre obtained its urban focus, the *Place des Victoires*, originally Place Louis XIV. The square was planned by the leading architect of the period, Jules Hardouin-Mansart, and was designed in quite a novel way. Instead of remaining a relatively isolated space such as the Place des Vosges, it was designed to connect several important directions within the urban texture: the Rue des Fossés Montmartre (Rue d'Aboukir), determined by the old city wall of Charles V, the Rue Croix des Petits Champs leading straight south towards the Louvre, and the Rue de la Feuillade leading west to the new districts north of the Tuileries. The circle was the only form which could be used for this purpose, and the Place des Victoires thus became the prototype for a series of great circular urban spaces throughout Europe. The Place des Victoires, however, is not a regular *rond-point*. The Rue des Fossés Montmartre which comes from the Porte St. Denis and links the square with the ring of boulevards as well as the main road leading north is used as an axis superimposed on the circular pattern. It ends in the cour d'honneur of the Hôtel de la Vrillière (Hôtel de Toulouse). The two other streets

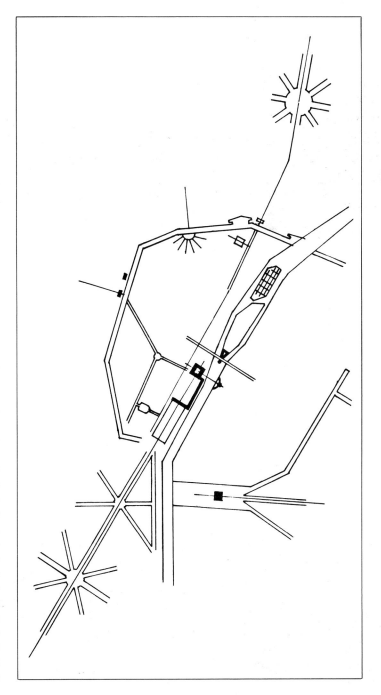

mentioned above branch off symmetrically to this axis. The whole composition is centered on an equestrian statue of Louis XIV (1686).[45] A uniformly articulated wall surrounds the space. It consists of a rusticated ground-floor and an Ionic giant order embracing two floors. The solution is of Berninesque origin, but the character is lighter and less plastic than in related Roman examples. The system is only applied to the wall facing the square, while the lateral walls along the streets have a simpler articulation. The *space* is thus the constitutive element of the composition, rather than the surrounding buildings, an idea which goes back to Michelangelo's project for the Capitoline Hill in Rome.

This basic fact is still more evident in the second of the royal squares built during the reign of Louis XIV, the *Place Vendôme* or Place Louis le Grand, which was built as a focus for the new districts in the western part of the city. A first project was made by Hardouin-Mansart in 1685, and parts of the façades were built *without houses behind them*. Originally a series of public (or royal) buildings were planned: academies, a library, the royal mint and embassies, but in 1698 the plan was abolished and the façades were torn down. Hardouin-Mansart made a new, smaller project consisting of a rectangular space with cut-off corners, namely an octagon with unequal sides. Again façades were put up (1699-1708) and the plots behind were sold to individual buyers. The Place Vendôme, thus, somewhat repeats the general solution of the Place des Vosges. The closure of the space, however, is stressed by the cut-off corners and by the strong and regular rhythm of the wall articulation. At the same time the shape is stretched longitudinally in accordance with its north-south axis which originally linked the nearby churches of the Capucines and the Feuillants. The solution represents a characteristic Baroque synthesis of centralization and ongitudinality, of closure and interaction with the environment. The wall articulation repeats the general system of the Place des Victoires, but the bays have a more slender proportion and the details are richer. The center was marked by an equestrian bronze of Louis XIV as a Roman emperor.[46]

The four royal squares of Paris are variations on a common theme. Basically they are intended as *spaces*; they are not dependent on particular *buildings* as are the Roman piazze,[47] but are conceived as "urban interiors." The continuity of the boundary wall, therefore, is essential, as well as the definition of a center. The general theme is varied by the choice of shape and by the relationship to the surroundings. The squares of Paris are thus based on four simple geometrical forms: the triangle, the square, the circle and the rectangle. Inevitably, they reflect the rational and systematic attitude of the society for which they were made. Royal squares were also introduced in other French cities, such as Dijon, where Jules Hardouin-Mansart created a semicircular space in front of the Palais des Etats de Bourgogne (1686).

Whereas the royal squares gave Paris a new internal structure, the ring

48. André Le Nôtre, Paris, Tuileries
(engraving by Perelle).

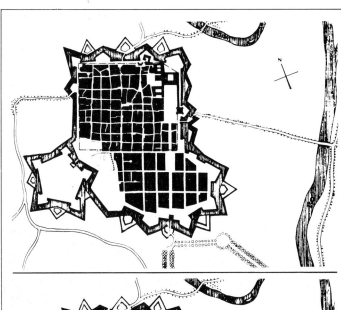

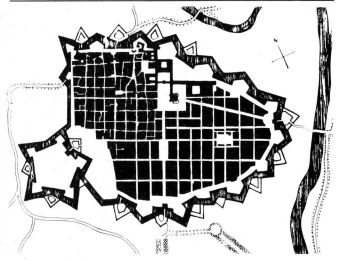

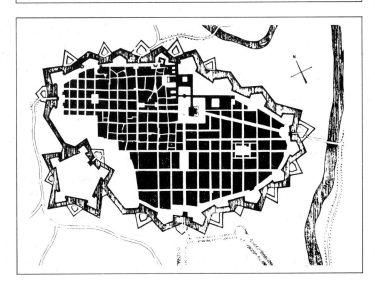

49. Turin, plan showing the first extension towards the south and plan after the second extension (from Atti del X Congresso di Storia dell'Architettura, Turin, 1957).

50. Turin, plan of town in the second half of the eighteenth century, after the third extension.

52-54. *Turin, Piazza S. Carlo,*
views.

55. *Amedeo di Castellamonte,*
Turin, Piazza Vittorio Veneto with
Via Po.

56. *Amedeo di Castellamonte,*
Turin, Via Po.

57. *Turin, topographic plan of town*
and environs (print by Baillieu).

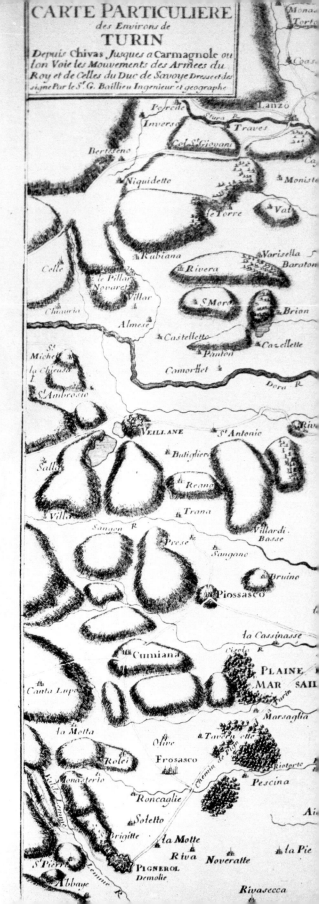

58. *Ascanio Vitozzi, Turin,*
S. Maria al Monte dei Cappuccini.

cennes was also planned and in part executed. A system of radiating paths was thereby initiated, which expresses the role of Paris as the capital city of the whole of France. The radiating roads and avenues were linked together by the ring of boulevards which defines the area of the city without closing it in. The boulevards of Louis XIV are thirty-six meters wide and consist of a main thoroughfare as well as narrower lateral streets. Where they cross the radiating roads, triumphal arches were erected, namely purely symbolic city-gates expressing the basic content of the spatial system.[48]

During the reign of Louis XIV, the basic structure of Paris was defined. Its systematic character is apparent and constitutive elements are spatial nodes, paths and regularly programmed districts. The buildings were planned in relation to this system, and therefore do not have any strong, plastic individuality. Rather than masses, they appear as surfaces which define the urban spaces and their continuations such as the characteristic cours d'honneur. The dynamism of French seventeenth-century urbanism thus lacks the dramatic quality of the Roman Baroque. Its emphasis on the systematic aspect led to an articulation based on a regular and correct use of the classical elements. We may, however, still employ the term "Baroque," inasmuch as there is present a strong wish for integration, continuity and "openness." Whereas Rome is the typical "sacred city" of the Baroque, Paris forms its "secular" counterpart.

Turin

The capital city of Piedmont is situated midway between Rome and Paris, and, in fact, its history is closely related to both. When Turin became the capital of the duchy of Savoy towards the end of the sixteenth century, it was still a small town having the square shape of the original Roman *oppidum*. Continuing the political restoration started by his father Emmanuel Philibert, Duke Charles Emmanuel I (1562-1630, duke from 1580) initiated the transformation of Turin into a Baroque capital city. At the same time, however, Piedmont was under the influence of the Counter-Reformation. The two main "forces" of the epoch met, therefore, and formed a singular synthesis, unifying the sacred and the secular aspects.[49]

The old town was structured by an orthogonal system of streets with a municipal square in the center. Joined to the eastern side of the city-wall, there was a castle, originally a Roman city-gate, transformed during the Middle Ages. Duke Charles Emmanuel naturally took this castle as his point of departure, commissioning his architect, Ascanio Vitozzi, to make it the center of a regular piazza (1584).[50] To concretize its function of "center," Vitozzi planned to surround the piazza with a new radially organized town. The idea was dropped, however, for a better adaptation to the existing orthogonal system, and on this basis a city extension towards the south and the east was initiated. This development lasted most of the sev-

of boulevards and the centrifugal axes created a new relationship to the environment. The ideas behind these innovations stem from garden architecture, and reflect a new attitude to landscape in general. As we will show later, the first decisive examples are found in Italy, but the French development was mainly the work of a single man: André Le Nôtre (1613-1700). In 1637, Le Nôtre was appointed gardener of the Tuileries, and during his long and incredibly active career he had his home there. The existing gardens were planned in the typical Renaissance way, forming a succession of "static" squares and rectangles (1563). Le Nôtre transformed the whole pattern thoroughly, introducing a system of axes and a variety of differently shaped spaces. Above all, he opened the area towards the west, creating a long avenue (the Champs Elysées) which ended in a large *round-point* (the Etoile). A similar axis leading eastwards from the Porte St. Antoine to Vin-

IX. Turin, S. Maria al Monte dei Cappuccini.

enteenth century, but we should point out that its general course was determined when Vitozzi created the *Piazza Castello*. This square was surrounded by uniform façades having an articulation based on continuous horizontal lines and rhythms. The enclosed character was stressed by rusticated arcades on the ground-floor. Shortly before his death (1615), Vitozzi laid out a new street leading south from the piazza, the Via Nuova (today Via Roma), which was intended to function as the main axis of a new district, the Città Nuova. The fronts of this street were designed as a continuation of the walls of the square, introducing thereby the idea of a homogeneous system for the whole city. He also indicated a new Ducal Palace at the starting point of the axis, with a courtyard opening on the Piazza Castello. The general horizontal continuity of the articulation was only broken by the new façade of the old castle which was given emphasis by strong vertical pilasters.

The work of Vitozzi was continued by his follower Carlo di Castellamonte, who was a ducal architect from 1615 till his death in 1641. From 1621 onwards, Carlo di Castellamonte carried out the city extension towards the south. He continued the orthogonal system of streets, and introduced a new secondary focus for the district: the Piazza Reale (today *Piazza San Carlo*), which was integrated with the Via Nuova and received a rectangular shape in accordance with the direction of the street. The square was centered on an equestrian statue, and had the character of a true place royale.[51] Compared with the French squares, however, there is one important difference: where the Via Nuova leaves the piazza, two symmetrical churches mark the corners, a solution somewhat similar to the twin churches of the Piazza del Popolo in Rome.[52] The "sacred" element thus participates fully, just as it does in the Piazza Castello. The new Palazzo Ducale (later, Palazzo Reale), is directly joined to the cathedral of Turin, and together they form a singular focus, where the simple, urbanistically determined surfaces of the palace contrast with the plastic dome and campanile of the church.[53] Throughout the history of Baroque Turin, in fact, we find sacred and secular elements brought together to form a rich and expressive counterpoint.

The son of Carlo, Amedeo di Castellamonte, faithfully carried on the work started by Vitozzi and his father. First he built the new Palazzo Ducale (1645-58), which was related to the square in front in a very interesting way. The rusticated arcades of the piazza were continued to form a screen-wall between the urban space and the cour d'honneur of the palace. Its central gateway was crowned by a tower-like pavilon, which served to show the most holy relic of Turin, the *SS. Sindone* or Holy Shroud.[54] Amedeo di Castellamonte furthermore planned a new large city extension to the east, towards the river Po (1659). Also here the orthogonal system was developed, and the district centered on another royal square, the *Piazza Carlina*. Its east-west axis continues westwards to join the Piazza San Carlo. A particular element in the new city extension, however, is a large

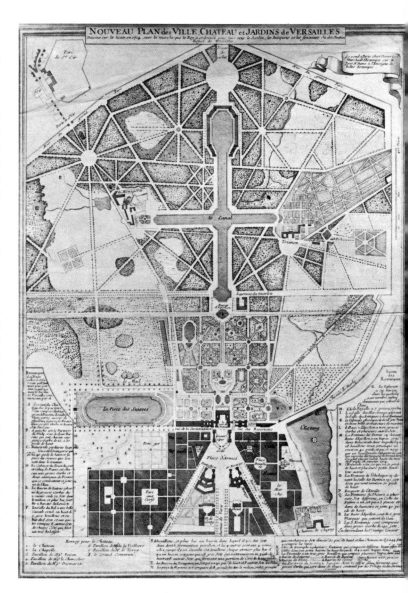

NOUVEAU PLAN de la VILLE, CHATEAU et JARDINS de VERSAILLES

60. *Versailles, schematic diagram.*

61. *Louis Le Vau, Versailles, Royal Palace, garden façade.*

62. *André Le Nôtre, Versailles, gardens, the main axis.*

63. *Versailles, general view (seventeenth-century engraving).*

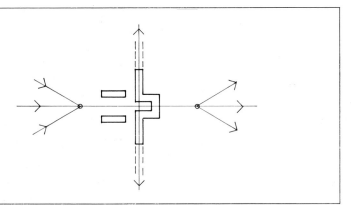

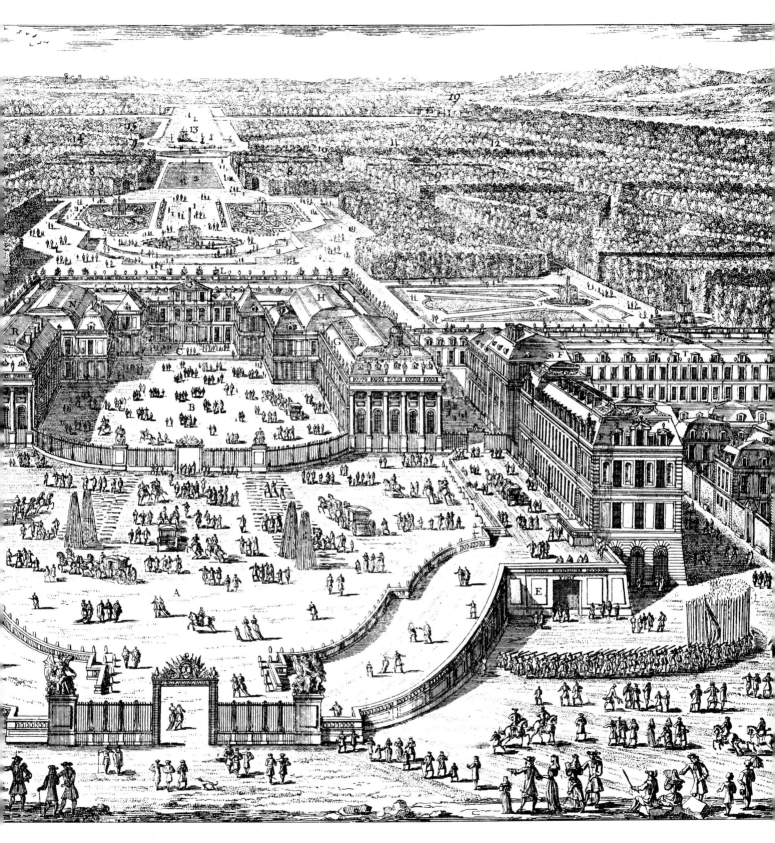

51

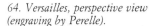

64. Versailles, perspective view (engraving by Perelle).

street crossing diagonally through the general pattern to connect the Piazza Castello with the Porta di Po, a splendid city-gate by Guarini (1676).[55] The construction of *Via Po* was initiated in 1673 after a plan by Amedeo di Castellamonte. Its uniform façades, with arcades on the ground-floor, define the most magnificent seventeenth-century street in existence. Towards the Po, the street terminates with an open exedra, which, seen from the outside, appears as a kind of "urban cour d'honneur." Rather than closing itself off, therefore, the city is opened to the environment, at the same time as it receives the visitor. The motif was repeated several times during the following centuries, particularly by Juvarra at the Porta di Susa (Quartieri Militari) and the Porta Palazzo, although the semicircular plan was never directly imitated. The works of Juvarra arose in connection with the last Baroque extension of Turin (after 1706), this time towards the west and again on the same pattern, even including a royal square: the Piazza Savoia.

We then see how Baroque Turin grew around the Piazza Castello that historically, politically and religiously formed the center of the city. To the north, however, the area was not extended. We find here the gardens of the Palazzo, which are linked with the open countryside. The solution is related to the contemporary layout of the gardens of the Tuileries,[56] but whereas Paris was made an open city, Turin had to maintain its fortifications until the Napoleonic period. Its theoretically open Baroque structure was thus always confined within a ring of bastions. This structure, however, is certainly more homogeneous and systematic than in any other capital city of the seventeenth century. It is mainly due to the fortunate circumstance of the well-preserved Roman street-pattern which was taken as a point of departure and fully integrated in the Baroque city. We may assume that the Roman layout was used intentionally to symbolize the importance of the new Turin and its glorious past. The hierarchical structure of the Baroque city is also particularly evident in Turin. The Piazza Castello functions as the primary focus, the old city has a secondary focus in the Piazza Palazzo di Città which obtained its final articulation as late as 1756,[57] and the new districts are all related to a new square. The piazze were linked by main thoroughfares, most of which led into the countryside. The districts as such were planned and built according to the same ideal of uniformity and continuity that we met in Paris.

The plan of Baroque Turin thus clearly expresses the ideal system of absolute monarchy, and its spatial structure has the French character of a horizontally extended network related to a main center of "content." "The urbanistic elements that go to make up a city, be they large or small, must all combine to become an integral part in the single, great vision of the city's organism; just as we find, for example, in the parallel sociopolitical organization of the Nation, that each individual has his place in a definite social class or category within a unified, pyramid-structured State, on the summit of which stands the Monarch."[58] In Turin, however,

65. *Domenico Fontana, Rome,*
Villa Montalto (contemporary
print).

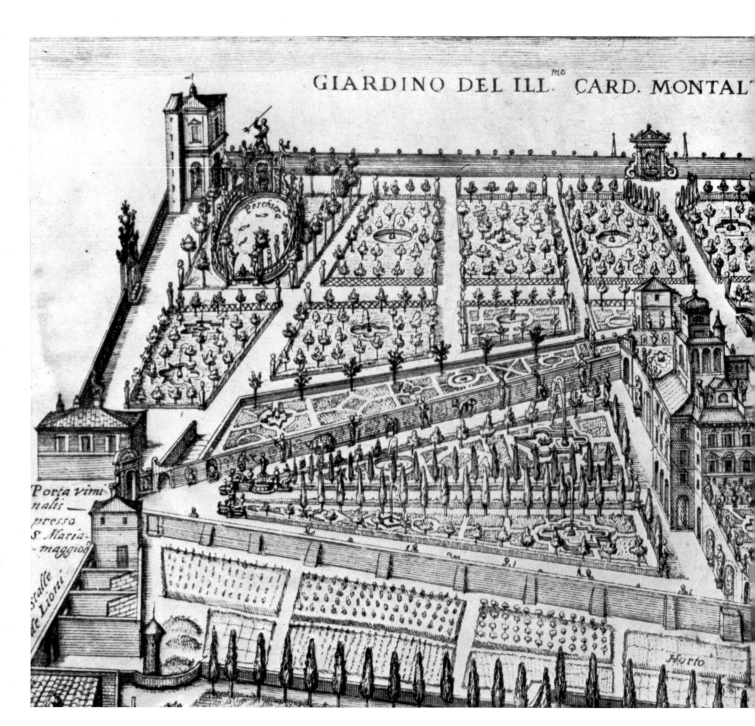

GIARDINO DEL ILL.^{mo} CARD. MONTAL

54

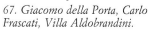

66. D. Barrière, Frascati, Villa
Aldobrandini plan.
67. Giacomo della Porta, Carlo
Frascati, Villa Aldobrandini.

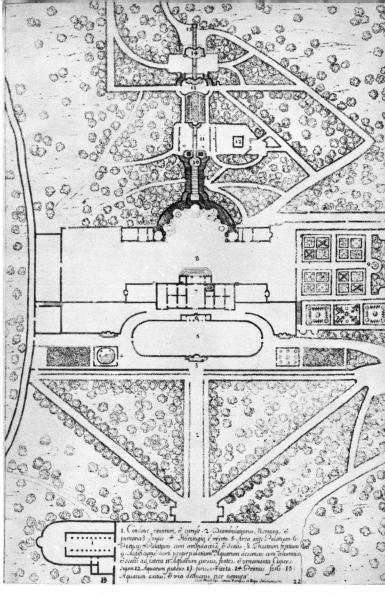

68. *Giacomo della Porta, Carlo
Maderno, Villa Aldobrandini,
bird's-eye view.*

69. *Louis Le Vau, Château de
Vaux-le-Vicomte, view from the
entrance side (engraving by Perelle).*

70. Louis Le Vau, André Le Nôtre,
Château de Vaux-le-Vicomte, the
castle seen along the main axis.

this secular system contrasts with the vertical towers and domes of the churches. A print from the eighteenth century, where Turin is seen from the east, gives an almost medieval impression of densely placed vertical elements. "For the world of faith the bell-tower is the most important of all vertical structures and acquires the character of a protective element; in its shadow one feels safer, the sound of its bells spreads over the faithful beneath, and its spire, reaching up to heaven, carries with it the symbols of religion." Turin thus represents a singular synthesis of the plastic-expressive and the spatial-systematic properties which we have found to be typical of Rome and Paris respectively.

This "double" character is also found in the surroundings of the city. Vitozzi contributed to both aspects. He built the church of S. Maria al Monte dei Cappuccini on a high rock at the foot of the hills along the Po, initiating thereby the creation of the "sacred landscape" of the Baroque Age, which culminated with the pilgrimage churches and convents of eighteenth-century Central Europe.[59] But he also took part in the planning of secular residences around Turin. Both aspects were developed by Castellamonte, father and son. Amedeo planned a small *ideal city* in connection with the ducal country residence, the Venaria Reale (1660-78).[60] The main axis of the layout is directed on the cour d'honneur of the palace, but on its way it crosses a transverse axis determined by two symmetrically placed domed churches. The plan confirms the great urbanistic talent of Castellamonte, and represents one of the most interesting ideal schemes of the seventeenth century. Like the surroundings of Paris, those of Turin were structured by a system of radiating roads and geometrically ordered gardens, but the landscape was also marked by the domes of the sanctuaries. Both aspects were developed during the eighteenth century and culminated with the great creations of Juvarra: the Basilica di Superga and the Stupinigi Palace. Finally we should mention the beautiful Piedmontese landscape which contributes to make Turin a truly great city.

Conclusion

Our short survey of seventeenth-century urbanism has demonstrated how the basic ideas of centralization, continuity and extension were concretized in different ways according to the particular situation, namely the socio-cultural system as well as the existing architectural and topographical circumstances. Some characteristic themes have been singled out, such as the symbolic square or "focus," the directional street or "path" and the uniform, subordinate district. In most cities of the period, these elements appear without real systematic integration. In a few cases, however, ideal plans were executed on a smaller scale. The most famous, and most typical, is *Versailles*.[61] We shall return to the palace later, but should in this context say a few words about its general urban properties and its relation to the landscape.

The urban development of Versailles started in 1661 with the extension

71. André Le Nôtre, Château de
Vaux-le-Vicomte, gardens, aerial
view.

72. Louis Le Vau, André Le Nôtre,
Château de Vaux-le-Vicomte, view
from the garden (engraving by
Perelle).

of the Royal Palace by Le Vau. The gardens were planned by Le Nôtre who supervised the works for more than thirty years. The total scheme may be considered the result of the simultaneous or successive contributions of Le Vau, Le Nôtre and Jules Hardouin-Mansart. The palace occupies the very center and its long wings divide the area into two halves: the gardens on one side and the town on the other. The latter is structured by three main avenues radiating away from the center, the Avenue de Paris, the Avenue de Saint-Cloud and the Avenue de Sceaux. Secondary streets and squares are planned on an orthogonal grid. The layout of the gardens shows a system of radiating paths and *rond-points*. Both halves are thus characterized by infinite perspectives centered on the palace. The entire surrounding landscape is taken into possession by the seemingly limitless system. The modest Notre-Dame church by Hardouin-Mansart has an asymmetrical location, and does not constitute any vertical accent. Instead Hardouin-Mansart planned to crown the palace with a dome to glorify the Monarch "by divine right."[62] "It is," says Baudelaire, "the natural solemnity of an immense city." Versailles represents the very essence of the seventeenth-century city: domination and definition, but also dynamism and openness. It is therefore something more than an expression of absolutism; its structure has general properties which give it the capacity of receiving other contents. And today, in fact, Versailles is visited by innumerable persons who experience an enrichment of existence which was once reserved for Louis XIV alone.

The gardens of Versailles represent the culmination of a development that started more than a hundred years earlier. The Early Renaissance garden still retained its medieval character of *hortus conclusus*. It was, however, geometrized to express the idea of an ideal nature, forming thereby a complement to the ideal city of the epoch. During the sixteenth century, this concept of static perfection was substituted by the idea of a mysterious and fantastic world consisting of a variety of "places." "The idea of 'regular' nature was now superseded by that of 'capricious' nature, full of 'inventions' and the unpredictable... the idea of a garden as a wonderful, fantastic place, perhaps even magical and enchanted, led to the breaking down of walls and fences, and to the transformation of the garden into a group of different places, each designed in relation to human feelings."[63] In several villas of the sixteenth century, we recognize, however, the beginning of a definition of "basic characters" which were to have a fundamental importance for further development: the decorative garden consisting of flower *parterres*, the extension of the function of dwelling in a *bosquet* made up of hedges and other "tamed" elements of nature, and the introduction of free nature in a *selvatico* ("wilderness").[64] In the *Villa Montalto* in Rome, built in 1570 by Domenico Fontana for Sixtus V before he became Pope, all these elements were present, as well as a new pronounced desire for spatial integration. From the side entrance near S. Maria Maggiore, a trident branched off to define the *palazzetto* and its

XI. Vaux-le-Vicomte, exterior view.

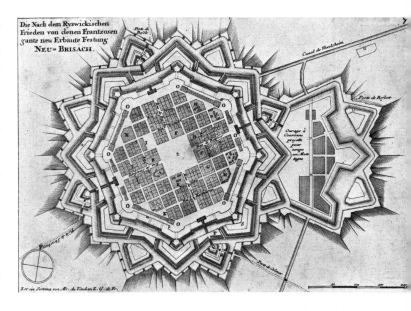

lateral parterres. The main axis continued through the building, crossing a transverse axis and ending at a distant *point-de-vue*. The scheme was repeated at the *Villa Aldobrandini* at Frascati by Della Porta and Maderno (1601-02, 1603-06), where the main axis is emphasized by the tall, central *risalti* of the palace.[65] In both villas, however, the relationship between the meaningful "domains" mentioned above and the system of nodes and paths is somewhat undecided. This is also due to the characteristic location of the Italian garden *casino* in the middle of the total area, in lieu of a transition from the urban world to nature beyond.

The further development of the Baroque garden is mainly due to André Le Nôtre, who more than anyone else realized the Baroque idea of space on the levels of city and landscape.[66] In spite of their infinite variety, his gardens are based on a few simple principles. The main element, naturally, is the longitudinal axis. It forms the "path" which leads the beholder towards his "goal": the experience of infinite space. All the other elements are related to this axis; the palace which divides the path into two different halves, the arrival from man's "urban" world through the "open" courtyard, and the departure into infinity defined as a gradual passage through the still "civilized" world of the parterres, the "tamed" nature of the bosquet, and the "natural" nature of the *selvatico*. Transverse axes and radiating patterns are introduced to indicate the general open extension of the system.[67] To make this extension still more effective, the natural topography is transformed into series of flat terraces, and large surfaces of reflecting water contribute to the experience. The fountains, basins and canals also introduce a dynamic element in the whole composition. One experiences an echo of the open ocean, always changing with the weather. The programmatic work of Le Nôtre is the garden of Vaux-le-Vicomte (1656-61). The trident of the Italian villas is here turned around to concentrate on the entrance, and after having followed the longitudinal axis through the palace and the main part of the garden, the movement again radiates away to form another *patte-d'oie*, a motif which was considered Le Nôtre's trademark. In several respects the layout is original. The parterres and bosquets are not placed behind each other but next to each other, giving the space along the main axis a splendid width. In Vaux-le-Vicomte, the limits of the Italian gardens have dissolved. Rather than defining space by boundaries, Le Nôtre used an open but regular system of "paths." Little wonder that his works were called *jardins d'intelligence*. In Versailles the same basic scheme is employed, only on a much bigger scale and with more variety, particularly in the bosquets where we find spaces having names such as *Salle verte*, *Salle de danse*, *Salle du conseil*, *Salle des festins*. The *selvatico* is still present in the Grand Parc although it has become quite tame, making it easy for the hunting parties to get quickly from one place to another. The whole area is structured by a great canal, indicating the main directions of the layout.

We have already mentioned the importance of Le Nôtre's ideas for urban design. Usually, however, the spatial system had to be confined within a ring of fortifications. During the seventeenth century the character of these changed considerably. Because of the more potent artillery, the bastions had to be made lower and wider, and earthworks were introduced which created a more gradual transition between the town and the surrounding landscape, although the physical separation was stronger than ever. The innovations were mainly due to the French military architect, Sébastien Le Prestre de Vauban, who designed a series of ingenious fortifications as well as new towns.[68] The best known is the well-preserved Neuf-Brisach (1698). We should, however, repeat that the idea of the Baroque city is open extension, and that the fortifications no longer formed part of the basic space conception.

Introduction

We have already discussed the basic architectural intentions that were brought forth by the Roman Counter-Reformation. Down to the end of the seventeenth century most of the important innovations were due to Italian architects.[1] During this period, however, a diffusion took place that brought the new ideas to the entire Catholic world. In the different countries, Roman forms met with local traditions, and a process of symbiosis and synthesis began which led to the creation of regional Baroque typologies. In most countries this process found culmination during the eighteenth century. During the whole of its development, however, we may also discern a general architectural trend which lay in the gradual working out of variations on the original intentions. We have already referred to the desire to arrive at a unification of the traditional longitudinal and centralized schemes, and the resulting formation of "centralized longitudinal plans" as well as "elongated centralized plans." For this purpose new spatial problems were tackled, such as the integration of spatial elements. We have furthermore mentioned the new relationship between the church and its environment, which also brought forth a more pronounced spatial interaction. The process was very complex; we may, however, distinguish between *combinations* of existing types and elements on the one hand, and the *synthetic development* of new types on the other.[2] As the process does not follow a simple chronological path, we will treat the basic intentions regardless of their being earlier or later in time. The names of the same architects will therefore appear in more than one place. More attention is given to the Italian scene, and in particular to Borromini and Guarini, who more than anyone else arrived at fertile results. The contributions of other countries will be treated more briefly in the last chapter of this book, except for some particularly important French examples. We will also discuss the problem of the Protestant church. During the seventeenth century, in fact, Protestant church architecture was still hesitant. The development of a particular typology belongs to the eighteenth century,[3] although some of the basic intentions may be traced back to the seventeenth century, or even before.

The Traditional Themes and Their Transformations

The longitudinal plan of the church of *Il Gesù* exercised an immediate influence. As a typical example, we may mention the *Madonna dei Monti* in Rome by Giacomo della Porta (1580). The plan shows a conventional longitudinal disposition with dome and transept. A strong wish for spatial integration, however, is present. The nave is wide and short (three bays only), the transept is shallow and the dome dominates the moment one enters.

The resulting unitary space is circumscribed by a continuous cornice that runs unbroken around the whole space.[4] The façade represents a further development of the theme introduced in Il Gesù. The ensemble is simplified, but the articulation has the same purpose: the accentuation of the center of the façade, i.e. the longitudinal axis of the church as a whole. All the details contribute to this effect: the blank lateral bays which are defined by a half pilaster towards the inside, the increase in plastic decoration towards the middle, the break in the entablature, and the interruption in the central bay of the string-course running under the capitals. The façade, thus, becomes a large "gate," and the interior space of the church interacts with the urban environment. As a whole, the Madonna dei Monti is a very subtle work which has so far been given too little attention. Within the limits of the architectural language used during the last decades of the sixteenth century, it represents an accomplished combination of longitudinal and centralized plan, and a convincing relationship between interior space and exterior plastic form. This synthesis does not bring about a weakening of the two traditional aspects so that they approach each other, but strengthens them individually. The longitudinal axis dominates the movement already before we enter the church, not because the building has been made longer, but because all the elements of the composition—space as well as masses—are understood as a function of the axis. At the same time, however, the effect of the dome is enhanced; to understand this one might compare it with the small domes of Quattrocento churches. The Madonna dei Monti thus consists of three strongly emphasized elements: the "gate," the "path" and the "goal," architecturally concretized by the façade, the nave and the dome. All Mannerist ambiguities and conflicts have disappeared; the three elements "collaborate," at the same time as they are strengthened individually. Giacomo della Porta has created a work which better than most others expresses the basic intentions of Early Baroque architecture: persuasive emphasis and formal integration.

During the following decades, a considerable number of churches of the same type were built in Rome.[5] The most important with regard to size and architectural quality is *S. Andrea della Valle*, initiated in 1591 by Giacomo della Porta and completed in 1608-23 by Carlo Maderno.[6] The façade was added 1656-65 by Carlo Rainaldi. The plan of S. Andrea della Valle in general resembles that of Il Gesù. There is, however, one important difference: the lateral chapels accompanying the nave are more shallow and considerably higher. A tendency towards increased spatial integration is present. Another innovation is the strong vertical integration by means of bundles of pilasters whose movement breaks through the entire entablature and continues in broad transverse ribs. The strong and repeated horizontals, however, secure a coherent space definition. The general effect is skeletal; the vigorous primary system seems to be immersed in an open space which is not given *a priori* as in Renaissance architecture, but comes into being through the movement of the plastic system and the light it allows through. As an organism, S. Andrea della Valle may be considered less advanced than the Madonna dei Monti; it still comprises, for instance,

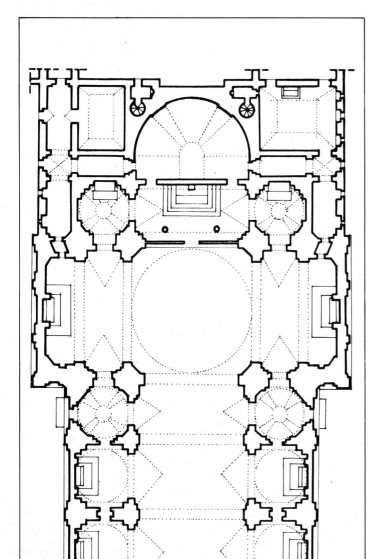

75. Giacomo della Porta, Carlo
Maderno, Rome, S. Andrea della
Valle, plan (D.A.U.).

76. Rome, S. Andrea della Valle.

four small secondary domes surrounding the main center, a remnant from
additive Renaissance grouping. This is probably due to the fact that S. Andrea is a very large church. Innovations are more easily carried out in smaller buildings, also for technical reasons. But with regard to articulation, S.
Andrea represents a great step forward towards Baroque continuity and
plasticity.[7] This also holds true for the façade originally planned by Maderno, where coupled half-columns and columns create a certain rhetoric emphasis. A general vertical continuity is present, which is carried on in the
dome.[8] The façade, built by Rainaldi, is fairly faithful to the model, but
the verticality is strengthened by more breaks in the entablature as well as
the cornice of the crowning pediment.[9]

The basic problems of the Early Baroque longitudinal church are not
exhausted, however, without mentioning the completion of St. Peter's by
Maderno (1607-12). The centralized plan of Michelangelo had been subject to severe criticism on functional grounds. In 1595 Mucante wrote:
"The new church of St. Peter's is really unsuited for the celebration of
Mass; it was not constructed according to ecclesiastical discipline; the
church will therefore never become apt for celebrating any sort of holy
functions decently and conveniently."[10] Michelangelo's project also did
not incorporate the necessary secondary spaces, such as chapels, sacristy,
narthex and, above all, benediction loggia. After Camillo Borghese had
been elected Pope in 1605 as Paul V, he attempted to correct these shortcomings. In 1607 a competition was held between the leading Roman
architects. Carlo Maderno was chosen, and on July 15, 1608, the foundation stone for his new façade was put *in opera*. In 1611 the Papal blessing
was given for the first time from the new benediction loggia, in 1615 the
vault of the nave was finished and in 1626 the nave was consecrated. The
nave and façade by Maderno are probably the most discussed and criticized works in the history of architecture. Le Corbusier wrote: "The
whole design (of Michelangelo) would have risen as a single mass, unique
and entire. The eye would have taken it in as one thing. Michelangelo completed the apses and the drum of the dome. The rest fell into barbarian
hands; all was spoilt. Mankind lost one of the highest works of human intelligence... The façade is beautiful in itself, but bears no relation to the
Dome. The real aim of the building was the Dome: it has been hidden! The
dome was in a proper relation to the apses: they have been hidden. The
portico was a solid mass: it has become merely a front."[11] This statement
well illustrates the problem Maderno had to face and the intentions of Early Baroque architecture. Le Corbusier evidently understands the project
of Michelangelo as it was intended: "a single mass, unique and entire, "
that is, a "thing" complete in itself, a symbolic *a priori* form without any direct and immediate relation to the urban environment and to the beholder. By adding the functionally determined nave and façade, Maderno
made the church become "...the instrument of a mass cult, with a propa-
gandistic purpose, but founded on the ideological premise that the com-

◁ 77. Rome, St. Peter's, central nave.

78. Paris, Val-de-Grâce,
(contemporary print).
79. François Mansart, Paris,
Val-de-Grâce, plan.

munity of the faithful, or rather, the Christian ecumene constitutes the very body of the Church, and is not just a spectator but also minister of its rites. Maderno's long nave undoubtedly destroys the dramatic unity of Michelangelo's single, tormented mass, but it also extends the basilica in terms of urban space, and thus develops the monument's urbanistic function..."[12] We thus understand that the introduction of a longitudinal axis was an essential demand of the Counter-Reformatory epoch to make the church become an active participant in its spatial environment, thereby expressing the role of the Church in the world. The formal unity of St. Peter's as it stands today, therefore, only becomes manifest if we intend *this* meaning, rather than the ideal Renaissance concept intended in the statement of Le Corbusier. Paradoxically we may also say that the plan of Michelangelo facilitated the addition of a nave which would not have been the case if the project of Bramante had been carried out with all its secondary spaces. The centralized organism planned by Bramante is characterized by an additive growth in *all* directions; and that is probably the reason why he and his followers never seem to have settled the question of the functionally necessary nave.[13] When Michelangelo cut away the secondary spaces, a *concentration* was achieved which could be used as the goal of a longitudinal movement. With much ability, Maderno made the addition, repeating the interior articulation of Bramante and the exterior system of Michelangelo without any break. The aisles, however, are entirely his intention. They are characterized as a succession of strongly plastic and somewhat pompous *aediculae*, creating a rhetoric and persuasive effect. The façade is derived from Michelangelo's system, but the giant order shows a characteristic increasing plasticity towards the middle. A "normal" two-story basilica façade would have hidden what is still visible of the dome.[14] The planned campanili should have connected the excessive length we perceive today.[15]

We have so far described the development of the Early Baroque longitudinal church. It is characterized by an increasing emphasis on the movement in depth as well as the vertical axis of the dome. The two aspects are well *composed* in the best examples, but do not fuse to form any new synthetic form. The façades are always faithful to the traditional two-story scheme[16] introduced by Alberti in S. Maria Novella, but the single parts lose their independence in favor of a general accentuation of the central axis, namely the "entrance." For this purpose, an increase in plasticity towards the middle became normal.

The scheme was repeated throughout the seventeenth century, also outside Italy. As an important example, we may mention the church of *Val-de-Grâce* in Paris by François Mansart (1645).[17] The plan shows a nave consisting of three bays like the Roman churches discussed above, and a concluding dome surrounded by four secondary chapels. These chapels, however, are not connected to the nave and the transept as usual, but open directly into the crossing along the diagonal axes. To make this possible,

the piers carrying the dome have been considerably widened. As a result, the dome is increased in size and importance, an effect furthermore strengthened by the use of apses rather than transept and choir. With this solution, Mansart took an important step towards the plans of the centralized longitudinal churches of the Late Baroque. His wide piers, in fact, became most usual in the eighteenth-century churches of Central Europe.[18] The façade follows the Roman models, but a portico with free-standing columns and a triangular pediment introduces a certain "classical" note.

During the last decades of the sixteenth century and the first of the seventeenth, a considerable number of smaller centralized structures were built, and a new characteristic type of plan appeared: the longitudinal oval. The longitudinal oval represents the most obvious synthesis of longitudinality and centralization, and therefore satisfied the basic intentions of the period, practical as well as symbolic. It is not, however, very well suited for large buildings, also because of the technical problem of constructing a dome over a large oval space. Vignola was the first to build oval churches; in S. Andrea in Via Flaminia (1550), a rectangular space is covered by an oval dome, and in S. Anna dei Palafrenieri (1572) the whole space has become oval. The architect of Il Gesù thus created another prototype which became very important for the whole Baroque development.[19]

The pupils of Vignola, Francesco da Volterra, Vitozzi and Mascherino, made designs for oval churches, and the oval appeared over and over again as a basic form or a constituent element during the seventeenth and eighteenth centuries. In Rome the most important example from the early phase is *S. Giacomo degli Incurabili*, planned by Volterra in 1590 and finished by Maderno 1595-1600. Exceptionally large is the oval pilgrimage church of *Vicoforte* near Mondovì in Piedmont by Vitozzi (1595-96).[20] Being a complete and "special" shape, the oval offers few possibilities of variation. In seventeenth-century architecture, therefore, the oval was often used as a point of departure for more complex organisms, in particular by Borromini. The longitudinal oval is one of the basic Baroque forms, because of its unification of movement and concentration, of linearity and radiation. Its clear but irrational character was well suited for serving the expressive purpose of the Roman Church.

During the whole epoch, however, we also find centralized chapels based on more conventional models such as the square, the circle or the octagon. An increasing desire for persuasive decoration and articulation is evident already in the *Cappella Paolina* in S. Maria Maggiore by Flaminio Ponzio (1605-11) and the *Cappella Salviati* in S. Gregorio al Celio (1600) by Volterra and Maderno. In the latter, full columns are placed in the corners to receive the thrust of the pendentives. The real motivation, however, is obviously a wish for a richer, more plastic articulation. Among the later centralized chapels we may single out the splendid *Cappella Lan-*

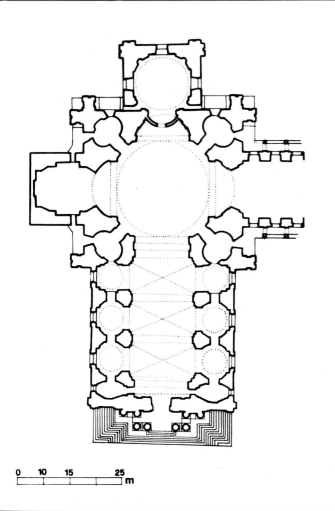

```
0    10    15        25
|____|____|_____| m
```

cellotti in S. Giovanni in Laterano by Giovanni Antonio de Rossi (c. 1675).[21] The chapel is formed by the interpenetration of a cylinder and a hemisphere. The dome becomes thus what is known as a "Bohemian cap." A slight axial direction is created by a shallow recess for the altar. Diagonally placed three-quarter columns, which carry a strongly projecting piece of entablature, give a pronounced vertical direction which continues in ribs ending in the ring of the lantern. This structure is accentuated by splendid stucco work, contrasting thus with the plain surfaces of the "filled-in" walls. The total organism is perceived as a vertically unified baldachin enclosed by secondary walls, a solution which was to have the greatest importance for the ecclesiastical architecture of the eighteenth century in Central Europe.

Few of the medium-size structures with a normal centralized plan built in or near Rome during the seventeenth century are as original as the Cappella Lancellotti. Bernini's *Assunta* in Ariccia (1662-64) is obviously derived from the Pantheon. The simple and regular interior, however, is transformed into a Baroque "mystery in action" by the plastic decoration, as has been admirably demonstrated by Wittkower. "The church is dedicated to the Virgin and, according to the legend, rejoicing angels strew flowers on the day of her Assumption. The celestial messengers are seated under the "dome of heaven into which the ascending Virgin will be received; the mystery is adumbrated in the Assumption painted on the wall behind the altar."[22] The exterior shows the church as part of a typically Baroque urban setting. It faces the Palazzo Savelli-Chigi and is flanked by symmetrical porticoes with coupled pilasters and straight entablatures. The great volume of the church is preceded by a more richly articulate portico with a triangular pediment and arches between single pilasters. A Baroque interplay of space and mass, reduced to its essentials, is thereby created. The church in Ariccia clearly represents the simple and great manner of the mature Bernini. His church in nearby Castel Gandolfo (1658-61) is based on a conventional Greek cross plan. It has, however, a strongly emphasized verticality, which is achieved by the general proportions as well as the articulation of the dome where ribs overlap a pattern of coffers. In its setting, the church introduces a vertical axis to the longitudinal urban space of Castel Gandolfo. The most important church by Bernini, however, is *S. Andrea al Quirinale* (1658-70).[23] Its plan is indeed original: a *transverse* oval, cut through by a "longitudinal" axis defined by a strongly marked entrance and a correspondingly important presbytery.[24] Instead of using the long axis of the oval for achieving an "easy" longitudinality, Bernini thus introduced a pronounced tension between the main directions, at least seemingly. A closer look at the plan shows that the spatial importance of the transverse axis has been neutralized by making it run against solid pilasters rather than into chapels. The movement is thus blocked up, and we experience two radiating "stars" that accompany the main movement from entrance to altar, rather than a conflict of direction. The analo-

69

gy with Piazza S. Pietro is obvious. The importance of the main axis is stressed by the columned aedicula in front of the altar recess. "And here, in the concave opening of the pediment, St. Andrew soars up to heaven on a cloud. All the lines of the architecture culminate in, and converge upon, this piece of sculpture. More arrestingly than in the other churches the beholder's attention is absorbed by the dramatic event, which owes its suggestive power to the way in which it dominates the severe lines of the architecture."[25] The relationship between outside and inside is also solved in a very original way. A small piazza is formed in front of the church by two quadrant walls which have the same diameter as the circles defining the interior space.[26] These walls are joined to the volume of the church where the great, flat aedicula façade is attached. The aedicula, thus, appears as a gate between two spaces which are variations on a common theme. The transition is enriched by a semicircular portico that projects from the façade into the piazza. S. Andrea al Quirinale demonstrates the possibilities of a Baroque transformation of a simple theme. It represents, however, a special solution rather than a contribution to the development of a new typology. Seen together, the churches of Bernini illustrate his preference for clearly expressed, elementary volumes. It is hardly any accident that the "classical" master among the architects of the Roman Baroque has given us designs for churches based on all the fundamental shapes of the epoch.[27] This general approach should come to exercise a strong influence elsewhere in Europe, in sacred as well as secular architecture.

Whereas the churches of Bernini show a traditional division between the dome and the space below by means of a continuous entablature, Carlo Rainaldi attempted a stronger vertical fusion in his circular church of *S. Maria dei Miracoli* at the Piazza del Popolo (1661-63). Here we find a drum that is treated as an ambiguous zone of transition, being penetrated by tall arches in the main axis. A certain longitudinality is thereby also created.

Among the more original solutions of the centralized church in Italian Baroque architecture, we may single out *SS. Trinità*, in Turin by Vitozzi (1598). Here a circular plan is divided into *three* sections, probably for symbolic reasons. The result is an evident break with the traditional, static character of centralized spaces. Similar symbolic plans are found in Baroque churches of Central Europe, especially in connection with the Trinity.[28]

The classical properties of the circular church were well suited as an expression of the basic intentions of French seventeenth century architecture. The *Church of the Visitation* in the Rue St. Antoine in Paris was built by François Mansart (1632-34) for the Filles de la Visitation de Ste. Marie.[29] It shows a normally disposed centralized plan with open chapels on the main axes and small closed ones on the diagonals. All the chapels have an oval shape, transverse to the axis. The way the larger chapels are joined to the main space is quite revolutionary: instead of being "added"

81. Giovanni Antonio de Rossi, Rome, S. Giovanni in Laterano, Cappella Lancellotti, detail of vault.

82. Gianlorenzo Bernini, Ariccia, S. Maria dell'Assunzione (engraving by Falda).

83. Ariccia, S. Maria dell'Assunzione, interior (engraving by Falda).

84. *Rome, S. Andrea al Quirinale, interior of dome.*

85. *Gianlorenzo Bernini, Rome, S. Andrea al Quirinale, diagram.*

86. *Rome, S. Andrea al Quirinale, plan (from De Logu).*

87. *Rome, S. Andrea al Quirinale, view of façade.*

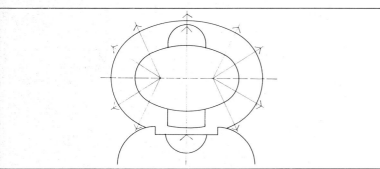

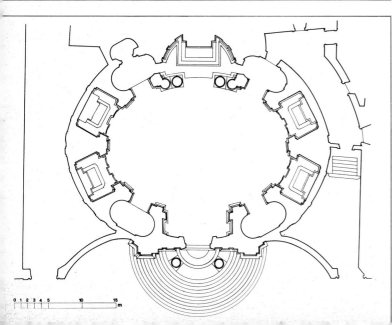

as complete volumes, they are interpenetrated by the circular space in such a way that they become incomplete. To our knowledge this is the first example of a true Baroque interpenetration of spaces.[30] The church also shows original features: the dome is cut off at a certain height, and another smaller dome is inserted below the lantern, so that increased verticality is thereby achieved. The façade is designed as a large arch, into which a smaller aedicula is inserted. The simple and unified scheme satisfies the basic intentions of the Baroque church façade, but contrasts with the complexity of contemporary Roman fronts. Only with Bernini's S. Andrea al Quirinale (1658) does Roman architecture arrive at a correspondingly synthetic solution.[31] The church of the Visitation exercised a strong influence, but the idea of spatial interpenetration was hardly understood before Guarini arrived in Paris in 1662. In fact, the first interpenetrations of spaces in the work of Guarini are found in Ste. Anne-la-Royale in Paris (1662-65).[32]

So far, we have discussed examples which do not represent any real attempts at the creation of new types. Before we arrive at the fundamental contribution of Borromini and Guarini, however, we must discuss some buildings containing ideas that introduce interesting new possibilities of a certain importance for later development. The first of these consists in strengthening the longitudinal axis of a centralized organism by joining together *two* domed spaces, whereby the first corresponds to the nave of the traditional longitudinal church. The idea goes back to the sixteenth century; as an example we may mention the Madonna di Campagna near Verona by Sanmicheli (1559-61),[33] where a presbytery with an irregular Greek cross plan is added to an octagonal "nave." The idea was taken up by Lorenzo Binago when building *S. Alessandro* in Milan (1602). Here the main church consists of a large five-dome group, resembling Bramante's plan for St. Peter's. To the east a smaller Greek cross with saucer dome has been added. The bay of transition between the main dome and the dome of the chancel is common to both Greek crosses, thereby creating a characteristic Baroque interlocking of spaces. A strong longitudinal movement results, but at the same time the center is emphasized by an increased diameter and by columns carrying the arches of the crossing.

A few years later we find the same basic idea in another Milanese church, the small *S. Giuseppe* by Francesco Maria Ricchino (1607). The main space here approaches an octagon, as the piers on the diagonal axes are considerably widened to receive niches and *coretti*. Also here the main space is distinguished by columns. The presbytery is joined to the octagon by means of a common Composite order as well as similar wall articulation. In genaral, S. Giuseppe represents a surprisingly mature example of a type that was to become very important during the eighteenth century in Central Europe.[34]

In Italy, the type culminated with Baldassare Longhena's *S. Maria della Salute* (1631-48). The church was erected as an *ex-voto* after the plague in

1630, and as such naturally received a centralized plan.[35] To the main octagon, however, is added a domed sanctuary which has apses on the transverse axis and an opening screened by the altar in the middle, resembling thus the centralized part of Palladio's Redentore. It is to Wittkower's merit to have pointed out the architectural qualities of S. Maria della Salute.[36] He thus indicates the Late Antique and Byzantine ancestry of the octagon surrounded by an ambulatory, and the Early Renaissance and Palladian models for Longhena's articulation by means of grey stone for the structural parts and whitewash for the walls and fillings. "In contrast, however, to Florentine procedure, where color invariably sustains a coherent metrical system, Longhena's color scheme is not logical; color for him was an optical device which enabled him to support or suppress elements of the composition, thereby directing the beholder's vision."[37] In fact, the two main spaces of S. Maria della Salute are joined together by optical means. "In spite of the Renaissance-like isolation of spatial entities and in spite of the carefully calculated centralization of the octagon, there is a scenic progression along the longitudinal axis... In S. Maria della Salute, scenery appears behind scenery-like wings on the stage. Instead of inviting the eye—as the Roman Baroque architects did—to glide along the walls and savour a spatial continuum, Longhena constantly determines the vistas across the spaces."[38] This particular Venetian character is also evident in the exterior where two closely spaced domes form a picturesque group. The façade shows the adaptation of Palladio's giant order to a centralized building. Its members (giant and small) repeat those of the interior, so that a coherence based on similar *motives* is created. The large central arch also repeats those inside, at the same time as it gives emphasis to the longitudinal axis. S. Maria della Salute thus illustrates how basic Baroque intentions could be given a convincing "regional" interpretation.

Another regional interpretation of the same theme is offered by the main work among French centrally-planned churches, the *Dôme des Invalides* by Jules Hardouin-Mansart (1680-1707). As the church was built on the main axis of Libéral Bruant's *Hôtel des Invalides* (1670-77), in communication with Bruant's chapel, a pronounced longitudinal movement was needed. Louis XIV, however, also wanted a worthy monument crowned by a dome. Hardouin-Mansart made a design based on the classical sixteenth-century scheme as developed by Michelangelo for St. Peter's. The centralized plan well fitted the building task in question, as well as the site between the two wings of the Hôtel. To this traditional scheme Hardouin-Mansart added a spacious sanctuary, of approximately oval shape, which opens on the pre-existent chapel. The needed longitudinal axis was thereby created.[39] Hardouin-Mansart's solution, however, also differs from the plan of Michelangelo in other important respects. The arms of the main Greek cross are relatively shorter, so that the whole building appears as a square block. The secondary domes at the corners are joined to the main circular space by means of openings in the diagonals, a solution

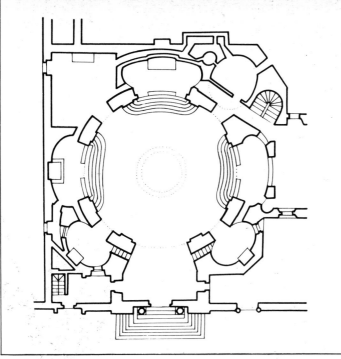

89. *François Mansart, Paris, Church of the Visitation, plan (from Blunt).*
90. *Paris, Church of the Visitation.*

91. *Paris, Church of the Visitation, interior looking upward.*

derived from F. Mansart's Val-de-Grâce. As a result, an increased integration of mass and space is achieved. This integration mainly serves a strongly developed verticality, which is accentuated by the employment of cut-off domes. The exterior shows a corresponding articulation. The façade, thus, builds up plastically towards the center, and the dome obtains increased height through the introduction of an attic between the drum and the cupola proper. Strong buttresses are placed in the diagonals (where, in fact, they are structurally most correct), depriving the dome of its usual "static" and "perfect" appearance. This strong vertical dynamism culminates in a diagonally oriented lantern crowned by a pointed *flèche*. Without doubt, the Invalides is one of the most convincing of the centralized structures of the Baroque epoch, forming a singular synthesis of classical architecture and Gothic verticalism defined by curved arcades and four smaller domed structures. A splendid *place* in front of the church, was unfortunately never built.

Another possibility for creating an elongated centralized plan consists in making the arms of a Greek cross differ (without, naturally, arriving at a Latin cross). This theme was taken up by Rosato Rosati in *S. Carlo ai Cantinari* in Rome (1612-20).[40] By shortening the transept and by adding an extra bay and an apse, Rosati gave the Greek cross a pronounced longitudinal direction. The effect is emphasized by the *oval* chapels between the arms which have their main opening on the nave. At the same time, however, the center is given primary importance by the tall dome which rests on strongly projecting piers, while the arms are articulated by flat pilasters. The piers are covered with similar pilasters, whose yellow color creates an impression of a continuous system surrounding the entire space. The space thus has a unified and total character, in spite of the longitudinal axis. As a whole, S. Carlo ai Catinari is a convincing example of Early Baroque planning. The church had a certain influence on following developments. The church of the *Sorbonne* in Paris by Lemercier (1636-42) is evidently derived from S. Carlo ai Catinari.[41] At the Sorbonne, the main axis is longer, and the lateral chapels have two openings on the nave, indicating rudimentary aisles. A certain basilical effect is thus present. The dome, however, is placed in the very center, making the lateral façade symmetrical, as necessitated by its forming a wall to the courtyard of the University.

The theme of the elongated Greek cross found its most convincing High Baroque interpretation in *SS. Luca e Martina* by Pietro da Cortona (1635-50).[42] In 1634, Cortona was elected *principe* of the Accademia di San Luca, and the following year he started the rebuilding of the church of the academy. As his point of departure, he took a circular plan resembling the designs of Michelangelo for S. Giovanni dei Fiorentini. Allowing the dome to rest on full columns, Cortona emphasized the central space, and he made the chapels behind appear as a continuous ambulatory by means of radially disposed dividing walls. A strong wish for plastic and spatial inte-

92. *Lorenzo Binago, Milan,*
S. Alessandro, plan (from Baroni).
93. *Francesco Maria Ricchino,*
Milan, S. Giuseppe, plan.

94. *Milan, S. Giuseppe, interior.*

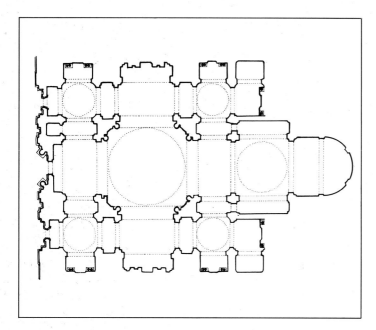

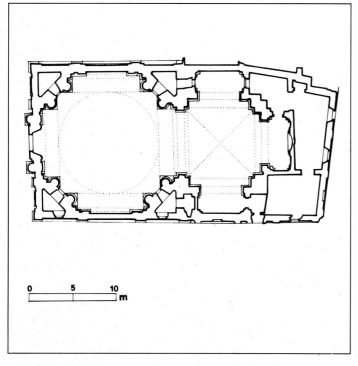

```
0        5        10
|__|__|__|__|__|__|
                m
```

gration is evident. During the process of planning, Cortona obviously tried to arrive at a truly continuous space boundary. The result was a Greek cross plan with slightly elongated main axis; here the bays, in fact, are wider than those of the transept, and the apses are semicircular (those of the transept are flattened). The differences, however, are hardly perceptible in the interior. The space has a singularly unified character determined by the rich plastic modelling of the bounding wall and the lack of coloristic differentiation. The basic element employed is the Ionic column, which is varied to express differences of structure and enclosure. Full columns appear under the dome and in the apses, indicating a primary structure. Between the columns the wall protrudes or recedes. The intermediary bays, thus, are given a certain transverse direction by projecting pilasters which define the connection with secondary volumes behind, while the apses are completely "open": the members appear as a skeleton covered on the outside by a thin secondary wall-surface. The same "openness" is found in the semidomes above the apses, as well as in the main dome where a pattern of vibrating, star-like coffers appears behind the structural ribs. A singular, meaningful interaction of mass and space is achieved. This also holds true for the organic relationship between interior and exterior. The exterior walls, in fact, are complementary to the spaces inside, the famous curved façade indicating the apse behind.[43] The main order employed also repeats the members of the interior, and the columns flanking the entrance express the openness of the apse. In all façades the curved central part appears between orthogonally disposed piers which serve as a determined frame of reference to the dynamism of the main volume. The building, in fact, seems to be *alive*; like a muscular body it breathes, contracts and expands. The elongation of the main axis and the flattened transept are not fixed forms, but seem to be the result of a process happening here and now. SS. Luca e Martina, thus, better than any other example expresses a Baroque *transformation* of a traditional theme. Rather than making the church a stage for persuasive naturalistic decoration (Bernini), Cortona gave "presence" to the building itself, and thereby realized a truly Baroque architecture.[44]

In the examples mentioned above, a centralized plan was taken as the point of departure, and a more or less pronounced longitudinal axis was introduced by various procedures. If we begin with a longitudinal organism, the problem of introducing a center arises. The simplest solution consists in the establishment of a transverse axis of symmetry. The first notable attempt at creating such a "biaxial" organism is due to Girolamo Rainaldi. In 1620 he built the interesting church of *S. Teresa* in Caprarola.[45] The organism is a simple rectangular volume covered by a large barrel vault. In both ends we find the same motif: a shallow recess divided into three openings by freestanding pillars. The wider opening in the middle is arched, whereas, the lateral openings have a straight architrave. This architrave continues into the central opening where it stops against the blank outer

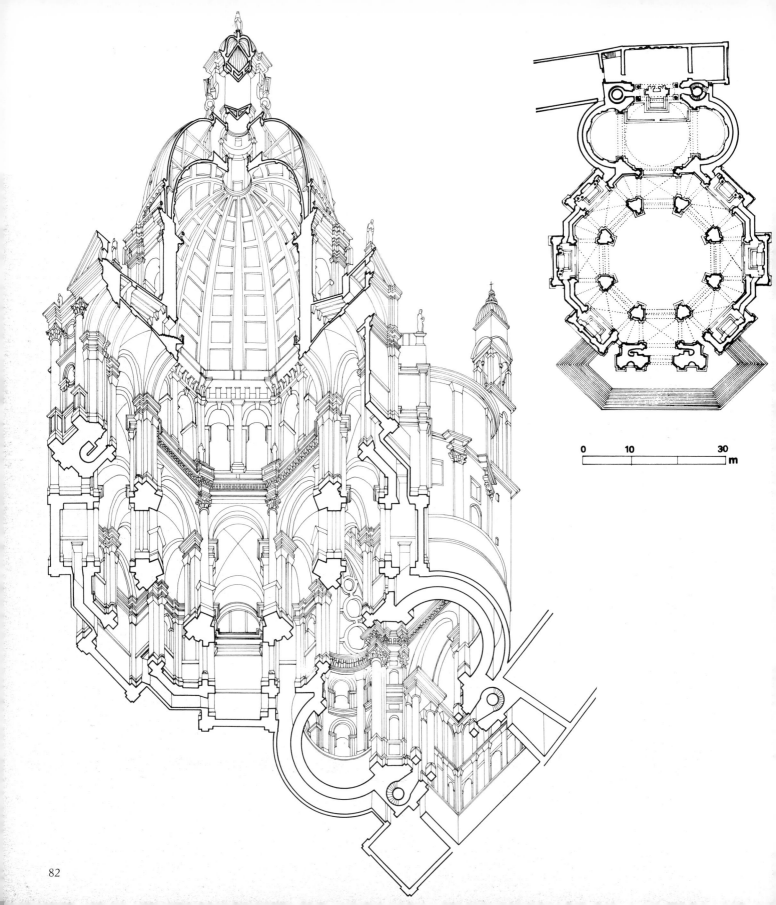

82

95. Venice, S. Maria della Salute,
axonometric projection (D.A.U.).
96. Baldassare Longhena, Venice,
S. Maria della Salute, plan (from
L'Architettura, I, 1955).

97. Venice, S. Maria della Salute,
cornice.

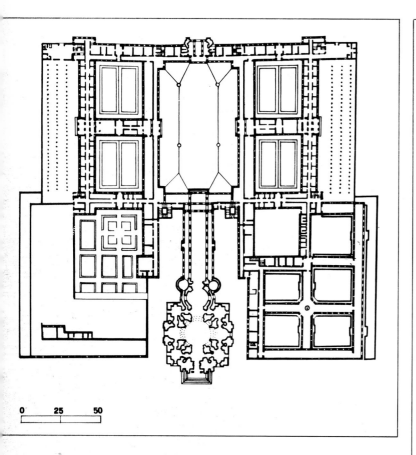

98. Libéral Bruant, Jules Hardouin-
Mansart, Paris, Hôtel des Invalides,
plan (from Luçart).

99. Jules Hardouin-Mansart, Paris,
Dôme des Invalides, axonometric
projection (D.A.U.).

100. Jules Hardouin-Mansart, Paris,
Dôme des Invalides (contemporary
engraving).

0   25   50

101. *Paris, Dôme des Invalides, interior.*

102. *Paris, Dôme des Invalides, exterior.*

103. Rosato Rosati, Rome,
S. Carlo ai Catinari, plan.
104. Rome, S. Carlo ai Catinari,
façade.

105. Rome, S. Carlo ai Catinari,
interior of dome.

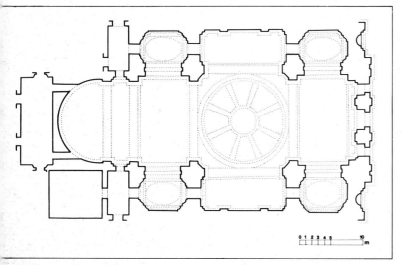

wall, which is thereby characterized as a secondary "filling." Exactly the same motif is repeated in the center of the lateral walls, as these are longer, extra bays are left at the ends, which are conveniently used for the confessionals. These bays are integrated in the system by means of the architraves mentioned above. A strong centralization is therefore created, while at the same time the space retains its general longitudinality. Its unified character is stressed by a strong cornice circumscribing the whole interior. Girolamo Rainaldi is generally considered a minor architect, but in S. Teresa he created an original combination of longitudinal and centralized schemes. The articulation also prefigures ideas that were to flourish during the eighteenth century, in particular the characterization of the main axes as connections between interior and exterior. In fact, arches break through the main architrave and frieze here, and where they meet the outer wall, blank filled-in surfaces express the "openness" of the scheme.[46] We should also mention the general transparency of the inner system.

In the small church of *S. Maria in Publicolis* in Rome by Giovanni Antonio de Rossi (1640-43), we find a bi-axial nave, but here a presbytery covered by a transverse oval saucer dome on pendentives has been added. The bi-axial type is thereby fused with the scheme based on a succession of two centralized units, a very fertile idea which was of considerable importance in future developments. In Rome we find, in fact, two important churches that have domes added to centralized naves: S. Maria in Campitelli by Carlo Rainaldi (1656-65) and S. Maria Maddalena, which was designed by Giovanni Antonio de Rossi the year of his death (1695). Both churches count among the masterpieces of Roman Baroque architecture.

For *S. Maria in Campitelli*, Carlo Rainaldi took a longitudinal oval to which he joined a circular presbytery covered by a dome with lantern. The scheme is fairly normal but the articulation is very interesting indeed, showing a further development of ideas from his father's S. Teresa as well as from Cortona's S. Luca. All the spatial elements are defined by an entablature (oval or circular) carried on columns. At the same time, the columns flank the main axes along which the spatial elements are organized. The elements touch each other and form an "open" system, which has been used to give emphasis to the longitudinal axis, where a full circle has been added. Similar circles are indicated on the transverse axis, but here they are reduced to lens-shaped chapels. Only on the diagonals of the main space are solid piers introduced, which contain secondary openings and *coretti*. The solution has fundamental properties in common with the spatial system of Kilian Ignaz Dientzenhofer, and may be considered one of the most advanced conceptions of the Roman Baroque.[47] The façade is also interesting, showing a two-story screen of columns in front of the wall, indicating thus the general spatial transparency of the project that comes surprisingly close to the *Zweischaligkeit* of eighteenth-century church architecture in Central Europe. In the execution, however, Rainaldi changed the project. All the essential parts of the first project are pres-

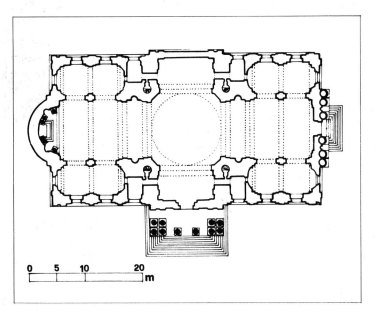

ent, but the oval nave has been transformed into a bi-axial hall. The longitudinal movement in depth is thereby considerably strengthened and, in fact, the interior appears as a succession of monumental aediculae, and the theme of the aedicula also characterizes the highly rhetoric façade. The change in approach was probably determined by the particular building task in question. S. Maria in Campitelli was erected after the pestilence as a votive church and particularly to house a miraculous Madonna. The architectural space, therefore, is *directed* on the image in the apse, and the column is used as a symbol of faith, rather than as a structural member. "One must not talk, therefore, of an optical illusion, or of the representation of an imaginary space... but of the visualization of content or ideological meanings intimately connected with the practical and devotional needs of the building. For the first time the Baroque concept of art as persuasion was applied to architecture... With its architectural forms it succeeds in producing a collective emotion... If examined from the point of view of the 'movement of the affections,' we find this is the pathos Campitelli's church arouses."[48] The church of Rainaldi, thus, does not represent a theoretical ideal, but concretizes an individual situation.

S. Maria Maddalena by De Rossi[49] represents a worthy conclusion to the ecclesiastical architecture of the Roman Seicento.[50] In the plan all the traditional types are brought together. We find the Latin cross interpreted as a succession of two centralized organisms, and the first of these may be understood as a bi-axial nave as well as a radiating oval. The essential contribution consists of the spatially unified form of the nave, which is based on a continuous succession of narrow and wide bays. The first and the last are parallel to the longitudinal axis, while the three middle ones define a transverse dilatation of the space. The transverse axis, however, has only secondary importance as it ends in narrow bays containing confessionals. The "diagonal" directions are emphasized by tall arches which break through the entablature. By means of this wall-articulation, De Rossi managed to give the nave spatial independence, at the same time as it is organically integrated with the domed unit behind. The building fulfills the double task of being a Congregational church and a sanctuary for a venerated Madonna.

In the works discussed above, we have seen how the traditional longitudinal and centralized schemes were transformed during the seventeenth century to meet the Baroque desire for a synthesis of center and extension, integrating thereby the building in a general, ideologically founded context. A real systematization, however, was rarely achieved by the architects we have mentioned so far. With "systematization" we mainly imply a method of spatial organization that allows for the solution of individual tasks within the general aim of formal integration and persuasive accentuation. The works discussed above represent modifications or combinations of traditional types and elements. Some of these combinations, however, were to have a particular importance for the sacred architecture

109. Pietro da Cortona, Rome, SS. Luca e Martina, plan (from De Logu).

110. Rome, SS. Luca e Martina, diagram.

111. Rome, SS. Luca e Martina.

112. Rome, SS. Luca e Martina, dome.

113. Rome, SS. Luca e Martina, interior, view of dome and vaults.

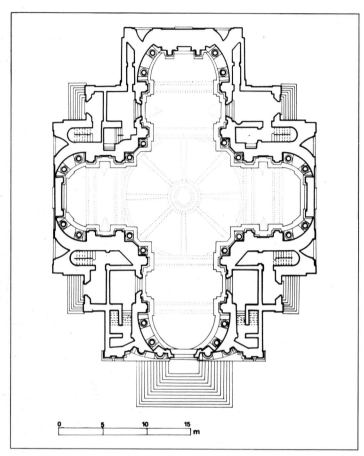

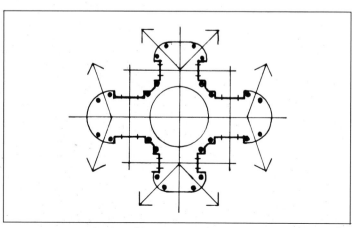

114. *Girolamo Rainaldi,*
Caprarola, S. Teresa, plan.

115. *Carlo Rainaldi, Rome,*
S. Maria in Campitelli, plan of
the first oval project.

116. *Rome, S. Maria in Campitelli,*
diagram of oval project.

117. *Rome, S. Maria in Campitelli,*
plan (from Ferraironi).

118. *Rome, S. Maria in Campitelli,*
exterior.

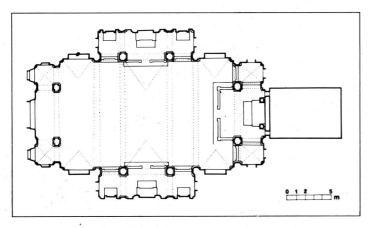

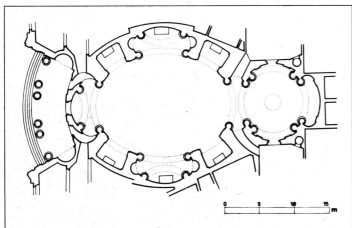

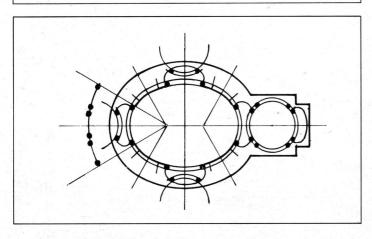

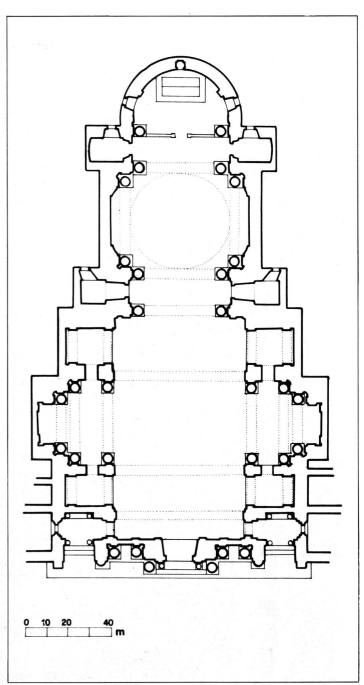

119. Rome, S. Maria in Campitelli,
view of interior towards the altar.

of the eighteenth century, such as the introduction of a "rotunda" at the very center of a longitudinal organism (S. Carlo ai Catinari, etc.), the spatial activation of the diagonal axes in a domed crossing (Val-de-Grâce), the succession of two centralized units (S. Giuseppe, Milan), and the centralization of a longitudinal space by means of bi-axiality (S. Teresa, Caprarola). We also find some attempts at developing a more general method of spatial organization mainly in the interpenetrations of François Mansart, and the suggestion of an "open" grouping in the first project for Rainaldi's S. Maria in Campitelli. Of a more general importance was the Baroque classicism of Bernini that aimed at the definition of one dominant character, and the organic dynamism and complementary relationship between inside and outside of Pietro da Cortona.

Towards Synthesis and Systematization
In the works of Francesco Borromini, we encounter a fundamentally new approach to the problem of architectural space. Until then, space had been understood as an abstract relationship between the plastic members that were the real constituent elements of the architectural form, although their location was determined by meaningful types of spatial distribution. The need for a new expressive intensity during the Early Baroque phase, therefore, was mainly satisfied by a richer instrumentation: doubling of columns, combination of pilaster and column, giant order, strong and repeated breaks of entablature and pediment, etc., or by an expressive, illusional decoration. Borromini broke with this tradition and introduced *space* as the constituent element of architecture. For Borromini space was something concrete that could be shaped and directed, rather than an abstract relationship between plastic anthropomorphic forms. He thereby concretized the philosophical concept of *res extensa*. "He is not content with an empirical verification of the psychological values of distance, proximity, or of the interference of compositional elements; he proclaims the need for a method that will permit the architect to work on space with the same energy with which Renaissance architects dealt with volume and linear structures by applying the canons of classical proportions..."[51] The spaces of Borromini are complex totalities that are given *a priori* as indivisible figures. With all the means at his disposal, he tried to stress this character, above all by the continuity of the bounding walls. The novelty of Borromini's approach must have been felt by contemporaries, as is testified by the long description of his church of S. Carlo alle Quattro Fontane by Juan de S. Bonaventura. Talking about the visitors who came every day to see the church, he says: "...and when they are in the church, they do nothing but look above and all around them, for everything therein is so disposed that one thing leads to another..."[52] By the architects of his time, however, Borromini was considered a *stravagante*, who created bizarre and chimeric forms. Today it is not easy to understand this negative judgement. Borromini's architecture in many respects seems more

simple and logical than the often rhetorical works of his contemporaries, and we also react positively to his sincere use of building techniques and materials. Considering the classical tradition, however, Borromini's architecture was indeed revolutionary, and opened up new fertile possibilities for the future.

The first work to display Borromini's basic intentions is the *Cappella del SS. Sacramento* in S. Paolo fuori le Mura. The chapel was built by Maderno in 1629 shortly before his death. His relative Borromini was assisting, and we have reason to believe that Borromini had a decisive influence on the solution.[53] The simple rectangular space has rounded corners and a system of regularly placed pilasters that continue through the entablature by means of slight breaks to form flat ribs that transform the vault into a skeletal "net." There are no pilasters in the corners, the concave shape of which are carried on in the vault to create a strong vertical continuity and to give a certain diagonal orientation to the space, an orientation that is concretized by diagonal vault-ribs. The solution comes surprisingly close to the system of Borromini's *Cappella dei Re Magi* in the Palazzo di Propaganda Fide built after 1660, and generally considered his architectural testament. The essential innovations of the SS. Sacramento chapel are the uniform and perfectly continuous wall articulation and the vertical integration. The space, therefore, is defined as an indivisible whole, a character that is furthermore stressed by the "centralization" created by the diagonal directions mentioned above.

In Borromini's first independent commission, the convent and church of *S. Carlo alle Quattro Fontane* or "S. Carlino" (project 1634), we find the same intentions carried through with several variations. The cloister (1635-36) is circumscribed by a continuous system of rhythmically placed columns. *There are no corners* in the usual sense of the term, as the narrow bay of the wall system is carried on in convex curves where the corners would have been. With the simplest possible means, thus, Borromini has succeeded in creating a unified spatial "element." In the convent we find several rooms where the same intentions are illustrated, such as the old refectory (today the sacristy) where the cornice is concavely curved over a normal corner. The transition between the two elements is taken care of by a cherub with outstretched wings, a motif used over and over again by Borromini to solve this type of problem. In the church (1638), the basic themes are repeated to form a much richer variation, illustrating Borromini's interest in giving each individual space an appropriate psychological character. Virtually no plan has been analyzed more often than that of S. Carlino, and the smallness of the space is often illustrated by saying that it could be housed within one of the piers carrying the dome of St. Peter's. What is usually pointed out when describing S. Carlino is the geometrical complexity of the plan. We do not have to repeat here the authoritative analysis of Portoghesi,[54] but wish to point out the basic novelty of the design by quoting Wittkower: It is important to realize that in S.

Carlo and in later buildings, Borromini based his designs on geometric units. By abnegating the classical principle of planning in terms of modules, i.e. in terms of the multiplication and division of a basic arithmetical unit (usually the diameter of the column), Borromini renounced a central position of anthropomorphic architecture. In order to make clearer the difference of procedure, one might state, perhaps too pointedly, that in the one case the overall plan and its divisions are evolved by adding module to module, and in the other by dividing a coherent geometric configuration into geometric sub-units."[55] In other words, the space is intended as a *unit*, which may be articulated but not decomposed into *independent* elements. The spatial unit of S. Carlino, however, is rather complex. The point of departure was the traditional longitudinal oval, as well as a stretched Greek cross scheme. These are *fused* rather than combined, creating as a result a bi-axial organism. All of these schemes are "hidden" within a continuous, undulating boundary defined by a rhythmically disposed "colonnade" which is continued all around the space (a variation on the theme of the cloister) and an unbroken entablature. The movement of the entablature, however, expresses the traditional schemes which are contained in the solution. The bays on the diagonal axes, thus, are defined as piers carrying the arches of the dome. They are pierced by doors leading into secondary spaces, such as the Cappella della Madonna which is characterized as a hexagonal unit circumscribed by a continuous boundary. The piers in the diagonals are the structural elements within the whole, having a straight entablature and columns with capitals different from the others. They have, in fact, active standing volutes, whereas the other "secondary" columns have normal Composite capitals. We see, thus, how Borromini differentiates the function of the single elements within the unitary whole. We could also add that the piers are joined to the flanking bays by means of continuous mouldings over the door and under the arches of the main axes. These bays, however, also relate to the apses, so that an ambiguous interpenetration of wall units is attained, contributing further to the general spatial integration.

Vertically, S. Carlino shows a more conventional organization based on arches and a ring carrying an oval dome. The vertical continuity is less strong than the accomplished coherence of the horizontal movement. We may, however, point out the interesting transformation which occurs when we proceed from the complex circumference of the main space to the oval dome. In the lantern a new transformation takes place, making the eight sides become convex as if they were pressed inwards by the space outside. The spaces of Borromini, thus, are not static units, but flexible entities that may take part in a more comprehensive spatial interaction. This flexibility is expressed by means of the movement of the bounding surface. Rather than dividing space according to relations such as "before-behind," Borromini's undulating wall makes the space expand and contract, creating changing "outside-inside" relationships. The Baroque

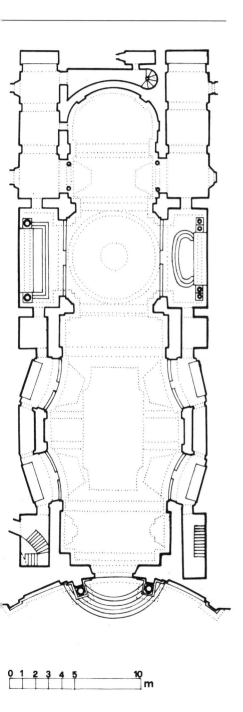

120. Giovanni Antonio de Rossi,
Rome, S. Maria Maddalena, plan.
121. Rome, Santa Maria
Maddalena, interior.

0 1 2 3 4 5   10
m

122. *Francesco Borromini, Rome, S. Carlo alle Quattro Fontane, plan (from Portoghesi, 1967).*

123. *Rome, S. Carlo alle Quattro Fontane, reconstruction of the aspect of the convent before Borromini's work (from Portoghesi, 1967).*

124. *Rome, S. Carlo alle Quattro Fontane, axonometric drawing (from Portoghesi, 1967).*

XIII. *Rome, St. Peter's, interior.*

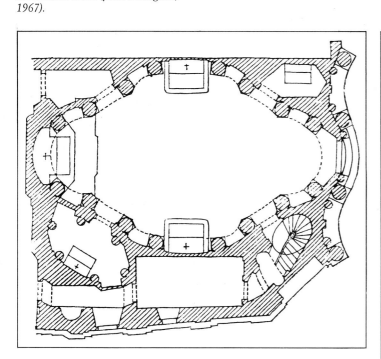

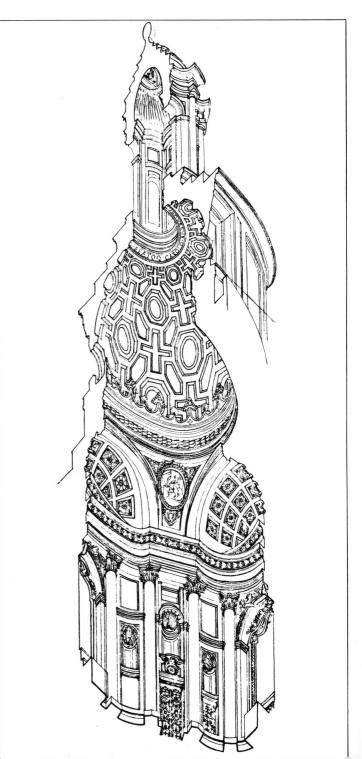

XIV. Rome, S. Carlo alle Quattro
Fontane, dome.

125. Rome, S. Carlo alle Quattro
Fontane, plan of convent and
church (Vienna, Graphische
Sammlung Albertina).

126. Rome, S. Carlo alle Quattro   ▷
Fontane, façade.
127. Rome, S. Carlo alle Quattro
Fontane, detail of façade.

128. Rome, S. Carlo alle Quattro
Fontane, view from the lantern.

129. Rome, S. Carlo alle Quattro
Fontane, detail of façade.

130. Rome, S. Carlo alle Quattro
Fontane, interior.

XV. Rome, S. Ivo alla Sapienza, dome.

XVI. Turin, SS. Sindone, dome.

131. Rome, S. Carlo alle Quattro
Fontane, interior, view of the
dome.

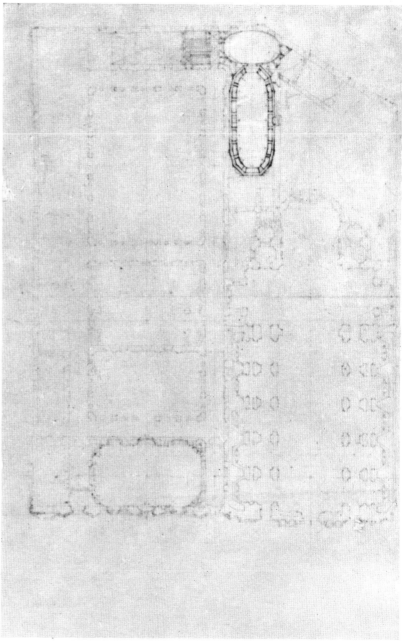

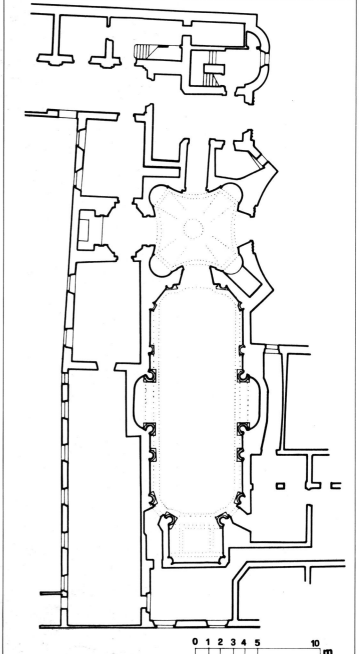

137. Rome, Oratorio dei Filippini,
axonometric drawing (from
Portoghesi, 1967).

138. Rome, Oratorio dei Filippini,
plan (from Portoghesi, 1967).

139. Francesco Borromini, Rome,
S. Maria dei Sette Dolori, plan.

0 1 2 3 4 5   10
                    m

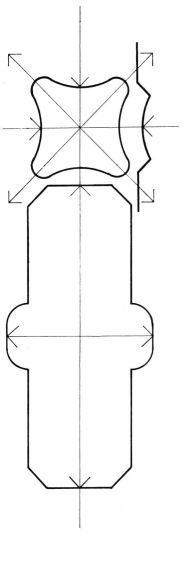

140. *Rome, S. Maria dei Sette Dolori, diagram.*

141, 142. *Rome, S. Maria dei Sette Dolori, detail of exterior and interior.*

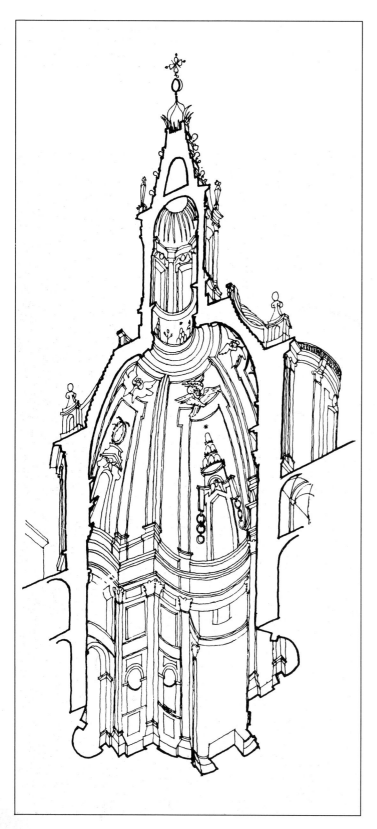

143. *Francesco Borromini, Rome, S. Ivo alla Sapienza, axonometric drawing (from Portoghesi, 1967).*

desire for spatial interaction, therefore, is fulfilled in a new general way, and as a consequence Borromini was able to do away with the particular episodes of interaction cultivated by his contemporaries. This variability in Borromini's form is also evident if we consider the façade of S. Carlino, added 1665-67. Its undulating movement may be understood as a result of the meeting of interior and exterior "forces": the expansive space inside and the directed movement of the street in front. At the same time, the façade varies the movement of the wall sections of the interior. The whole composition, thus, may be understood as variations on a "wall theme," which is a function of the basic space-dynamism introduced by Borromini.[56] And the façade prepares for the basic properties of the interior.

The next main work of Borromini, the *Casa e Oratorio dei Filippini* (1637), was a large commission that gave Borromini the occasion to plan an extensive group of different spaces. We need not describe here the complex history of the *casa*,[57] but should try to arrive at the basic intentions. The plan has a wonderful clarity, in spite of the problem of adapting to the existing Chiesa Nuova and its large sacristy. Taking functional demands as his brief, Borromini incorporated the sacristy between a *cortile* and a *giardino*, creating a succession of main spaces flanked by two long corridors. The *oratorio* proper should have concluded the succession towards the piazza in front of the church, as shown in one of Borromini's preliminary drawings.[58] Because of minor practical difficulties, the oratorio had to be moved out of the axis, introducing an irregularity in the plan. All the main spaces are treated as integrated spatial units defined by a continuous wall articulation and rounded corners. The oratorio, which represents a further development of the ideas from the Cappella del SS. Sacramento, has a bi-axial disposition, determined by the altar on the longitudinal axis and the planned entrance from outside on the transverse axis. The space, however, is unified by means of a continuous series of pilasters and by cut-off corners where the pilasters are placed diagonally.[59] The vault shows a complete net of interlacing ribs, and as a whole the system has a pronounced skeletal character. The central part of the façade, which should have corresponded to the oratorio proper, has a concave curvature. Borromini himself has given us the explanation: "… when designing this façade I had in mind the human body with arms outstretched, as if embracing all who entered there, which body with outstretched arms is divided into five parts, that is, the breast in the middle, and both arms in two parts each…"[60] The building, thus, should *receive* the visitor, in other words, interact with the urban space in front. In addition to this general property, the exterior shows an abundance of novel features. The pediments of the windows and doors introduce most of the synthetic forms that were to characterize the Late Baroque architecture of the eighteenth century, the main gable of the façade is a synthesis of triangle and segment, and above all, the main entablature is *continuously transformed* into the traditional scroll that links the wings and the main part of the façade. The principle of flexibility and

144. *S. Ivo alla Sapienza, elevation and section of dome and lantern (Vienna, Graphische Sammlung Albertina).*

145. *Francesco Borromini, Rome, Palazzo della Sapienza, plan with S. Ivo alla Sapienza and Biblioteca Alessandrina (Vienna, Graphische Sammlung Albertina).* ▷

metamorphosis is thereby applied to the single forms, making them subject to change according to their position in the totality. The building is also adapted to the urban spaces around by means of change of articulation and texture, although cut-off or rounded corners indicate that the building is a totality placed within a continuous exterior space.

In 1642 Borromini was asked to build a smaller, somewhat similar building, the convent for the *oblate agostiniane* with the church of *S. Maria dei Sette dolori.* As the work remained unfinished, we shall merely point out a few essential features. Spatially S. Maria dei Sette Dolori represents a first attempt at making several spaces *mutually interdependent.* To date, Borromini had used a rather conventional, additive procedure when grouping spaces. In S. Maria dei Sette Dolori the church, the vestibule and the space in front of the concave façade determine each other reciprocally. Where one contracts, the other expands and a pulsating effect results that changes space from being mere extension into an active "field" of forces.[61] This principle of *pulsating juxtaposition* was to have a fundamental importance for the further development of Baroque architecture. It must be distinguished from the principle of spatial interpenetration. Instead of penetrating into each other, the spatial elements expand and contract as if they were made of elastic material. The principle of pulsating juxtaposition also leads to a *complementary* relationship between interior and exterior. The interior of the church is bi-axially organized. In spite of its elongated shape, it has a fully unified character, due to the continuous colonnade defining the space, as well as the encircling entablature with rounded corners. The principle of metamorphosis is particularly evident, as the entablature without any break is transformed into an arch or a scroll according to the situation. Unfortunately the vault was completed later, and its inferior design hardly does justice to the magnificent space below.

In 1642, Borromini also initiated what is generally considered his principal *opus,* the church of *S. Ivo* in Rome's old University, the *Sapienza.* The situation here demanded a centralized structure inserted at the end of the existing courtyard.[62] Borromini, however, was not satisfied with adopting one of the traditional schemes, such as the octagon or the Greek cross, and invented instead one of the most original organisms in the entire history of architecture. S. Ivo indeed makes us remember his proud words: "I would not have joined this profession with the aim of being merely an imitator."[63] The plan of S. Ivo is developed around a hexagon, and shows an alternation of apses and recesses with a convex fond.[64] The complex shape resulting, however, is unified by a continuous wall articulation and an engirdling entablature. The six corners of the hexagon are characterized as being of primary structural importance, having double pilasters, while the apses and recesses have single ones. And, in fact, over these corners, ribs rise vertically to "carry" the ring of the lantern, while the other ribs only form large frames around the windows of the dome. Thus, again, we encounter the principle of differentiation and transformation within an inte-

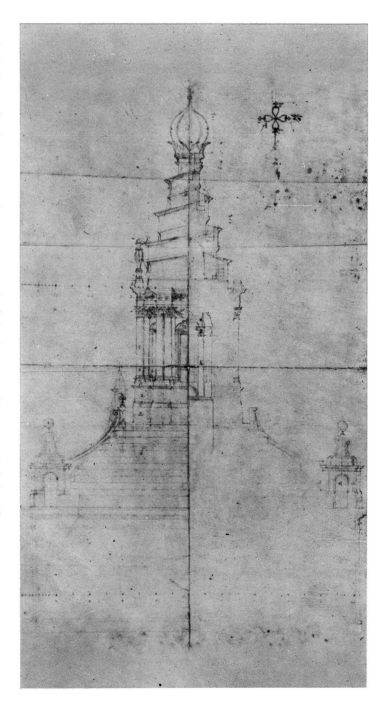

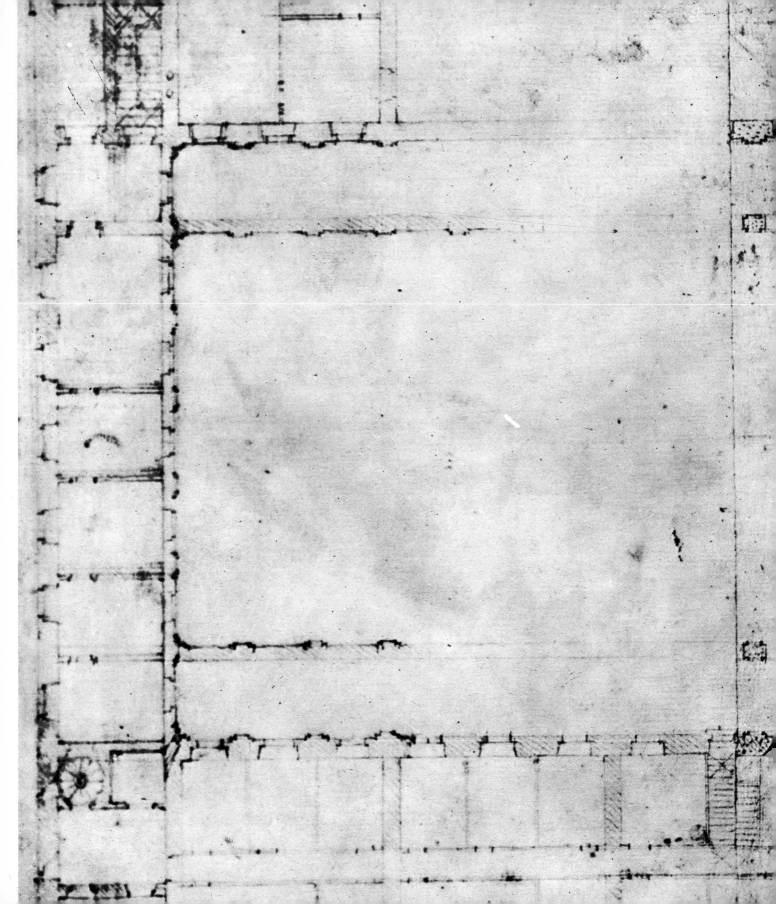

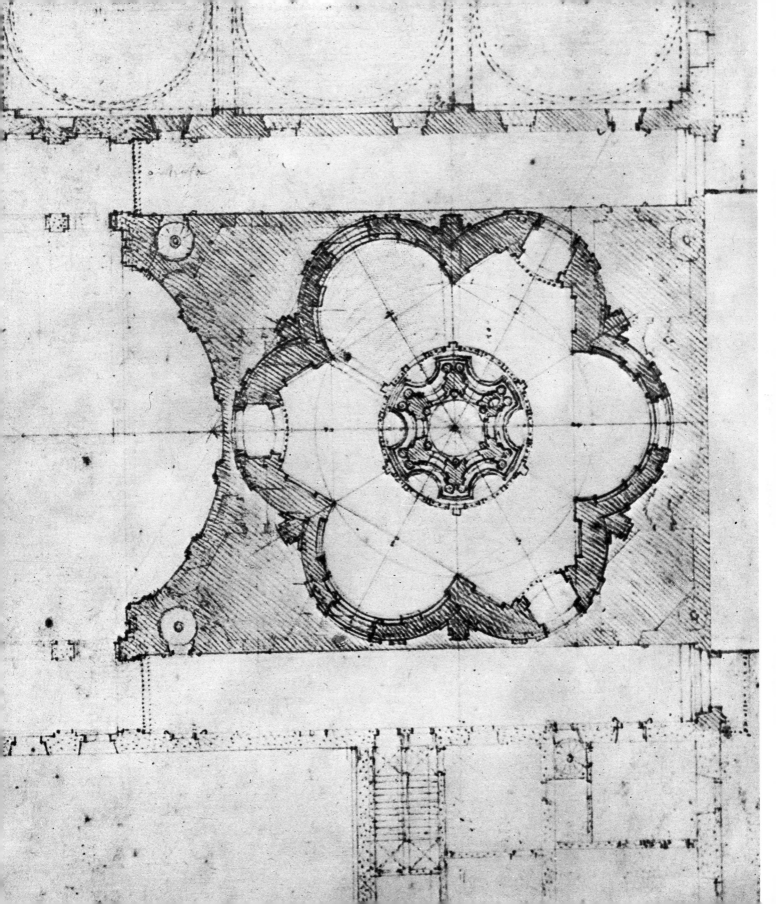

146. *Rome, S. Ivo alla Sapienza,*
view from court of the Palazzo
della Sapienza.

147. Rome, S. Ivo alla Sapienza, detail of dome.

grated totality. The basic invention of S. Ivo, however, is the idea of attaining vertical continuity by carrying the complex shape of the ground plan without interruption into the dome. The dome, therefore, has lost the traditional character of static enclosure. It seems rather to be undergoing a constant process of expansion and contraction, a process that gradually comes to rest towards the circular ring under the lantern. The inside of the lantern, however, has convex sides, and the vertical transformations introduced in S. Carlino have become part of a continuous form. Indeed, S. Ivo is one of the most unified, total spaces in the history of architecture, in spite of its rich and novel shape. The exterior is in general complementary to the interior space. The six "structural" corners appear in the drum as bundles of pilasters, while the walls between them have the character of expansive membranes, contrasting with the concave exedra below. The concave sides of the lantern form another contrast to the dome below and the spiral that ends the incredibly dynamic, vertical composition. More than any other work, S. Ivo must have inspired Borromini's contemporaries to consider him a "Gothic" architect. It is mainly a centralized organism, but being based on the triangle and the hexagon rather than the square or the circle, it has, none the less, a dynamic character that is never found in traditional centralized structures where one "side" corresponds to the opposite. S. Ivo also contains a slight longitudinal direction from the exedra in front of the entrance to the altar, a direction which Borromini orginally wanted to stress by means of an open screen of columns behind the altar, forming part of a circular space that interpenetrates with the main apse. Because of its very special solution, S. Ivo did not find any direct following, [65] and yet there is hardly any building that more convincingly expresses the basic intentions of Baroque architecture.

In a few other buildings and projects, Borromini had the occasion to give further evidence of his basic intentions. Most important is his last research into space, the *Cappella dei Re Magi* in the Palazzo di Propaganda Fide.[66] Again we find a bi-axially organized hall, with rounded corners and a skeletal system of pilasters and vault ribs. The walls have almost disappeared, and the lower part of the chapel actually opens onto recesses in such a way that the entire transparent structure seems immersed in space. The giant order of pilasters is connected with a net of diagonally disposed vault ribs creating a complete "Gothic" system. Its dynamic character is expressed in the swelling bases of the pilasters, and the strong vertical continuity. The main architrave and frieze are thus reduced to small fragments over the pilasters, separated by large windows. And still, horizontal coherence is secured by the cornice and a secondary architrave over the openings to the lateral recesses and the small presbytery. The Propaganda Fide chapel represents a magnificently clear synthesis of Borromini's basic intentions: longitudinality and centralization, horizontal and vertical continuity, uniformity of structure and spatial "openness."

All the churches and chapels discussed above are on a relatively mod-est scale. Borromini's only chance to design a large church came in 1646 when Pope Innocent X commissioned him for the restoration of the great Early Christian basilica of *S. Giovanni in Laterano*. The task, however, did not give Borromini much freedom. The structure of the old basilica was to be preserved, and the work had to be finished for the Holy Year in 1650. Borromini secured the endangered structure by encasing pairs of the existing columns inside broad pillars. The pillars he covered with a giant order of pilasters, rhythmically disposed to allow for arched openings to the aisles. Borromini intended to vault the nave, and to join the walls by diagonally disposed ribs, similar to those he introduced a few years later in

117

152. *Rome, S. Ivo alla Sapienza,*
view from the lantern.

153. Rome, Palazzo di Propaganda Fide, Cappella dei Re Magi, section (Vienna, Graphische Sammlung Albertina).

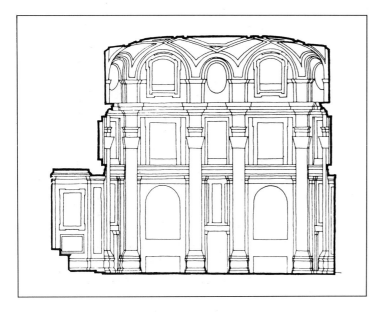

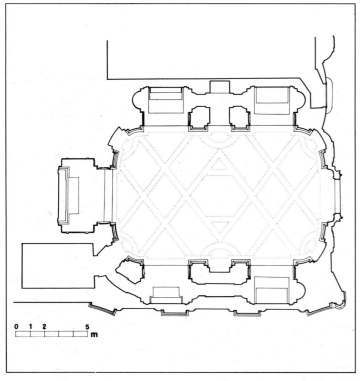

the Propaganda Fide chapel. The costly enterprise had to be abandoned, and the church still has its coffered ceiling from 1564.[67] Although the existing system is a fragment, S. Giovanni in Laterano possesses one of the most magnificent naves in existence. The solution of the entrance wall shows us that it was intended as a unified space with cut-off corners and a pronounced horizontal and vertical continuity. Between the main pillars, the system is characterized as being "open": the entablature is interrupted, and large openings merge with the spaces beyond. The aisles are intended as a succession of baldachins, namely small centralized units with concave corners that continue into the vaults. The larger vaults are "Bohemian caps." S. Giovanni gives us indications as to how Borromini would have tackled the problem of a large church. Remembering his ideas from S. Maria dei Sette Dolori, it is clear that he would have created a group of mutually interdependent spaces, employing the principle of pulsating juxtaposition. Guarini, in fact, made the idea a reality.

The contribution of Borromini did not lie in the development of new types. The concept of fixed types could not really satisfy the Baroque desire for immediacy and participation in particular contexts, namely the desire for creating extended, living organisms. He invented rather a *method* of handling space. By this means, he was able to solve the most varied tasks, creating buildings that are particular and general at the same time. Basically his method is founded on the principles of continuity, interdependence and variation. His spaces, therefore, have the character of a dynamic "field" determined by the interaction of outer and inner "forces," and the wall is the critical zone where these forces meet.[68] It is important to stress that the forces have psychological implications. The changing inside-outside relationships of Borromini, in fact, represent psychic processes,[69] just as his fusions and transformations of the traditional anthropomorphic forms (i.e. the classical orders) make the static psychological categories of the past break down. Bernini felt this when he called the works of Borromini "chimeric." Borromini thereby also intended a historical synthesis of a new kind. His wish for unity does not only concern the spatial, but also the temporal dimension. First of all, Borromini made *space* become the concrete constituent element of architectural design. While the space of Bernini is "a stage for a dramatic event expressed through sculpture," to use the words of Wittkower, Borromini made space itself become a living event, expressing the situation of man in the world.

In the works of Guarini, the general method proposed by Borromini is systematically worked out. The activity of Guarini well expresses the open world of the seventeenth century. Travelling for his Order, the Theatines, he planned or built churches in Messina, Paris, Turin, Nice, Vicenza, Prague, and Lisbon, as well as several smaller towns in Italy. Present in Rome from 1639 to 1647, he must have been deeply impressed by the construction of Borromini's first buildings, and he probably passed through Rome later during his travels. Unfortunately, most of the churches of

Guarini have disappeared. But we have his own treatise *Architettura Civile* which gives us information about his intentions and solutions,[70] as well as other literary and philosophical works that indicate the profound symbolism and complex synthesis of Guarini's architectural creations.[71] In our own context, we may characterize the importance of Guarini with the word *systematization*. Borromini's idea of making space the constituent element in architecture was taken over by Guarini who systematically composed with *cells* which were organized according to the principle of pulsating juxtaposition.[72] In fact, Guarini considered the pulsating, undulating movement the basic property of nature, saying: "The spontaneous action of dilation and contraction is not governed by any principle, but is present throughout the whole living being."[73] The Baroque ideas of extension and movement, thus, are given a new dynamic and vitalistic interpretation. Guarini's first major work, *S. Maria della Divina Provvidenza* in Lisbon (1656-59?),[74] is permeated by an undulating movement, which makes even the pilasters of the nave quiver. In its general disposition, the plan is conventional, showing a basilical layout with transept and apse. The longitudinal axis is defined by a succession of domes, but a wish for spatial fusion, however, is present which is without precedent in the history of architecture. The units constituting the nave and the transept grow together to form a continuous movement, and it is impossible to say where one unit stops and the other starts. The fusion is achieved by making the walls as well as the vault undulate, and by omitting all dividing lines. It is therefore not in context to talk about an "interpenetration" of spaces that presupposes a clearer definition of the participating cells.[75] The particular solution of the church corresponds to its dedication, as explained by Guidoni: "Divine Providence is the force that constitutes and informs the fragments of the world from within."[76] The church in Lisbon represents an early general approach to the problems. In his following projects, Guarini worked out more precise methodological tools.

This is particularly evident in the two solutions for a church *senza nome*, which develops the ideas from S. Maria della Divina Provvidenza. The project is a fascinating study of the problems of spatial interpenetration and pulsating juxtaposition. The aisles are composed according to the latter principle, whereas the nave, the crossing, the transept (right half) and the apse interpenetrate. The aisle of the right half interpenetrates with the units of the nave, and its cells are complete, regular elements. The right half also shows a full complementary relationship between interior and exterior. In fact, it has a higher degree of organic coherence than the left half. More than any other project of the seventeenth century, Guarini's church "without a name" demonstrates how a large church could be constructed following the principles hinted at by Borromini.[77]

Instead of employing interpenetration and pulsating juxtaposition to solve certain "critical" transitions within the building, Guarini develops the entire organism on the basis of these principles. He is therefore the cre-

158. Rome, Palazzo di Propaganda
Fide, Cappella dei Re Magi,
interior.

159. Francesco Borromini,
S. Giovanni in Laterano, section,
Cod. Vat. Lat. 11257 (Rome,
Biblioteca Apostolica Vaticana).

160. S. Giovanni in Laterano,
project for the wall of the central
nave, Cod. Vat. Lat. 11258 (Rome,
Biblioteca Apostolica Vaticana).

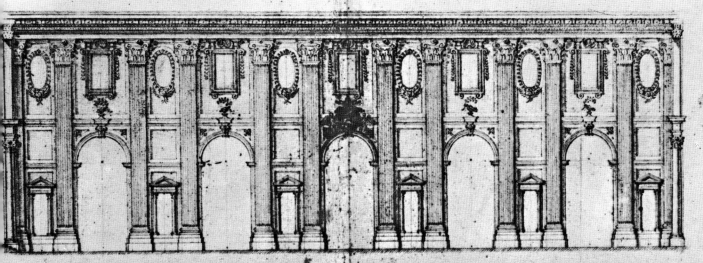

161. Rome, S. Giovanni in Laterano, interior, detail of central nave.

162. Rome, S. Giovanni in Laterano, interior, aisle.

163. Rome, S. Giovanni in Laterano, interior.

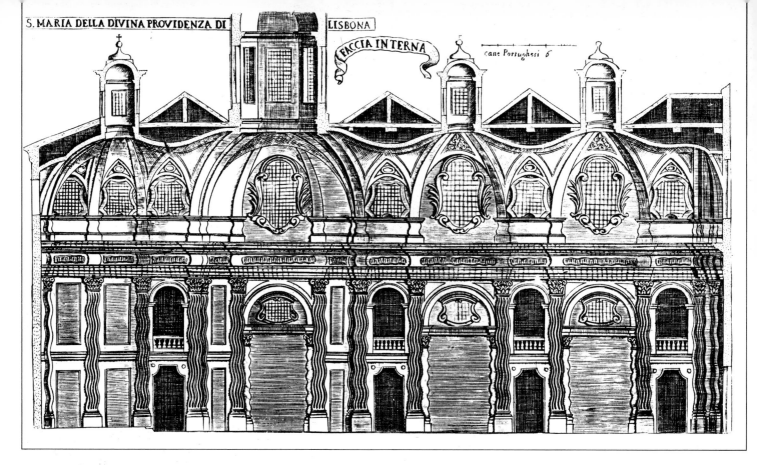

S. MARIA DELLA DIVINA PROVIDENZA DI LISBONA

FACCIA INTERNA

Cane Portughesi 6

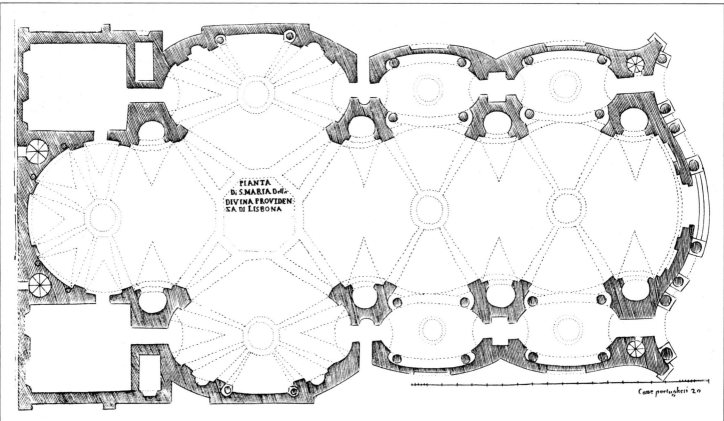

PIANTA
DI S. MARIA Della
DIVINA PROVIDEN
SA DI LISBONA

Cane portughesi 20

164. Guarino Guarini, Lisbon,
S. Maria della Divina Provvidenza,
section (from Architettura Civile,
Plate 18).

165. Guarino Guarini, Lisbon,
S. Maria della Divina Provvidenza,
plan (from Architettura Civile,
Plate 17).

166. Guarino Guarini, Messina,
Church of the Padri Somaschi,
section and plan (from Architettura
Civile, Plate 30).

ator of the first true groupings of spatial cells. Both principles express a desire for spatial continuity and "openness." In both cases, therefore, the
plastic form is reduced to a *skeleton* which is covered or filled in by secondary membranes, creating a complementary relationship between interior and exterior. Guarini's further works demonstrate how his method
could be applied to varying situations and tasks, generating solutions
which seem to represent particular cases of an open system of possibilities.

In Guarini's church for the *Padri Somaschi* in Messina (1660-62), we encounter another important aspect of his architectural invention: the vertically developed, centralized organism. The hexagonal plan shows an interesting grouping of interdependent cells (notice the triangular spaces at
the corners with internally convex sides). The pronounced skeletal effect
of columns and arches, reducing the wall to a mere skin separated from the
primary structure, makes the system appear as part of a general extension,
giving thereby a fundamentally new interpretation to the centralized
plan.[78] To this horizontal extension, a strongly emphasized vertical axis
forms an expressive contrast. It consists of a superposition of domical
structures. The first is based on a system of interlacing ribs, allowing for
large windows and a central opening on which a smaller, more conventional dome rests. The interlacing ribs are obviously related to Gothic
architecture as well as certain Hispano-Moresque domes.[79] The radically
new type of dome resulting became a major motif in Guarini's architecture. The domes, in fact, are his most evident inventions. "They seem the
result of a deep-rooted urge to replace the consistent sphere of the ancient
dome, the symbol of a finite dome of heaven, by the diaphanous dome
with its mysterious suggestion of infinity."[80] The domes of Guarini do not
assume the plastic continuity we have found in Borromini; they represent
rather a further development of the principle of vertical transformation.
After the first attempt in Lisbon, Guarini, in fact, suppressed plastic continuity, making his structures skeletal and diaphanous.

Ste. Anne-la-Royale in Paris (1662-65) shows a further development of
the vertical succession of spaces. A drum has been inserted, which consists
of a light inner screen of doubled columns and arches, and an outer wall
pierced by windows, namely a "double" wall of Gothic derivation. The
plan is based on an elongated Greek cross. The octagonal cells are articulated by diagonally oriented pilasters that combine with vault-ribs to
form a clearly defined skeletal system. Small walls are pierced by large
freely shaped windows, a solution found already in S. Maria della Divina
Provvidenza, obviously to express the structurally "open" character of the
bounding surface.

This vertically developed centralized scheme was repeated in several
other projects. Two of these were built, and have survived the vicissitudes
of history. After settling in Turin in 1666, Guarini was commissioned by
Charles Emmanuel II to finish the chapel of the *SS. Sindone*, or "Holy
Shroud," initiated by Amedeo di Castellamonte (1657).[81] The chapel was

129

167. *Guarino Guarini, Paris,*
Ste. Anne-la-Royale, section (from
Architettura Civile, Plate 11).

168. *Guarino Guarini, Paris,*
Ste. Anne-la-Royale, plan (from
Architettura Civile, Plate 9).

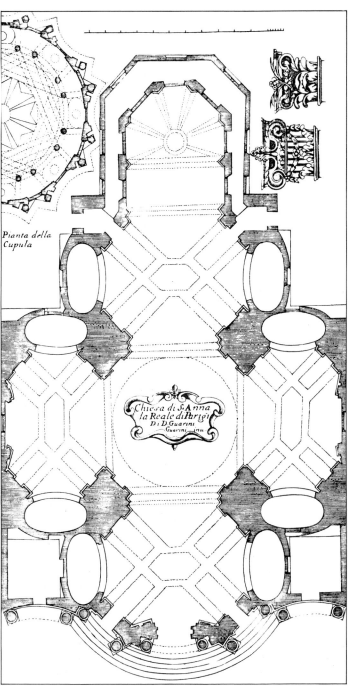

attached to the east end of the cathedral in close contact with the Ducal palace. A circular plan was adopted, but Guarini gave it a completely new interpretation. Having to incorporate three entrances, two from the church and one from the palace, he divided the circle into nine sections, spanning every two bays with a large arch, and using the remaining three for the entrances. As the two ramps leading up to the chapel from the cathedral meet the periphery of the chapel on an oblique angle, he introduced circular spaces of transition that interpenetrate the main space at the same time as they determine the convex shape of the stairs. A continuous movement is thereby created between the two levels. More than any other concept of Guarini, these circular vestibules testify to his skill in handling the problems of space, and to the possibility of solving difficult transitions by means of interpenetration.

The large arches already mentioned carry three pendentives instead of the usual four. They are pierced by large windows which are also found over the entrance bays, introducing thereby a regular rhythm of six elements, which from a puzzling counterpoint to the basic division of nine and three. The three arches carry the normal ring on which rests a most unusual dome. Its "drum" is pierced by large arched openings which form part of the inner shell of a "double" wall, related to the earlier solution in Ste. Anne-la-Royale. The arches of these windows carry a series of segmental ribs that are spanned from center to center of the six arches. Over the ribs a new series is spanned from center to center of the first ones, a procedure that is repeated six times, creating a system of thirty-six arched ribs that define six hexagons, three of which are turned 30° to the other three. Between the ribs, small windows are inserted, which make the whole structure diaphanous. The space ends with a large twelve-edged star, at the center of which the Holy Dove appears. The irrational character of the structure is stressed by the black marble that is repeated throughout. In fact, the chapel of SS. Sindone is one of the most mysterious and deeply stirring spaces ever created.[82]

Near the SS. Sindone, Guarini from 1668 onwards built the Theatine church of *S. Lorenzo*.[83] Here he was free to design a plan that may be considered his most fertile invention for the influence it was to have on the further development of ecclesiastical architecture. The centralized organism is developed around an octagonal space whose sides are convexly curved towards the inside. On the main axis a transverse oval presbytery is added, according to the principle of pulsating juxtaposition, so that a longitudinal axis is introduced. On the transverse axis similar spaces could have been added, but they have been omitted. The piers on the diagonals carrying the pendentives are transformed into a screen defining lens-shaped chapels. Their columns and arches correspond to those on the main axes, creating the effect of a continuous skeletal structure surrounding the space. The plan, thus, demonstrates the application of the principle of pulsating juxtaposition to a centralized grouping of cells. In principle, the sys-

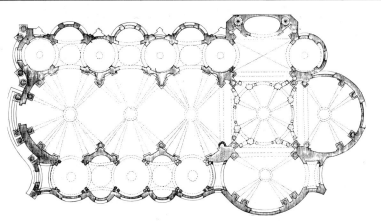

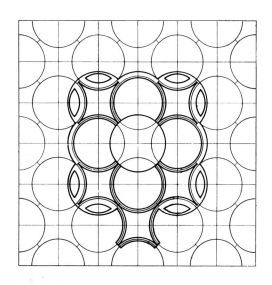

tem is "open," but Guarini has only used some of the possibilities for adding secondary spaces, thereby creating what has been called a "reduced centralized building."[84] The vertical development of the space is related to the solution planned for the church of the Padri Somaschi in Messina, with the difference that both domes are constructed by means of interlacing ribs.

After S. Lorenzo, Guarini planned four other centralized churches that were never built. *S. Gaetano* in Nizza (c. 1670) should have been a relatively small building on a pentagonal plan. The vertical direction is strongly emphasized and a certain desire for simplification is evident. Larger and more complex is the solution proposed for the pilgrimage church in *Oropa* (c. 1670?). A large octagonal space with externally convex sides is surrounded by a ring of oval chapels that are joined to the main space by means of transitory cells shaped like concave lenses. A pulsating juxtaposition is thus created. The skeletal structure is simplified, so that the curved wall-membranes gain in importance. These are pierced by large openings, and on the ground-floor all eight axes are characterized as "open" in view of the large aediculae. The Oropa church is one of Guarini's strongest and clearest designs, giving convincing emphasis to horizontal radiation as well as vertical growth.

Two other centralized projects illustrate a somewhat different approach. *S. Filippo* in Casale (1671) and *S. Gaetano* in Vicenza (1674) do not show the same vertical emphasis, but represent rather a further research into the problems of horizontal organization of cells. S. Filippo is developed over an infinitely extended grid of pulsating cells—circular and square with internally convex sides. The spatial system is defined by a transparent skeleton consisting of freestanding columns, which is closed in by a thin outer membrane. In the extended grid Guarini introduces a circular center defined by a dome which interpenetrates with the four surrounding circular cells. The combination of an infinitely extended pulsating pattern and an emphasized center makes S. Filippo one of the most radical and forward-looking of Guarini's designs.[85] S. Gaetano is related to S. Filippo. The circular cells on the main axes, however, have been substituted for ovals and the corners are closed off by the introduction of circles that interpenetrate with the ovals. (A similar "closure" of the form was achieved in S. Filippo by the addition of small lens-shaped recesses.) The vertical development shows a more varied transformation than the relatively simple dome of the former project. The central square with internally convex sides is thus transformed into a small circular ring on which a larger circular dome consisting of two shells is superimposed. These shells should have been decorated with illusional frescoes. A vertical contraction and expansion of space is thereby indicated that prefigures the "syncopated" spaces of Cristoph Dientzenhofer. In the projects for S. Filippo in Casale and S. Gaetano in Vicenza the general pulsating movement intended by Guarini is realized by the consequent use of "exact" methods

XVII. Turin, S. Lorenzo, dome.

XVIII. Turin, Immacolata
Concezione, dome.

of spatial articulation. During the last years of his activity, Guarini again applied his method to longitudinal organisms. The church of the *Immacolata Concezione* in Turin (1673-97) shows a succession of three centralized units; the first and the third are circular, whereas the middle one may be interpreted as a rectangle or a hexagon. The interpenetrations create a strong spatial integration.

In general, the scheme may be interpreted as a rectangle or a hexagon. The interpenetrations create a strong spatial integration. In general, the scheme may be characterized as bi-axial, but a marked longitudinal rhythm of expansions and contractions is present. The façade repeats the curvature of Borromini's S. Carlino, indicating an interaction between interior and exterior. The use of the classical orders is more conventional than in other works of Guarini, probably because the church was finished after his death.

In the project for *S. Maria Altoetting* in Prague (1679), the same scheme is varied and enriched. The first and the third unit have become transverse ovals that interpenetrate with a larger, irregular oval in the middle, and with lateral oval recesses. A presbytery has been joined in pulsating juxtaposition. All the spatial interrelations are clearly defined, and the solution as a whole represents a mature and convincing achievement.[86] The third of Guarini's late longitudinal projects. *S. Filippo* in Turin (1679), is also based on the succession of three large, centralized spaces. Symmetrically disposed narthex and presbytery create a certain biaxiality. All the main units are accompanied by secondary chapels. Interpenetrations or pulsating juxtapositions do not occur but the diagonally oriented structural members that are repeated throughout the whole organism create none the less a strong spatial integration. The skeletal effect is pronounced and the outer walls are perforated by large, freely-shaped windows. Those of the clerestory have a *casula*-like shape which appeared already in S. Maria della Divina Provvidenza.

We have demonstrated how Guarini's general approach could be applied to large and small centralized and longitudinal churches. His points of departure were the conventional types of the epoch, such as the Greek cross, the circle, the octagon, the Latin cross or the sequence of domed units. Instead of aiming at a *synthesis* of these schemes as attempted by Cortona and Borromini. Guarini defined the spatial elements or *cells* common to all the schemes, whereupon he *combined* them into a coherent whole by means of interpenetration and pulsating juxtaposition. He thus never arrived at "new" complex spaces like those of Borromini; his achievement consists rather in the development of "open" spatial *groups*. The method of Guarini has a certain mechanical character. It is an *ars combinatoria*, as envisaged by the philosophers of the Baroque Age. Like Borromini, Guarini also aimed at a combination of previously distinct characters and contents, of science and art, thought and feeling. In his *Architettura Civile*, he says: "Though it depends on Mathematics, Architecture is

174. *Guarino Guarini, Vicenza,*
S. Gaetano, plan and section (from
Architettura Civile, Plate 26).

175. *Guarino Guarini, Turin,*
S. Filippo Neri, section (from
Architettura Civile, Plate 16).

176. *Turin, S. Filippo Neri, plan*
(from Architettura Civile, Plate 14).

177. *Guarino Guarini, Turin,*
Cathedral, chapel of the SS.
Sindone, plan (from Architettura
Civile, Plate 2).

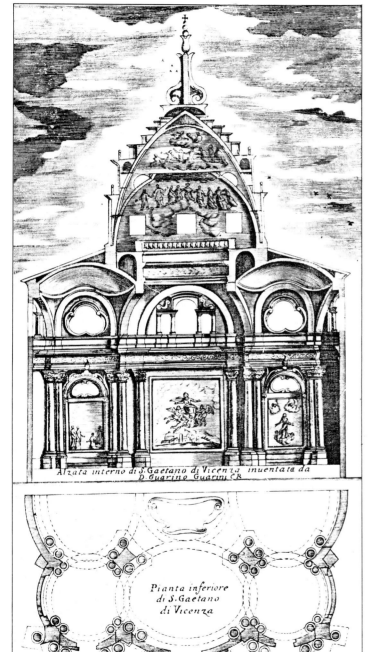

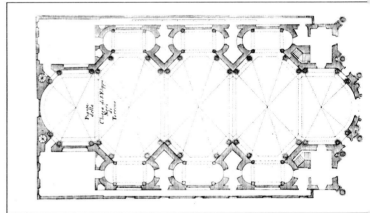

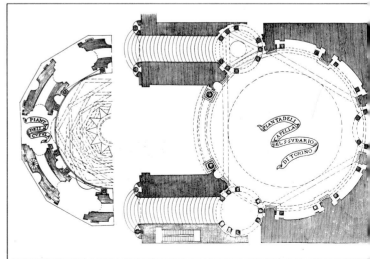

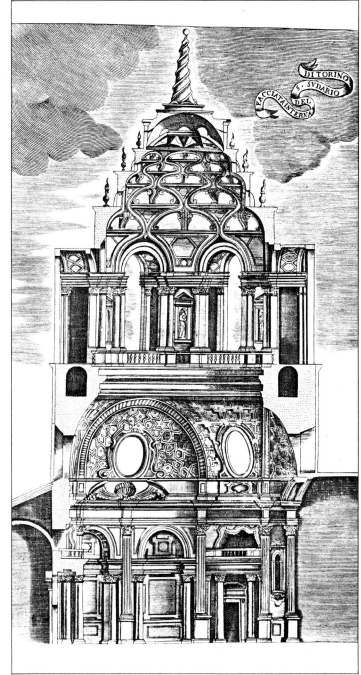

178. Turin, Cathedral, chapel of the SS. Sindone, axonometric drawing (D.A.U.).

179. Guarino Guarini, Turin, Cathedral, chapel of the SS. Sindone, section (from Architettura Civile, Plate 3).

180. *Guarino Guarini, Turin, Cathedral and chapel of the SS. Sindone, domes.*

181. *Turin, Cathedral, chapel of the SS. Sindone, interior of dome.*

182. *Guarino Guarini, Turin,
S. Lorenzo, section (from
Architettura Civile, Plate 6).*

183. *Turin, S. Lorenzo, plan
(from Architettura Civile, Plate 4).*

184. *Turin, S. Lorenzo, dome.*
185. *Turin, S. Lorenzo, perspective
reconstruction of Guarini's project
(from De Bernardi Ferrero).*

FACIES INTERNA

S. LAVRENTII TAVRINI

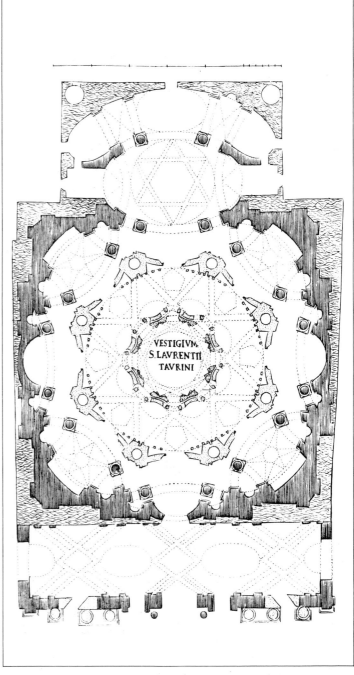

VESTIGIVM
S. LAVRENTII
TAVRINI

186. Turin, S. Lorenzo,
axonometric drawing (D.A.U.).

nonetheless an Art aiming to please, which does not wish to disgust feeling for reason's sake..."[87]

Conclusion

We have seen that the basic types of Baroque ecclesiastical architecture go back to Renaissance models, significantly modified during the second half of the sixteenth century. The longitudinal plan, thus, was centralized by means of bi-axial schemes or by the introduction of a pronounced center. The eventual mastering of this problem can be observed from the first attempt in S. Teresa in Caprarola to the accomplished solution in Guarini's project for S. Maria Altoetting in Prague. The centralized plan was elongated by "stretching" the basic form (longitudinal oval, elongated Greek cross), by adding a second centralized unit, or by "reducing" the transverse axis. Guarini's S. Lorenzo may be mentioned as an advanced example. In both cases the result may have a combinatory or a synthetic character. During the Early Baroque phase, a simple combination of types (i.e. large units) was normal, whereas Guarini arrived at much more flexible combinations by decomposing the types into general spatial elements or "cells." Borromini, on the other hand, aimed at a synthetic fusion that was scarcely attained by anybody else. In general, both the longitudinal and the vertical axes were emphasized; the first by transforming the façade into a dominant "gateway" to the *theatrum sacrum* of the interior, and the altar into another gate to the illusory space of a devotional image; the second by stretching the proportions or by indicating a vertical "growth" of superimposed elements, ending in another heavenly image. In both cases the church is more actively related to its environment. The "open" longitudinal axis makes it a part of urban space, while the vertical accentuation expresses its role as a "focus." Hardouin-Mansart's Invalides, with the planned *place* in front, is a characteristic example. A strong desire for general spatial integration is evident. This desire brought about the transformation of the building into a transparent skeleton, while the secondary spaces lost their independence and became part of an open system. Interpenetration, interdependence ("pulsating juxtaposition") and a complementary inside-outside relationship are characteristic means used to attain the intended integration. These means were invented during the High Baroque phase by architects such as François Mansart, Pietro da Cortona and Borromini, and were systematized during the second half of the seventeenth century by Guarini. The spatial continuity is often accompanied by plastic continuity, particularly in the works of Borromini.

Plastic continuity also means that previously distinct elements grow together to form new synthetic wholes expressing a fusion of traditional characters and contents. Forssman has pointed out that church interiors are usually Corinthian. He quotes Scamozzi, who says: "Indeed, of all the Orders none is so praiseworthy and beautiful as the Corinthian... The ancients used this Order to decorate the façades and interiors of their Tem-

ples, in their desire to show that only the noblest and excellent things are fitting for the Gods... We can equally say that this Order represents sincerity of soul, that which is due to the Majesty of the highest God."[88] During the Baroque Age, the richness of the Corinthian was used as a point of departure for making the church a comprehensive synthesis of symbolic forms, past and present, an *imago mundi* expressing the eternal and universal role of the Church.[89] The classical columns and the dome represent then the stability of the basic dogmas of the system, while the illusional decoration and dramatic use of light create a "frozen theater," aiming at persuasion and transportation. In general, sacred architecture "has the

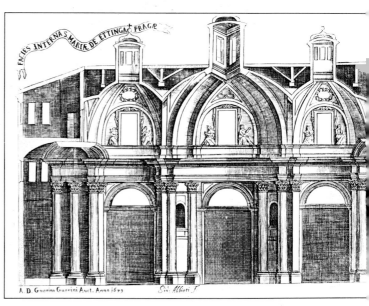

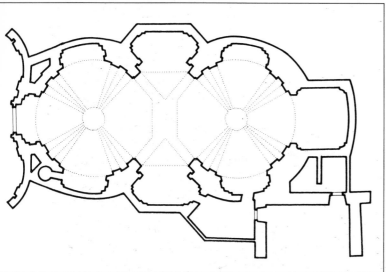

task of preparing the human soul for a life to be lived in a single dimension, in a space without terrestrial limitations."[90] Bernini is the great inventor of the Baroque *theatrum sacrum*. His *Cathedra Petri*[91] in St. Peter's furnishes a characteristic example. As an apotheosis of Popedom, it forms the natural "goal" for the longitudinal "path" of the main monument of the *Ecclesia Triumphans*. The persuasive dynamism of Bernini's architecture is primarily created by decoration, whereas Borromini and Guarini made architectural form itself the carrier of the expressive content. In the Late Baroque architecture of Central Europe, the two alternatives were fused into a last, exuberant synthesis.

Introduction

In the first chapter we reviewed basic seventeenth-century secular architectural types: the city-palace and the villa (château), also demonstrating that they tended towards a synthesis. The city-palace was opened up, as illustrated by the horseshoe-shape of the French hôtel, and the villa became typified, with the same scheme as its formal base. This development, however, was conditioned by local factors such as climate and life style, and therefore took a different course in different countries. In Italy the block-shaped palazzo has a tradition reaching back to Antiquity, and it is well adapted to the climatic conditions since it closes the sun out. Its massive character is also in agreement with the Italian feeling for plastic form and articulation. The palazzo therefore survived into the Baroque Age, although it underwent certain changes. In the North, the tradition was different. The more severe climate required more comfortable dwellings, which allowed the sun in wherever needed. Instead of closed blocks, we therefore find a joining together of outstretched wings and pavilions. The general layout was more flexible and more easily adaptable to the demands of comfortable living. During the seventeenth century French architecture, in fact, showed a growing concern for use and commodity, and the Italian palazzo was criticized for being "uncomfortable."[1] It is therefore convenient to divide our material into two sections, discussing first the Italian palazzo and subsequently the French château and hôtel. The contributions of other countries will be treated more briefly in the last chapter of the book.

A study of the palace has to include several of the general problems discussed in connection with the church, such as the organization of space, plastic integration, and the relation between the building and its environment. Functionally, however, the palace is much more complex than the church, and the general intentions are therefore expressed in a less direct way. A real spatial integration, for instance, is hardly possible, as the single units serve different purposes. The needs satisfied by the palace also comprise more variable factors than those of the church, giving the question of functional adaptation primary importance. The form of the Baroque palace, therefore, may be understood as the synthesis of the particular functional demands and the general wish for systematization of the epoch. It is commodious as well as representative and dominant.

The Italian Palazzo

We have already defined the palazzo as a "closed world." Basically it is a block centered on the courtyard (cortile), which is the real focus of the centripetal organism, and is therefore characterized as a space without directions enclosed by a uniform and continuous boundary.[2] The distribution of the secondary spaces, however, shows a certain differentiation, according to their practical functions and the surrounding urban spaces. There is usually *one* main entrance, allowing for efficient control and easy orien-

tation, and one main staircase is situated either to the right or the left when entering the cortile. A service entrance is usually found at the back, relating to the stables and coach-house. The ground-floor in general was used for services (and perhaps for shops on the primary street), whereas the main rooms are placed on the first floor or *piano nobile*. The rooms are linked together without much differentiation as to shape and size, although a main hall (salone) is usually present. A second floor with bedrooms and a mezzanine or attic with chambers for the servants completes the scheme. As to the use of the main rooms, it was decided by the furnishing of the occasional inhabitant, rather than by shape and position in relation to the urban surroundings. A surrounding gallery or loggia forms a functional and spatial transition between the courtyard and the rooms[3] and stresses the centripetal character of the organism.

The outside wall, on the contrary, formed a continuous, closed envelope. It was, however, differentiated *vertically* to express the changing internal spaces. The ground-floor, thus, was traditionally treated as a rusticated base that gave emphasis to the massive and solid character of the building. In the palaces of the Quattrocento the vertical articulation was taken care of through a decrease in the roughness of rustication from floor to floor, conserving thereby the massive unity of the block.[4] During the following century, an extensive experimentation with the classical orders took place, and they were used either to give dignity to the piano nobile or to create effects of complexity and contradiction.[5] In certain cases differentiation was achieved by the treatment of secondary elements, such as the window frames, rather than by the introduction of orders proper. This idea in particular was taken up by Antonio da Sangallo the Younger, who developed a type that is generally known as the Roman palazzo.[6] The type culminated with Sangallo's great *Palazzo Farnese* (1541-49). The organization of the Palazzo Farnese follows the general principles outlined above. The cortile shows a conventional superposition of orders,[7] whereas the façade is articulated by variations of the window frames and by groining. The succession of characters, however, is not the usual one, as the windows of the piano nobile are framed by small Composite columns, while the top floor is Ionic. The articulation, thus, is used to "express" the content of the building. The Palazzo Farnese represents the ideal of a complete, well-proportioned block that hardly interacts with its environment. Later, however, Michelangelo introduced a longitudinal axis which was intended to pass through the building, linking it spatially with the Villa Farnesina on the other side of the Tiber. He thus gave emphasis to the middle of the façade by a large window over the entrance, and he planned to open the back wall of the courtyard by introducing transparent loggias (1546-49). Michelangelo thereby invented two motifs that were to be of basic importance for the development of the Baroque palazzo.

During the following decades, the idea of lending support to the main axis of the palace was taken up by several architects. In the *Palazzo Caetani*

◁ *XIX. Rome, the Cathedra Petri.*

*XX. Chateau de Maisons, façade
toward the gardens.*

194. *Michelangelo, Rome, Palazzo Farnese, project for court (engraving by Ferrerio).*

195. *Martino Longhi the Elder, Flaminio Ponzio, Rome, Palazzo Borghese, court.*

196. *Giacomo della Porta, Rome, Palazzo Serlupi, façade (engraving by Falda).*

(Mattei-Negroni) in Rome (1564), the back wall of the cortile has been transformed into a one-story loggia connecting the two wings of a U-shaped building. Its Tuscan order forms a continuation of the articulation of the other sides of the cortile, so that an interesting counterpoint of enclosure and longitudinality is created. The solution may be due to Ammanati who had used a similar device in the cortile of the Palazzo Pitti in Florence (1560). The idea was taken over by Maderno in the adjoining *Palazzo Mattei* (project 1598 - finished 1618), which is generally considered the first truly Baroque palace in Rome. The direction of the cortile in the palazzo Mattei is furthermore strengthened by the absence of loggias on the sides. Here we find continuous walls whose articulation is limited to the development of a few of the horizontals from the loggias. The traditional centralized cortile has been abolished and a strong desire for movement in depth is evident.[8] Because of the corner position of the palace a transverse axis is introduced, directed on the splendid staircase, which is one of the most important innovations of Maderno. It has four flights instead of the usual two, and the landings are emphasized by saucer domes decorated with rich stuccoes. Spatially the solution points towards the great staircases of the High Baroque.

Less advanced, but more impressive, is the cortile of the *Palazzo Borghese*.[9] Here the three-story wings of the building are connected by an open two-story loggia, a solution attributed to Flaminio Ponzio (1607). The continuity around the courtyard is intact while at the same time the longitudinal movement is given direction by a fairly large garden. In the three examples mentioned, we cannot, however, talk about a real interaction between the building and the *urban* environment. The longitudinal axis implies an extension of the *private* domain, by spatially linking a garden to the cortile. But we may also talk about an "opening" on an illusive, ideal *landscape*.

As in the church, interaction with the urban domain takes the form of a new articulation of the façade, with a new emphasis on the central axis. The creator of the first Early Baroque church façades, Giacomo della Porta, also made the earliest attempts at solving the problems of the palace façade. By simply placing the windows closer together towards the middle, he managed to create an efficient concentration, and thereby abolished the static self-sufficiency of the traditional Roman palazzo. The unfinished *Palazzo Serlupi* (Crescenzi) of 1585 is a good example. He did not, however, arrive at any vertical integration of the façade, a problem that was tackled by Roman architects only much later.

All the examples mentioned above show a surprising lack of systematization of the plan. The rooms are linked together with no clear relationship to the main axes, and the symmetrical façades do not correspond to the distribution of the spaces behind them. In the Palazzo Farnese, for instance, the main salone is placed in the left-hand corner of the façade.[10] If we go outside Rome we find much more advanced solutions. In Palladio's

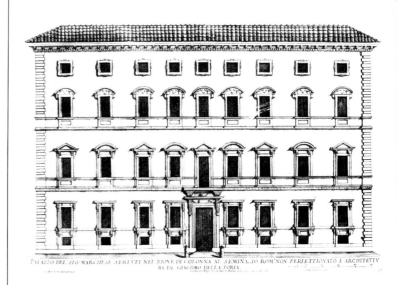

PALAZZO DEL SIG·MARCHESE SERLVPI NEL RIONE DI COLONNA AL SEMINARIO ROM·NON PERFETTIONATO E ARCHITETTVRA DI GIACOMO DELLA PORTA·

197. *Genoa, Palazzo dell'Università, vestibule, detail.*
198. *Francesco Maria Ricchino, Milan, Palazzo del Senato (Collegio Elvetico).*

palaces, staircases and salone are regularly disposed and the whole plan tends towards perfect axial symmetry, without, however, aiming at spatial integration in the Baroque sense. If we take a look at the late Cinquecento palaces in Genoa, we find a similar bias for regularity and also a surprisingly mature treatment of space. The great masterpiece is the *Palazzo Doria-Tursi* (Municipio) by Rocco Lurago (1564-66). Here a spacious vestibule is joined to the elongated cortile by means of a free flight of stairs. The cortile here is not enclosed at the back, but connected to the garden above by means of a great staircase. A strong movement in depth results, and the longitudinal axis becomes the organizing factor for the symmetrical plan. The salone, thus, is placed over the vestibule, and flanked by secondary staircases. The Palazzo Doria-Tursi represents an interesting combination of palace and villa. Towards the street we experience a typical city-palace, but the great staircase, however, led to a garden where only the upper part of the palace was visible, creating a more intimate scale.[11] The solution is determined by the sloping terrain, but the desire for spatial continuity is new and promising. In fact, the scheme was further developed in the *Palazzo dell'Università* by Bartolomeo Bianco (1634-38). Here the vestibule has been given the same width as the cortile (including the loggias) and the great staircase leading up to the garden has become completely transparent. The mass of the palace is therefore reduced to a U, resembling the main shape of the Roman palaces mentioned above. The spatial continuity, however, is infinitely stronger, and the plan shows a systematic regularity hardly found in Rome at this time. The wall articulation of the Genoese palaces is typically Mannerist, combining simple Renaissance arcades and complex experiments with interlocking rustication and orders.

From about the same period as the University in Genoa, we also have a few significant attempts at creating a more active relationship between the palace and its urban environment. In 1627, Ricchino built the façade of the *Collegio Elvetico* in Milan, making the central part *concave*, at the same time as he stressed the general continuity of the wall by means of an unbroken, strongly projecting cornice and a regular repetition of window frames. The building, thus, "receives" the visitor, that is, exterior space, in the way Borromini intended with his Oratorio façade ten years later. The meeting of exterior and interior on the main axis is marked by a strongly emphasized gateway and a convex balcony. The convincing solution confirms that the as yet little-known Ricchino must be considered one of the protagonists of Early Baroque architecture.

In 1625 Maderno was commissioned to construct the new *Palazzo Barberini* in Rome. A preserved drawing in the Uffizi shows that he first intended to build a large, square block with an arcaded cortile. The plan of Rome from 1625 by Paolo Maggi shows such a square block, but with projecting wings framing the façade towards the city. The executed palace, in fact, has such a cour d'honneur, and surviving documents show that its general shape must have been decided before January 1629 when Maderno

199. Carlo Maderno, Gianlorenzo
Bernini, Rome, Palazzo Barberini.
200. Rome, Palazzo Barberini, plan
(by Letarouilly).
201. Rome, Palazzo Barberini,
diagram.

died and Bernini took over the direction of the construction.[12] Borromini
served as an assistant to both, and his possible influence on the general
layout cannot be denied. During the planning the cortile was abolished,
transforming the palace into an "H." This layout was quite revolutionary
for a city-palace in Rome, and the first project proves that Maderno
originally intended to build a city-palace. The building-site, however, was
among gardens on the periphery of the town proper, and the idea must
have arisen to change the palace into a monumental villa suburbana. The
latter had been built on many different patterns, but a particularly fertile
type had been realized by Peruzzi in his lovely Villa Farnesina near the
Tiber (1509-10).[13] The entrance façade of the Farnesina has a cour d'honneur and an open loggia, while the garden front is a simple flat wall with an
exit in the middle. The resulting horseshoe-shaped plan was to become the
basic scheme of the villas and great residences of the Late Baroque. In the
Palazzo Barberini, the theme was taken over and further developed. The
entrance portico has three bays in depth whose width is gradually reduced
to create a strong concentration along the main axis. In the façade this concentration is expressed by a seven-bay *risalto* consisting of three floors of
superposed arcades. The portico leads into an oval *sala terrena* which opens
on a long ramp leading into the garden.[14] As the garden is on a higher level
than the entrance court, it is also linked to another oval room on the first
floor by means of a bridge. Between this oval room and the main façade,
we find the great double-height salone of the palazzo, symmetrically
placed on the main axis. The plan of the Palazzo Barberini, therefore, not
only contains the first truly Baroque movement in depth, but also a strong
bias towards systematization and a more practical disposition of the plan.
Spatially it shows a more dynamic interpretation of movement along a longitudinal axis than any of the French palaces of the seventeenth century.
The motif of the deep, contracting portico was never repeated again, although the plan in general was to have the greatest importance for the development of the Late Baroque palace outside Italy. In Italy, however, the
Palazzo Barberini remained a unique work, representing a synthesis of
types that did not correspond to the usual Italian building forms. Maderno,
Bernini, Borromini and Pietro da Cortona all contributed to make the Palazzo Barberini a unique manifestation of Baroque art, the latter mainly by
his magnificent ceiling in the Gran Salone, which he decorated with a
great fresco paying homage to Divine Providence and the Barberini Pope,
Urban VIII (1633-39). "The whole architectural composition is in movement and the figures dart between the painted entablatures, the mock cary-
atids, and the clouds. Decoration is no longer fable, but prayer and spec-
tacle."[15] Bernini included in the palace an open four-flight staircase which
foreshadowed the great staircases of the Late Baroque palaces.

The Palazzo Barberini demonstrates how a strong longitudinal axis is
the basic means introduced by Baroque architecture to organize the plan
of a building as well as its relationship to the urban environment. In his

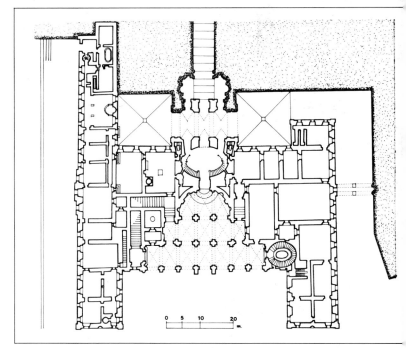

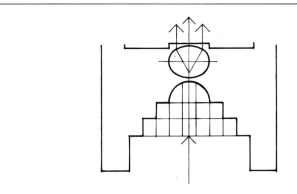

PROSPETTO E VEDVTA DEL PALAZZO DELLA CVRIA ROMANA PER RESIDENZA DE TRIBVNALI NVOVAMENTE FABRICATO SVL MONTE CITATORIO
VOLGARMENTE DETTO CITORIO DALLA SANTITA DI NS PAPA INNOCENTIO XII.

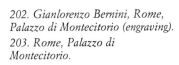

202. *Gianlorenzo Bernini, Rome, Palazzo di Montecitorio (engraving).*
203. *Rome, Palazzo di Montecitorio.*

204. *Gianlorenzo Bernini, Rome, Palazzo Chigi-Odescalchi, façade (engraving by Specchi).*

later secular works, Bernini gave further proof of this general intention. The construction of the *Palazzo di Montecitorio* for the Pamphili family was started in 1650, but work was interrupted in 1655 when the building had reached the first floor. Forty years later, the palace was completed by Carlo Fontana who changed the design of the portal.[16] In 1871 the palace became the seat of the Italian Parliament and later a large assembly hall was built within the former cortile. The plan by Bernini shows a symmetrical disposition in relation to a main axis which is emphasized by a great gateway, a spacious vestibule and a "U"-shaped courtyard flanked by two similar staircases. The systematization initiated in the Palazzo Barberini, thus, has been developed further. The very long façade is dominated by a central *risalto* and closed at both ends by slight projections. The different sections of the wall meet at obtuse angles, creating an effect of a large protruding mass. We see, thus, that the building is no longer intended as a well-proportioned block like the Palazzo Farnese, but is determined by the general urban situation. The ground-floor is characterized as a base by means of rustication and naturalistic rock formations at both ends, while the two floors above are tied together by tall pilasters which also serve to determine the five wall-units. The central axis was to have been emphasized by a gate flanked by atlantes carrying the balcony of a large window on the first floor. The simple and strong monumentality of Bernini's solution was to have a decisive importance for the development of the Late Baroque palace.

In the *Palazzo Chigi-Odescalchi* (1664-67), Bernini arrived at a further clarification of his intentions. The building had been started by Maderno, who was the architect of the cortile. Bernini added a new front, which may be considered the Baroque palace façade *par excellence*. Between two rusticated wings is placed a central *risalto* of incomparable grandeur. Again we find a giant order rising over a simple ground-floor, but here the pilasters create a regular rhythm alternating with richly ornamented windows. The *risalto* is accentuated by a strongly projecting cornice and a balustrade that was to have carried statues. The articulation expresses in a convincing way the closed character of the ground-floor, the festive openness of the piano nobile and the intimate privacy of the top floor. In general, the façade represents a truly Baroque interpretation of Serlio's concept of the "opera di mano" rising self-assertingly over the "opera di natura." Unfortunately the façade was made much longer in 1745, losing thereby its clear organization relative to a dominant central axis.

The palaces of Bernini show a strong desire for spatial systematization, as well as plastic integration horizontally and vertically. His endeavours culminated with the projects for the *Louvre* in Paris (1664-65). In 1664 Colbert, who had just become Surintendant des Bâtiments du Roi, decided to ask for advice from Italian architects as he was not satisfied with the plans of Le Vau. The original intention was to obtain projects from Bernini, Cortona, Rainaldi and Borromini, but the latter refused to par-

205. *Gianlorenzo Bernini, Paris, Louvre, main prospectus, first project (Paris, Louvre).*
206. *Paris, Louvre, general layout, second project (Paris, Louvre).*

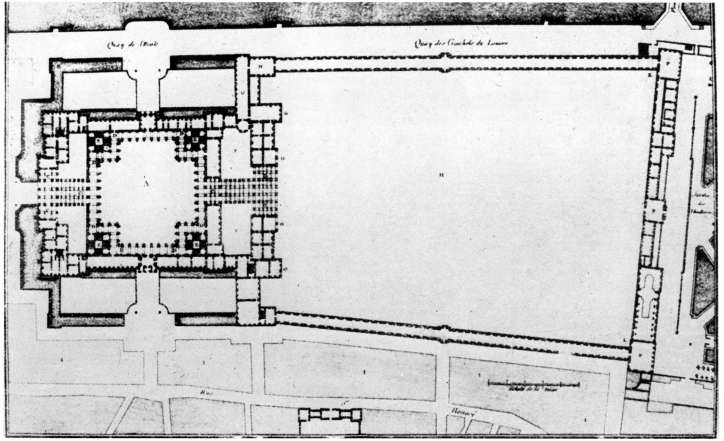

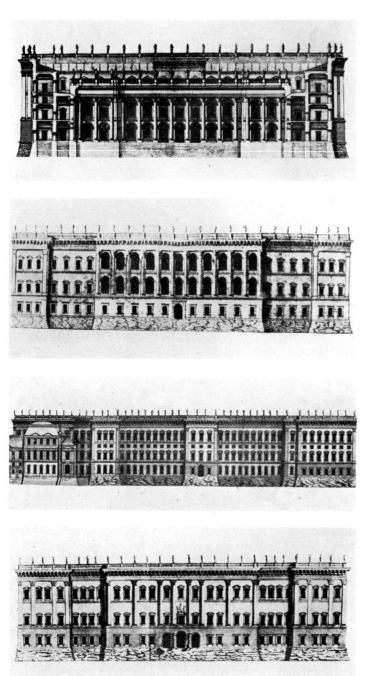

207. *Gianlorenzo Bernini, Paris, Louvre, section with elevation of the façade towards court, second project (Paris, Louvre).*

208. *Paris, Louvre, façade towards the Tuileries, second project (Paris, Louvre).*

209. *Gianlorenzo Bernini, Paris, Louvre, façade towards the Seine, second project (Paris, Louvre).*

210. *Paris, Louvre, façade towards the church of St-Germain, second project (Paris, Louvre).*

ticipate. The interest of the French soon concentrated on Bernini, and the projects of Cortona and Rainaldi were hardly considered. Before he went to Paris in April 1665, Bernini had sent in two projects, and during his six months' stay he worked out a third one, for which the foundation stone was laid on October 17th, three days before Bernini left France.[17] The following year, however, the interest of the King shifted to the rebuilding of Versailles, and the great project was abandoned. In 1667 the famous east façade was built on the project of François d'Orbay.[18] As he had to incorporate the existing structures, the projects of Bernini show a similar disposition around the great court of the palace. In the first project, he mainly concentrated on the design of the missing eastern section, whereas the third shows a considerably enlarged scheme where the existing structures around the courtyard are hidden behind two-story loggias and smaller courts have been added to the east and the west. Architecturally the first project is indeed a very radical invention. The main front basically may be interpreted as a further development of the cour d'honneur scheme from the Palazzo Barberini. Here the projecting wings have been connected with the central *risalto* by concave two-story loggias, and the *risalto* itself has become a convexly protruding volume, emphasized by a tall attic which gives height to the great oval vestibule.[19] The result is a strongly plastic ondulating façade, whose movement is unified by a continuous cornice and by a dominant giant order of semi-columns flanked by half pilasters.[20] The concave arms and the projecting but transparent central volume gives an unsurpassed feeling of interaction between exterior and interior space, and the simple and masterly articulation creates a magnificent grandeur. Two staircases are incorporated in the corners of the courtyard, one square and one round, echoing the disposition of the Palazzo Barberini. The project remains one of the greatest achievements of seventeenth-century architecture, indeed worthy of the building task in question. In the first Louvre project, Bernini demonstrated how spatial interaction could be created by means of the juxtaposition of simple volumes, and he proved that one of the most convincing interpretations of basic Baroque intentions lay in the clear statement of one great theme.

The east façade of the second project varies the solution of the first by making the central *risalto* concave. The loggias are abolished and a third story added by putting the giant order over a rusticated ground-floor. Spatially the solution is less convincing, as the movement of the front does not correspond to any clear interaction of volumes. The inclination towards a certain simplification is evident, a tendency that resulted in the straight façade of the third project, where the three-story disposition is retained and the whole solution may be considered a monumental variation of the theme of the Palazzo Chigi-Odescalchi. The main *risalto*, thus, is emphasized by columns that are more closely spaced towards the middle. In general, the façade has a relatively closed character, whereas the opposite western front should have had a wide *risalto* with open loggias on

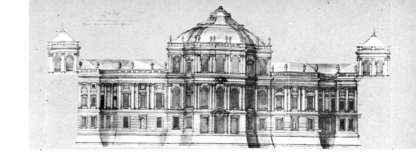

211. *Pietro da Cortona, Paris,*
Louvre, project for the garden
façade (Paris, Louvre).
212. *Francesco Borromini, Rome,*
Palazzo Carpegna, plan (Vienna,
Graphische Sammlung Albertina).

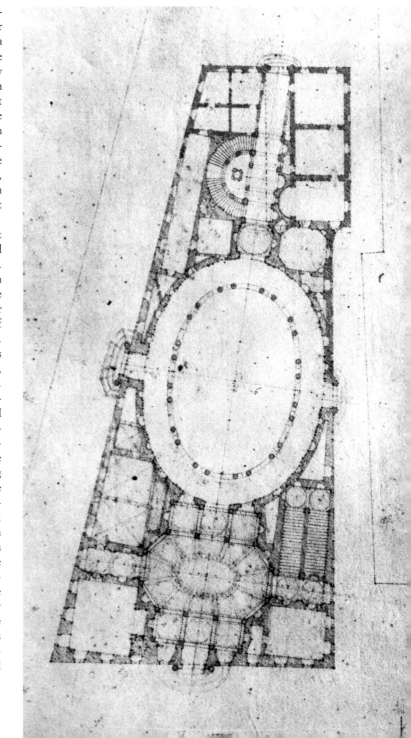

both the upper floors. The solution of the courtyard is one of the most interesting aspects of the project. By abolishing the third floor on the inner
side, Bernini could make a wall of two tiers only. He thereby achieved a
well-lit space of excellent proportions that certainly could have become
one of the most splendid courtyards in existence. As we have already
mentioned, his project was criticized on practical grounds, and the main
reason why it was never executed certainly lies in the fact that it did not
satisfy French taste and the French way of life. "Paris was saved the
doubtful honor of having within its walls the most monumental Roman
palazzo ever designed. Splendid though Bernini's project was, the enor-
mous, austere pile would forever have stood out as an alien growth in the
severe atmosphere of Paris. In Rome, the cube of the Palazzo Farnese,
the ancestor of Bernini's design, may be likened to the solo in a choir. In
Paris, Bernini's overpowering Louvre would have had no resonance: it
would have cast an almost sombre spell over the gaiety of the city."[21]

The existing parts of the Louvre consisted of a long series of rooms lit
from both sides, namely an *appartement simple*. Whereas Bernini added
loggias around the courtyard, creating an *appartement semi-double*.
Rainaldi and Cortona kept closer to the original plan of Le Vau which
proposed a new double wing to the east. Their projects, therefore, are
mainly of interest because of the wall articulation.[22] Rainaldi's design for
the main façade testifies to his love for the column. The three tall *risalti* of
the elevation, in fact, are decorated with superposed coupled columns.
The lower walls between the *risalti* have a giant order of single pilasters
and an attic. The whole design has a strained and overloaded character,
which contrasts with the simple monumentality of Bernini's projects.
One particular feature, however, must be mentioned: the *risalti* are completed by tower-like structures carrying naturalistic imitations of Royal
crowns. With this solution "Rainaldi's intention may have been to give elo-
quent expression to the idea of the divine origin of the absolute monarch's authority, an origin from which it drew prestige and dignity."[23] The
palace designed by Cortona is also dominated by a large dome resembling
a closed crown. Remembering the oval attic of Bernini's first project, one
might imagine that the program included a "crown."[24] Cortona also en-
countered difficulties in giving strength and unity to the large building;
vertically, thus, his main façade shows a rather disproportioned addition
of superimposed elements. The wide *risalto* in the middle manages to a
certain extent to keep the whole together. The opposite front towards the
Tuileries is more interesting.[25] A large oval volume in the middle protrudes into the garden. Lower wings are added on both sides, joining the
central volume and the long lateral galleries leading to the Tuileries by
means of interesting, ambiguous bays of transition that remind us of the
ingenious solution of S. Maria della Pace. The wall articulation illustrates
Cortona's interest in a rich play of light and shadow. In general the project represents an interesting synthesis of the French pavilion system and

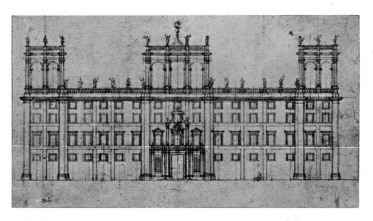

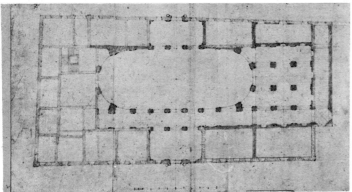

the Italian modelling of plastic volumes, a synthesis that prefigures certain works by Fischer von Erlach and Hildebrandt. About the same time Cortona designed a Chigi palace in Piazza Colonna in Rome which was never built. The solution of the front resembles the lower part of Borromini's S. Agnese in Piazza Navona, as well as Bernini's first design for the Louvre. The giant order, however, rises over a rusticated ground-floor which incorporates a large fountain with figures and artificial rocks, an idea that was realized in the Trevi fountain by Nicola Salvi almost seventy years later. Cortona's project demonstrates how certain basic motifs were becoming part of a general "vocabulary," such as the concave recess with a counter-movement in the center, and the giant order over a rusticated base.

Borromini also contributed significantly to the development of the High Baroque vocabulary. Although he never had the occasion to build a complete secular palace, his projects for reconstructions and his ecclesiastical palaces give us good information as to his intentions.

Between 1635 and 1650, Borromini prepared several projects for the rebuilding of the *Palazzo Carpegna* in Rome.[26] The most complete of his schemes shows a very interesting spatial composition. Along a longitudinal axis that runs through the whole palace, a series of unitary spaces follow each other, creating a magnificent movement in depth. The longitudinal axis is crossed by a transverse axis, to give the whole palace a bi-axial organization. The center is marked by a large oval cortile. We see again how Borromini takes space as his point of departure, arriving thereby at solutions that are at the same time more united and more dynamic than those of his contemporaries. About the same time (1645-50), Borromini made several studies for the Palazzo Pamphili in Piazza Navona, built by Girolamo Rainaldi (1650). Borromini's scheme again shows a quasi-oval cortile with vestibules on the minor axis, giving the palace a bi-axial disposition. His façade is centered on a strongly emphasized *risalto* which is crowned by a tall, transparent *belvedere*. Vertical integration is achieved by means of a giant order comprising all four stories. In general, the design is more advanced than anything else made up to that date. Borromini's most important large structures, however, are his ecclesiastical palaces, the *Casa dei Filippini* (1637) and the *Collegio di Propaganda Fide* (1647-64).[27] We have already mentioned the clear and systematic organization of the Casa dei Filippini and Borromini's attempt at creating a correspondence between the interior disposition and the exterior articulation. The irregular building site of the Propaganda Fide palace and existing structures along two sides did not allow for the development of a regular plan, but the articulation of the exterior illustrates the maturity reached by Borromini since the construction of the Oratorio. In fact, the Propaganda Fide palace represents his ultimate achievement, and a singular work within the history of Baroque architecture. The large block is characterized as one unitary volume by means of rounded cor-

217. *Guarino Guarini, Turin, Palazzo Carignano, plan (from Haupt).*

218. *Turin, Palazzo Carignano, diagram.*

219. *Turin, Palazzo Carignano, façade.*

220. *Turin, Palazzo Carignano, façade.*

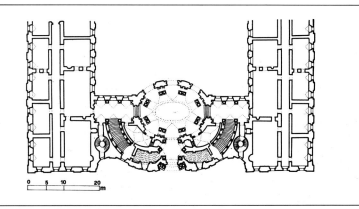

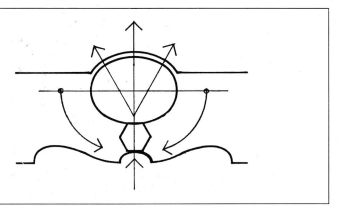

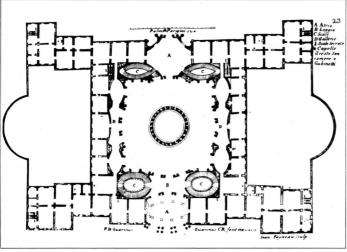

ners. The corner between Via di Propaganda and Via Capo le Case is a masterpiece of plastic articulation. The continuity of the boundary surface is stressed by stringcourses running around the corner, at the same time as each wall is defined by flat pilasters. Better than most examples it illustrates that articulation means a simultaneous separation *and* joining together. The main façade on the Via di Propaganda is an extraordinary work. Immense pilasters unify the austere wall. In the middle and on the ends they are obliquely placed, as if the system was changing under the pressure of slow but irresistible forces. Between the pilasters large plastic aediculae break through. The whole façade is a study in compression and dilatation, and expresses better than any other work of the epoch the role of the wall as the meeting-point of outer and inner forces. The window frames are Doric, but a surrealist Doric which includes flowers, garlands and palm branches. The capitals of the main pilaster stem from the triglyph as well as the Ionic *Kyma*, and carry a cornice on large brackets, instead of the normal entablature. In spite of its austerity, the façade shows a singular synthesis of characters.

A similar synthetic character is found in the building which represents the culmination of seventeenth-century Italian palace architecture: Guarini's *Palazzo Carignano* in Turin (1679-85). The palace was built as the residence of the prince of Carignano and became the seat of the first Italian Parliament in 1860. Guarini's project is based on a "U,"[28] but this well-known scheme gets a new interpretation thanks to the treatment of the central part of the building. Here we find a great oval "rotunda" that ends in a drum-without-dome, and protrudes convexly on both sides of the palace.[29] On the ground-floor, thus, it functions as a vestibule that brings together all the movements within the palace, as well as a trident radiating into the courtyard. On the piano nobile we find the main hall of the palace, with a cut-off dome inside the tall drum. Between the oval volume and the main façade curved flights of stairs connect the two levels. The façade has a complementary relationship to the interior spaces, at the same time as it forms one continuous undulating envelope. The center of the convex middle sinks in to receive a convex two-story aedicula, a variation on a theme from Borromini's Propaganda Fide palace. The articulation is based on two superimposed giant orders; the lower one a surrealist Doric, the upper one an equally free Corinthian. The surrealist decoration reaches its climax on the courtyard façade which is articulated by pilaster-bands closely set with stars.

In general the Palazzo Carignano has a true plastic monumentality, and the interdependence of the spatial units is a singular achievement in seventeenth-century palace architecture.

In another project, the so-called "Palazzo Francese," Guarini applied the principle of pulsating juxtaposition to the palace, creating a continuous undulating movement around the cortile. Unfortunately the idea was never again applied to a large secular building.[30]

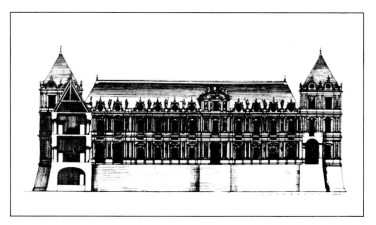

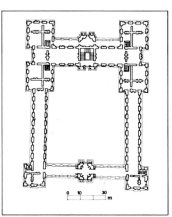

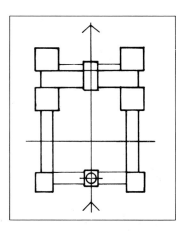

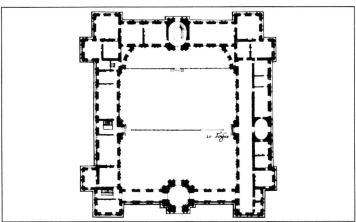

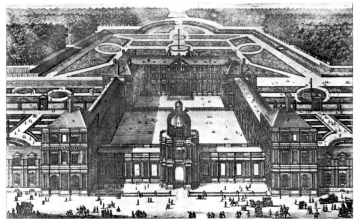

229. *Salomon de Brosse, Rennes,*
Palais de Justice.
230. *François Mansart, Château*
de Berny (engraving by Perelle).

231. *François Mansart, Château*
de Blois, Orléans Wing.
232. *François Mansart, Château*
de Maisons, view from the entrance
(engraving by Perelle).

233. Château de Maisons, view from the garden (engraving by Perelle).

159

The French Château and Hôtel

The large French dwellings of the seventeenth century have roots that are quite different from those of the Italian palazzo. Rather than the Roman *insula*, the hôtel was based on medieval prototypes which consisted of a series of units distributed around a spacious courtyard. We find this pattern in the country seats, as well as the larger town-houses such as the house of Jacques-Coeur in Bourges (1445-51). Certain tendencies towards a more regular layout were present, especially the placing of the main hall opposite the entrance which gave the courtyard a kind of axis, and at the same time created an intimate privacy unknown in the Italian palazzo. In general, the hôtel may be considered "the adaptation, the urban transportation of the nobleman's castle or the feudal country house."[31] Different geneses make the Italian and French palaces inversions of each other. In the Italian palace, the main part of the building faces the public world whereas the cortile is private. In the French hôtel, the cour d'honneur "opens" on the urban space in front, while the corps de logis is withdrawn and private. Different ways of life and social structures are thereby expressed. The inhabitants of the Italian palazzo may follow civic life from their dwelling; they participate,[32] but they still retain the individual identity symbolized by the enclosed block-like structure and the centralized cortile. The inhabitants of the hôtel do not participate in the civic milieu, but they are still subject to the dominated space on which their courtyard opens, and become parts of the general "system." During the sixteenth century, the ground-plans tended towards a more pronounced geometrization, under the influence of Renaissance concepts. This tendency is evident in Chambord (1519-50) where a medieval castle has become systematized, creating an organism whose general layout comes surprisingly close to that of the first palaces of the seventeenth century, such as the Palais du Luxembourg.[33] More revolutionary than Chambord, however, is the Château de Bury (1511-24) which has a "U"-shaped plan containing the corps de logis in the middle and lesser functions on both sides. The "U" is closed by a lower wall with arcades on the inside and a gate in the middle. The corps de logis opens on a garden through a central exit. A clearly defined longitudinal axis is thus created.

To illustrate the further development of the "U"-shaped plan, we may mention the Château de Villandry (1532), which has a fully developed cour d'honneur, and the splendid Château d'Anet by Philibert de l'Orme (1547-52),[34] where the longitudinal axis is emphasized by means of a monumental gateway and a tall *risalto* in the middle of the corps de logis, articulated by the superposition of freestanding Doric, Ionic and Corinthian columns. In his own house in Paris, De l'Orme applied the "U"-plan to a simple town dwelling. The court was to be closed by a transverse wing having a two-story façade on the street with an emphasized gate in the middle, while the center of the corps de logis was taken up by a chapel whose apse projected convexly into the garden.[35] In spite of many Mannerist traits,

Philibert de l'Orme was the initiator of French classical architecture, and in his *Architecture* he presented many worthwhile ideas, such as the application of the giant order to a house. This idea was adopted by Jean Bullant at the Château d'Écouen (c. 1560) and by Baptiste du Cerceau in the cour d'honneur of the Hôtel Lamoignon in Paris (1584), whose Mannerist articulation reflects the inventions of his father Jacques Androuet du Cerceau. In 1665 Du Cerceau the Elder designed the Château du Verneuil on a "U"-plan, and introduced a circular, domed vestibule in the middle of the enclosing screen-wall.

The man who was to unify all these ideas into what may be called a French Early Baroque architecture was Salomon de Brosse. During the second decade of the seventeenth century, De Brosse built three great palaces, the Château de Coulommiers (1613), the Château de Blérancourt (1614-19) and the Palais du Luxembourg in Paris (1615-24). The *Château de Coulommiers* is the more traditional, having a "U"-plan and a one-story screen-wall with a great domed vestibule closing off the fourth side.[36] While the "U" has two floors, the corners are marked by three-story tower-like pavilions. The articulation, however, shows a pronounced desire for unity and integration. The whole exterior is enveloped by a continuous system of coupled rusticated pilasters. The main axis is stressed by the introduction of half-columns on the vestibule as well as the *ressaut* of the corps de logis, which contains an oval staircase. The courtyard is also articulated by coupled half-columns. It has a bi-axial disposition and curved wall sections join the wings to the corps de logis. The Château de Coulommiers, thus, is a sensitively balanced composition where the individual volumes are separated, at the same time as they are united by the continuous bounding surface. The courtyard is varied and gives added importance to the wall system of the exterior, expressing an increased "openness." Its engirdling walls form an expressive contrast to the longitudinal axis. The *Château de Blérancourt* has no wings, but is reduced to the corps de logis. The plan becomes a kind of H, and the building as a whole interacts with exterior space in a way that may be compared with the Palazzo Barberini in Rome. Unlike the Italian palazzo, Blérancourt has defined square corner pavilions with voluminous roofs and crowning lanterns. Unity, however, is achieved by a continuous but varied wall articulation, employing a superposition of three orders. The corner pavilions are divided into two bays to reduce their formal independence, while the tripartite central *ressaut* is accentuated by a segment pediment. As a whole, the Château de Blérancourt is a very convincing work combining a Baroque feeling for space and volume with a simple and refined articulation that was to become the main characteristic of French classical architecture.

The third of De Brosse's châteaux, the *Palais du Luxembourg* in Paris, combines the plans of Coulommiers and Blérancourt. It was built for Marie de' Medici and became in 1642 the residence of Gaston d'Orléans ("Palais d'Orléans").[37] The palace has a corps de logis with corner pavilions

160

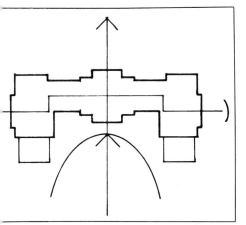

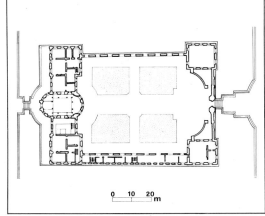

0 10 20
m

similar to Blérancourt, and wings and a domed vestibule similar to Coulommiers. The continuous articulation consists of coupled rusticated pilasters, but columns are only introduced to emphasize the main entrances. The corner pavilions contain complete *appartements* on each floor, a solution that represents an important step towards the functionally planned apartments of the later seventeenth century.[38] The unit consisting of a large room, two small rooms and a wardrobe became a standard. It introduced a new conception of commodity and privacy, and a more practical distribution of rooms than the *enfilades* of the old-fashioned *appartement simple*. The *enfilade*, however, always exerted a strong influence on the Baroque mind. Thus Madame de Maintenon said of her husband, Louis XIV: "With him only grandeur, magnificence, symmetry matter; it is infinitely worthwhile enduring all drafts which sweep under the doors if only these can be arranged facing each other."[39] The last palace of De Brosse, the *Palais de Justice* in Rennes (1618), was built for the Parliament of Brittany. This simple but sophisticated work may be called the first full-grown work of French classicism. A shallow cour d'honneur determines the shape of the façade. The wings are divided into two bays, and are thereby characterized as subordinate elements. They have a slightly more solid character than the central part, which consists of a row of large arched windows between coupled pilasters. The main axis is marked by coupled columns carrying an attic with a round pediment. The order rises over a closed rusticated base. The articulation clearly derives from Raphael's Palazzo Vidoni, but in Rennes the plastic quality of the Roman palace is gone. Instead we find a crisp and crystalline character which emphasizes surface and volume rather than plasticity and mass. The general shape comes close to Peruzzi's Farnesina, although it evidently has different roots.

The intentions of De Brosse were carried on and perfected by François Mansart. In his first châteaux, *Berny* (1623), and *Balleroy* (1626), the disposition departs still more from the traditional courtyard model, spreading a series of pavilions out along the transverse axis. At the same time, however, the main axis is given emphasis by means of a tall, tower-like *ressaut*. In Berny the wings are joined to the corps de logis by curved wall sections on the ground-floor as in Coulommiers, while Balleroy shows a gradual stepping forward of the wall-surface towards the middle. The simultaneous spreading out and coming together around a dominant axis leading through the building into depth creates a typical Baroque tension, less dramatic but more subtle than the contemporary Palazzo Barberini in Rome.

In the Orléans Wing of the *Château de Blois* (1635-38), Mansart introduced a shallow cour d'honneur where the wings again are joined to the dominant tripartite central *ressaut* by means of curved colonnades.[40] The superposition of three tiers of slender coupled pilasters (Doric, Ionic and Corinthian) and the tall windows create an exterior of unsurpassed elegance and sensitivity. In all three works Mansart shows how the basic spatial intentions of the seventeenth century could be combined with a restrained classical language of forms. The Château de Blois also contains the first truly grand staircase of the century, covered by a series of superimposed spaces. A vertical axis is thereby introduced into the extended organism of the palace.[41] The *Château de Maisons* is generally considered Mansart's masterpiece, and here, in fact, we find a synthesis of all previous ideas combined with a new richness of modelling and detail. The palace was built for René de Longueil, Président de Maisons, between 1642 and 1646.[42] In general, Maisons may be characterized as a building that is simultaneously fully articulated and fully integrated. The different volumes, having their roots in the French pavilion tradition, are clearly defined by means of steep roofs and *ressauts*. The wings, thus, have a certain independence, appearing as the arms of the corps de logis. They are, however, unified in a convincing way by means of dominant axial symmetry and a most effective continuous wall articulation. In fact, there are few buildings that have a more unitary character than the Château de Maisons. This is also due to the approximately bi-axial organization of the plan. We could interpret the plan as a regular bi-axial scheme that has been transformed, and now interacts with exterior "forces," namely the different spatial domains of entrance court and garden. On the garden side the wings only form slight *ressauts*, whereas they create a shallow cour d'honneur on the other side. This court is deepened by added oval one-story vestibules that are integrated in the total organism by the strong and continuous Doric entablature. The transverse axis is marked in the exterior by bipartite *ressauts* with triangular pediments. The axis, thus, is simultaneously defined and blocked. The main axis is emphasized by "double" *ressauts*, where the central part rises to three-story height, repeating the characteristic De Brosse theme of three superimposed orders. It is not easy to point out a building where centrifugal and centripetal movements, horizontality and verticality, or we might say "classical" and "Gothic" properties, have found a more convincing dynamic equilibrium. The tensions inherent in the general disposition are echoed in the pilaster rhythms that show a continuous condensation and dilatation, giving substance to the corners and joints, and opening to the spaces between. The modelling, however, does not have the plastic expression of Roman Baroque buildings. In spite of the inherent dynamism, its character remains crisp and restrained, precise and crystalline. The bi-axial vestibule repeats this general form although the articulating members show an original synthesis of Doric and Ionic characters. The laterally placed staircase has a strong vertical development, ending in a cut-off dome. With the Château de Maisons, François Mansart showed himself to be one of the most forceful personalities of the seventeenth century.

At about the same time that Maisons was being erected, Louis Le Vau built the *Château de Raincy* for Jacques Bordier, Surintendant des Finan-

238. *Schematic diagram showing
the layout of Italian and French
palaces.*

239. *Louis Le Vau, Château
de Vaux-le-Vicomte, diagram.*
240. *Château de Vaux-le-Vicomte,
façade.*

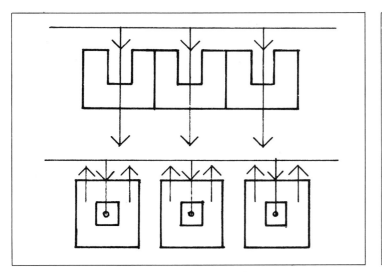

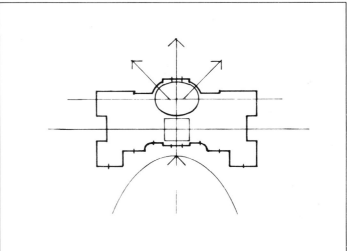

241, 242. *Château de Vaux-le-Vicomte, exterior views.*

243. *Salomon de Brosse, Jacques Lemercier, Paris, Hôtel de Liancourt, plan (from Blunt).*

244. *François Mansart, Paris, Hôtel de la Vrillière (engraving by Marot).*

245. *Paris, Hôtel de la Vrillière, plan (from Blunt).*

246. *François Mansart, Paris, Hôtel de Jars, plan (from Blunt).*

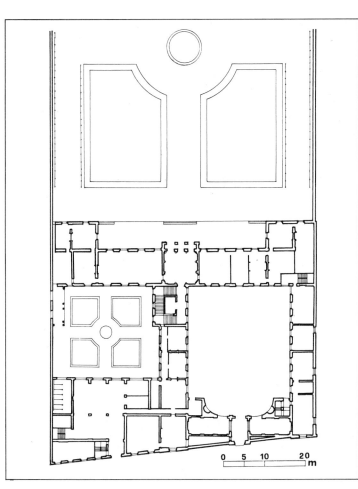

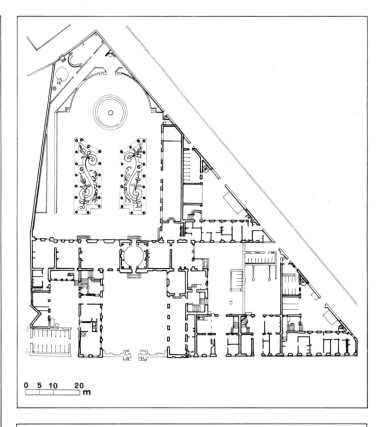

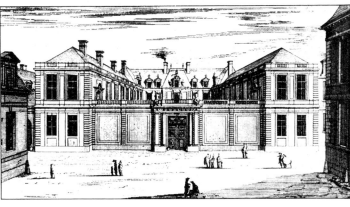

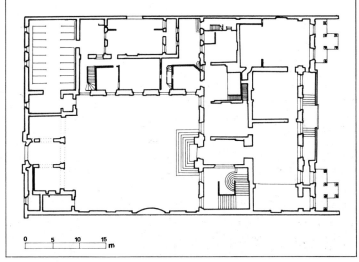

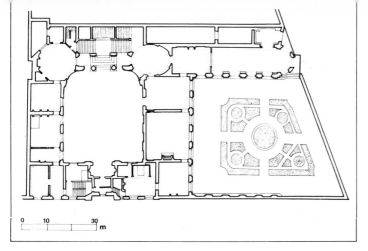

247. Louis Le Vau, Paris, Hôtel
Lambert, plan (from Blunt).
248. Paris, Hôtel Lambert, garden.
249. Paris, Hôtel Lambert, detail
of façade on the court.

ces (1645).[43] Raincy is based on the traditional "U"-scheme, and the court
is closed by a monumental gate and corner pavilions. The corps de logis,
however, is clearly defined as one unified volume, repeating somewhat the
general bi-axial disposition of Maisons. As a forecourt has been added, the
wings do not form any real cour d'honneur, they only project slightly more
than on the garden side. The main novel feature is a quasi-oval hall which
defines the longitudinal axis, protruding markedly on both sides of the
building. The wings are articulated by colossal pilasters which give them a
certain rigidity in contrast to the horizontal division of the corps de logis.
A flat, linear rustication as well as a continuous Doric entablature over the
ground-floor tie all the parts of the palace together. The general character
is simpler than in the works of Mansart, and the use of elementary, well-
defined volumes, as well as dominant motifs such as the giant order, creates a certain affinity with the style of Bernini.[44]

Twelve years after Raincy, Le Vau was given the opportunity of developing his ideas further, building the *Château de Vaux-le-Vicomte* for
Nicolas Fouquet, Surintendant des Finances (1657-61).[45] Vaux-le-Vicomte is without doubt the masterpiece of Le Vau, and one of the most important works within the history of the palace. It consists of three main
units: the palace proper, placed on an "island" surrounded by a moat, and
two base-courts flanking the main axis on either side of the entrance. A
strong movement in depth is thereby created, which continues on the other
side of the building, defined by the infinite perspective of Le Nôtre's
splendid garden. Several transverse axes are introduced, indicating a general "open" extension. The palace forms the focus of this space, a role that
is emphasized by the traditional (originally functional) motif of the moat,
and by a dome that is the very center of the composition. If we see the
layout as a whole, the palace island forms one large *ressaut* which projects
into nature from the human world of entrance and base-courts. This motif
is repeated on a smaller scale in the palace proper, where the round domed
volume forms the innermost meeting-point of the two "worlds." The palace, thus, receives the visitor in the cour d'honneur, leads him through the
symbolic center, and finally releases him into infinite space. This grand
conception is not a new invention, but rather a particularly convincing
synthesis of the basic intentions of seventeenth-century secular architecture. The palace may, like Maisons, be characterized as an organism that
is simultaneously articulated and integrated. The means employed,
however, are different. As one would expect after Raincy, Le Vau primarily works with relationships between volumes. In Vaux-le-Vicomte the
composition has become more complex. This is evident if we look at the
center of the building. Instead of consisting of one uniform volume, the
two sides facing the court and garden respectively have become differentiated, adapting to the functions of "reception" (tri-partite gateway and vestibule), "dwelling" (centralized grand salon) and "extension" (radiating
axes and curved *ressaut*). The grand salon is built over a transverse oval

250. Louis Le Vau, Paris, Hôtel
de Lionne, façade (engraving by
Marot).
251. Paris, Hôtel de Lionne, plan.

that creates a necessary counterpoint to the very strong longitudinal movement, at the same time as it indicates an active spatial relationship with the
wings of the palace. The introduction of a closed dome as an eminently
symbolic element is a courageous invention that may have contributed to
the rage of the King. The wings end in traditional corner pavilions, which,
however, have lost their independence, interpenetrating the main body of
the palace. Towards the court they are transformed into flat fronts that initiate a series of planes stepping back towards the entrance. All these
planes are bipartite and the last of them concave, to give emphasis to the
tripartite entrance. The volumes, thus, form part of a continuous wall-
movement, at the same time as they are defined as such by the steep roofs.
On the garden side the articulation is simpler, and the single units hardly
free themselves from the general continuity of the front. As in Raincy, the
corner pavilions are strengthened by giant pilasters. In general, Vaux-le-
Vicomte is a masterpiece of spatial composition. Le Vau did not have Mansart's sensitive capability for wall articulation and detailing, but his ability
in handling spatial relationships and volumes made him the most Baroque
of French architects.

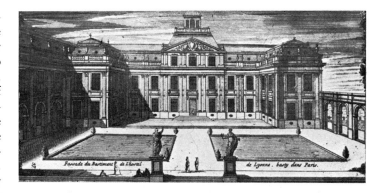

Vaux-le-Vicomte is also important for the practical disposition of the
plan. Traditionally the rooms of the palace were only accessible through
each other, forming an *enfilade* or *appartement simple*. We have seen that
the Italians used a lateral corridor for disengagement, creating thereby an
appartement semi-double. Only in the corners could the spaces be arranged
in a more practical way, as in the Palais du Luxembourg. In Vaux-le-
Vicomte, however, the whole corps de logis has been doubled, a solution
made possible by the introduction of a vestibule in front of the grand
salon.[46] The *appartement double* was thus created, an innovation that was
to have a fundamental importance for subsequent developments.[47] In combination with secondary staircases and other *dégagements*, the double corps
de logis allowed for a practical disposition of the rooms, giving each apartment its privacy. The basic intention was to attain convenience without
giving up representation. This wish was connected with the important role
of the woman in French society. In fact, it was often she who made up the
program for the architect, with whom she did not always agree.
Mademoiselle de Scudéry said: "Indeed, it is usual for these great houses
to be extremely uncomfortable! Architects dream so much about the exterior of things, for which they desire to be praised by foreigners, that they
hardly give a thought as to how these beautiful places may be made more
comfortable for the people who own them."[48] The desire for convenience
did not only bring about a more practical access to the various rooms, but
also a differentiation of use and space. The basic elements were the *anti-
chambre* for waiting and eating, creating a sort of "barrier" between the
entrance and the private world, the *chambre de parade* for reception and
entertainment, usually furnished with a bed as the master and mistress of
the house often received in their bedroom, the *chambre à coucher* for sleep-

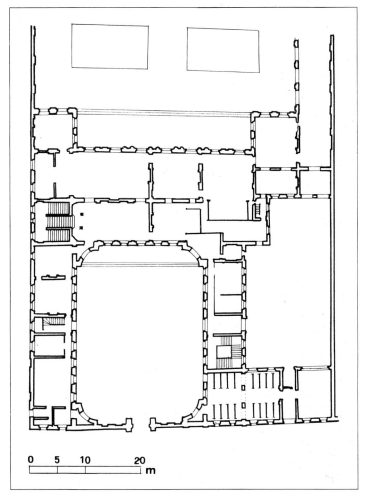

252, 253. *Louis Le Vau, Château de Versailles, courtyard.*

254. Jules Hardouin-Mansart, Château de Versailles, Galerie des Glaces.
255. Louis Le Vau, Château de Versailles, plan.

ing as well as reception, the *cabinet* for work and reception of business connections, and, finally, the *garderobe* for dressing and storage where the maid or valet slept, "for servants were no more separated from the life of the family than reception from living quarters."[49] In addition to the chambre de parade, the larger houses usually had a *salon* and perhaps a *galerie*. The *salle à manger* also appeared as a specialized room.[50] The ground plan, thus, became divided into many relatively small units. What the house might lose in grandiosity, it gained in charm and surprise. "Where would contemporary comedy be, without these hiding-places, screens, doors and secret stairways? And the countless surprises, the subterfuge, the comic situations, where would they be, were it not for the fact that the desire for comfortable living-space had divided up home life even in its smallest details."[51]

We have already pointed out that the château and the urban hôtel represent the same basic type. Because of the different situation, however, the hôtel developed certain particular traits. Usually the hôtels were built adjacently, having therefore only two façades. As a consequence, the plan often became more cramped than in the case of the freely situated châteaux. The impossibility of having a separate base-court in front of the cour d'honneur led to the development of two courts placed next to each other, an arrangement already found in the *Hôtel de Liancourt* (Bouillon) by De Brosse and Lemercier (1613-23). The main axis of the cour d'honneur therefore no longer corresponds to that of the garden, so that a certain confusion in the spatial relationships results.[52] The entrance axis of the Hôtel de Liancourt ended blindly, while the access to the corps de logis was found in the left-hand corner of the courtyard. It opened on the staircase, connected to the vestibule at the center of the garden front. The courtyard had a simple, classical wall-articulation with a Doric order of pilasters rising over a rusticated ground-floor. The façade looked like the front of a monumental château with projecting wings and a central *ressaut*. Its conventional articulation was based on a network of horizontal and vertical lines rather than classical members.[53]

Still more old-fashioned is the articulation of the courtyard in the *Hôtel de Sully* built by Jean du Cerceau (1624-29). The very deep and narrow building site determined a simple axial layout. More interesting is the *Hôtel de Bretonvillers* by the same architect. It was built between 1637 and 1643 on the eastern corner of the newly developed Ile St. Louis.[54] Again we find a displacement of the main axis due to the addition of a small base-court. The displacement, however, is very slight as the court-axis ends in the lefthand opening of the tri-partite central *ressaut* of the garden front. The central bay, therefore, is closed, while the right one opens on the main salon, so that a symmetrical façade is obtained. The courtyard is formulated in a new and interesting way, as the lateral wings have been separated architecturally from the corps de logis, which has two short wings of its own forming an inner cour d'honneur. The disposition is ob-

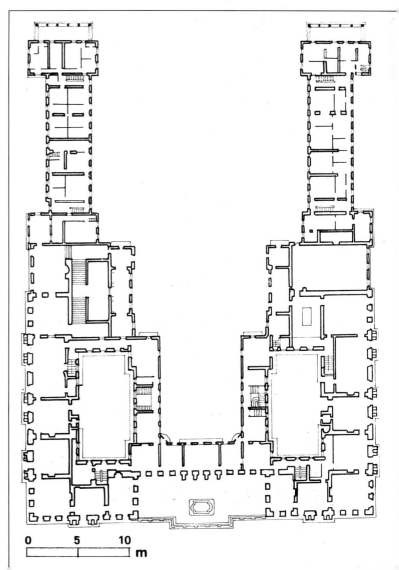

0   5   10
m

viously derived from the corner pavilions of the château, and points towards the freestanding hôtel of the eighteenth century.[55] A Baroque emphasis on volume results, which also determines the unified character of the façades which have unusually large windows. Along the northern side of the garden, a gallery has been added for protection from the adjacent buildings.

In 1635, François Mansart received his first commission for a private house in Paris, the *Hôtel de la Vrillière*.[56] The disposition is the usual one with three wings around a court that is closed by a wall. As in the Hôtel de Bretonvillers, a base-court has been added on the left side, bringing about a similar displacement of the main axis. We also find an analogous break in the side walls of the courtyard which separates the corps de logis from the wings. The articulation, however, is far more subtle than in the contemporary work of Du Cerceau. Mansart, thus, gave emphasis to the main axis by a wide *ressaut* which had a slightly taller roof than the wings on both sides, a solution he also applied on a grander scale in Blois. The *ressaut* defined a splendid domed vestibule. The wall-treatment shows Mansart's sensitive feeling for proportions and detailing, which made the Hôtel de la Vrillière the classical town-palace of the first half of the century. In 1648 Mansart began the construction of the *Hôtel du Jars*.[57] Again the disposition shows the characteristic displacement of the main axis. As a consequence, Mansart eliminated the central door to the garden, creating instead two exits from the lateral *ressauts*. The Hôtel du Jars may be the first palace where the corps de logis has been doubled. The *appartement double* made it possible to have the staircase in direct contact with the vestibule, behind a spacious garden salon. Again the corps de logis is separated from the wing, this time by an interruption of the roof, whereas the wall articulation is continuous.

The first important city-palace by Le Vau, the *Hôtel Tambonneau* (1639) consisted of a two-story corps de logis with one-story wings added.[58] The engraving by Marot shows a very simple wall articulation, which contrasts with the transparent central *ressaut*. Two tiers of columns are superposed under a pediment and a broken roof, which adds to the voluminous character of the building. In fact, Le Vau seems to have been the inventor of the so-called Mansard roof, where the steep Gothic slope is broken to allow for a better utilization of the volume. The broken roof became a characteristic feature of Late Baroque architecture, giving the buildings an almost sensual plasticity.[59] The garden front of the Hôtel Tambonneau had a giant order of Ionic pilasters. Le Vau, thus, adapted to the infinite extension represented by the garden, whereas the courtyard was divided into stories having a human scale.[60] The plan of the Hôtel Tambonneau is not preserved, but the bird's-eye view by Marot indicates that the corps de logis had a certain depth, i.e. it may have been built as an *appartement double*.

The most important of Le Vau's surviving city-palaces is the *Hôtel Lambert* (1640-44) built on the Ile St. Louis next to the Hôtel de Bretonvillers, on a similar site. The Hôtel Lambert shows a most ingenious adaptation of the standard scheme to a particular situation. As the complex is entered from the longer side, Le Vau could not carry through a longitudinal axis. The axis of the courtyard, thus, ends in a grand staircase where it crosses a transverse axis that leads out towards the landscape through an oval vestibule and a magnificent long gallery. A garden is incorporated between the gallery and the right-hand wing of the building. The narrow site did not permit the development of an *appartement double*, but the *bel étage* is put over a still more ingenious ground-floor, which even allowed for the exit of carriages in the corner of the courtyard. The courtyard is centered on the open volume of the staircase whose screen-wall is joined to the walls by means of rounded corners. A continuous Doric entablature engirdles the entire space. Virtually nowhere else has French architecture come so close to the conception of Borromini. The wall articulation shows a superposition of two orders, while the garden façade has giant pilasters.[61] Between these, the walls are completely opened by means of "French doors," namely, windows that reach the floor, another ingenious invention by Le Vau. In the *Hôtel de Lionne* (1661), Le Vau could bring all his ideas together and create a truly monumental city-palace.[62] The plan shows a displaced axis because of the introduction of a base-court next to the main courtyard. The corps de logis has two stories plus an attic, while the wings have two stories only. The courtyard is integrated spatially by means of concave corners and continuous entablatures. It has two superposed orders plus the attic, and the main axis is emphasized by a triangular pediment. The two-story garden façade is articulated by coupled giant pilasters (half-columns at the central *ressaut*) on the corps de logis and single ones on the wings. The plan forms an irregular "H" with an *appartement double* in the middle, which contains the first great tri-partite staircase of the type Balthasar Neumann was to use with so much success in Würzburg and Brühl. The simple volumetric relationships and clear articulation give the Hôtel de Lionne a convincing architectural quality. It belonged without doubt to the major works of the period.

After his success with Vaux-le Vicomte, Le Vau was commissioned to rebuild the *Château de Versailles* for Louis XIV (1664). He was ordered to preserve the old hunting-lodge built for Louis XIII in 1624, and in 1669 it was decided to envelop the old château in a new building which left the original court exposed.[63] The result was an immense almost square block with two wings attached to form a very deep cour d'honneur. The plan shows long *enfilades* on both sides of the old building and a large terrace between them. The garden façade, thus, consisted of two projecting wings and a deep recess over a continuous rusticated ground-floor. The *bel étage* was articulated by Ionic pilasters and columns carrying a tall entablature and an attic. An unusual feature is the employment of a flat "Italian" roof, a solution that is generally understood to be an echo of Bernini's project

256. Jules Hardouin-Mansart,
Château de Dampierre.

257. Jules Hardouin-Mansart,
Versailles, Château de Clagny
(engraving by Perelle).

256. Jules Hardouin-Mansart,
Château de Dampierre.

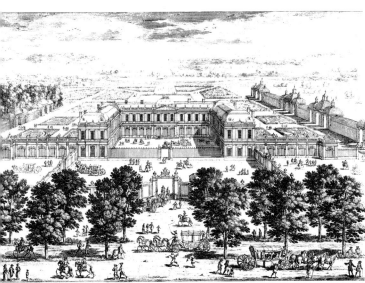

257. Jules Hardouin-Mansart,
Versailles, Château de Clagny
(engraving by Perelle).

for the Louvre. Le Vau's wings are still in existence but the terrace between them was substituted by Jules Hardouin-Mansart's Galerie des Glaces in 1678, so that the façade received a rather monotonous character. The monotony became still more accentuated when Hardouin-Mansart added long transverse wings, repeating the same wall system at a total length of over four hundred meters. It would, however, be unfair to judge Versailles as a well-proportioned complete volume. Here *extension as such* is the theme, and accordingly the building has been transformed into a simple repetitive system. The system consists of a transparent skeleton where the intervals between the pilasters are entirely filled in by large, arched windows.[64] Versailles therefore has the character of a glass house, and represents a link between the transparent structures of the Gothic period and the great iron-and-glass buildings of the nineteenth century. Its extension is "indeterminate," another characteristic property that prefigures certain modern conceptions. The complete block of Le Vau, thus, has been transformed into one large *ressaut*, which actively projects into the landscape. Seen in this context, the flat roof also becomes meaningful. The interpretation of Versailles as an expression of pure extension resolves the contradiction that has always existed between the fascination the building exerts on the beholder and the negative judgements given by architectural critics on the basis of "academic rules." In spite of its lack of traditional architectural qualities, Versailles concretizes the basic intentions of the Baroque Age, intentions that in particular were connected with absolute monarchy and therefore *ought* to be expressed here more than anywhere else. In fact, the whole grandiose layout has the bed of the sovereign as its innermost focus. Versailles is a true symbol of the absolute but "open" system of seventeenth-century France.

Before he worked out his great scheme for Versailles in 1678, Jules Hardouin-Mansart had built some smaller palaces where his characteristic approach was already evident. The small *Château du Val* (1674) is a one-story building consisting of a salon "où le Roi mange ordinairement au retour de la chasse" in the middle, a small apartment on one side and four rooms of varied shape "où est representée dans chacune une des quatre saisons" on the other. The elongated, narrow building is completely opened to the surroundings by series of arched French windows. The *Château de Dampierre* (1675) has a more conventional layout, but except for a central *ressaut*, the articulation mainly consists of the repetition of numerous uniform openings. The building, thus, is of indeterminate extension, but is kept together by a voluminous Mansard roof. Still more characteristic was the *Château de Clagny* built for Madame de Montespan (1676).[65] The plan shows a series of very long, narrow wings forming a layout which prefigures the solution of Versailles. A domed grand salon introduced a very efficient focus in the outstretched repetitive organism. We may say that Clagny, on a smaller scale, shows how Versailles would have been if Hardouin-Mansart had started from zero. In 1679 he built

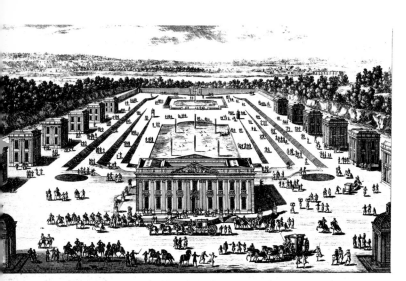

the *Château de Marly* as a place of entertainment for the King.[66] A centralized pavilion formed the focus and determined the strongly emphasized main axes. "Extension" was achieved by two lateral rows of small pavilions for the courtiers, which created a continuous rhythm of indeterminate duration. All the buildings were based on a similar repetitive system of pilasters. The ideas of Hardouin-Mansart culminated with the *Grand Trianon* in the garden of Versailles (1687). Here the very long narrow one-story wings simply consist of a uniform system of pilasters and columns carrying a straight entablature. The continuous rhythm is emphasized by arched French windows, and the flat roof contributes to the effect of infinite extension. We may conclude that all the secular works of Jules Hardouin-Mansart are based on the same formal principle, which concretized fundamental aspects of Baroque space.[67] To gain his end, Hardouin-Mansart had to reduce the elements to the essentials, i.e. he based the articulation on simple classical members. His open organisms differ from those of Guarini. They do not consist in the repetition of spatial "cells," but are constituted by a uniform structural system. He is often considered a classicist, although his general schemes have nothing in common with the classical ideal of a complete "perfect" form. Instead of being classical, the works of Hardouin Mansart come close to the twentieth-century ideal of "open," indeterminate organisms, and they illustrate how the Baroque in many ways prefigures modern architecture.

Conclusion

The essential "content" of the Baroque palace is continuous movement along a longitudinal axis. This movement actively unites the three basic "levels" of human life: the civic world, the private "place" and infinite nature. Common to Italian and French palaces is an emphasis on the main axis by means of symmetry and formal accentuation. The spaces of the building and its environment live in relation to this axis.

The most important design problem was the transition from one spatial domain to the other. In Italy the Baroque palace kept its enclosed block-like form, and the transition from the urban environment to the "inside," therefore, became a dramatic event which deprived the wall of its traditional character as a separating element. The Italian wall tends to concentrate its subordinate components around the main axis, or to become inflected as a result of the meeting of interior and exterior forces. The transition from the building to the garden (landscape) was less violent, as nature was conceived as an extension of the dwelling rather than a different domain. The cortile was therefore opened up whenever possible and a more regular distribution of the interior spaces was attempted to satisfy the general symmetry of the layout. The French palace never had the same enclosed character. From the very beginning, it was an "extended" organism. The early palaces of the seventeenth century still have an "additive" character.

For about fifty years there was a process of formal concentration and unification that ended with the uniform, repetitive structures of Jules Hardouin-Mansart, so that a new kind of general, open extension became possible. The French wall, therefore, tended to become a transparent skeleton allowing for a fusion of exterior and interior space. The plastic frames and pediments used to emphasize the figural character of the opening in Italian architecture were abandoned, and replaced by a uniform system of arches of equal height encompassing doors, windows, interior panelling, decoration and mirrors. The French window, in fact, is of decisive importance for the light and summery character of the French palace. The French palace was primarily the scene for the development of a new concept of comfortable living. In both countries articulation was based on the use of the classical orders for formal differentiation and unification, as well as for integrating the works in the great tradition of European humanism.[68]

Chapter Five
THE DIFFUSION OF BAROQUE ARCHITECTURE

Introduction

We have so far discussed the major building tasks of the Baroque Age. It remains to take a more general look at the contributions of individual countries and architects. In previous chapters we emphasized the *common basis* of the various manifestations. Firstly the general *esprit de système*, and secondly the leading building tasks as a common point of departure. We have also defined general formative principles resulting from the common existential basis, such as centralization and extension, which may be studied on different "levels" in terms of concrete spatial relationships. The common basis, however, was interpreted in many different ways, according to various circumstances and forms of life. We have, in fact, already pointed out that the seventeenth century was characterized by a great diversity. The differences were due to various factors.

Theoretically we could distinguish between five kinds of environmental determinants: physical, personal, social, cultural and historical. These factors obviously are interdependent, but may to a certain extent be studied separately.[1] The physical factors can be described in terms of climate, topography, resources, etc., and determine what is usually called "regional character," namely typified use of building materials, location and size of openings, and roof shapes. The personal factors stem from differences in needs and attitudes, and determine what is called "personal style." The client as well as the architect are relevant in this connection. The social factors may refer to social differences or to a way of life common to the members of a particular group. They determine the more general properties of a "milieu," such as separation or togetherness, but also formal distinctions which express a particular social role. The cultural factors consist in ideas and values, and determine "meanings" which are expressed through formal languages or "styles." All these factors obviously operate in the temporal dimension and are therefore historical. With historical factors in particular, we intend certain artistic influences, or extra-artistic events that initiate, accelerate or retard significant changes in the human environment. During the seventeenth century all these factors contributed to architectural development, according to the circumstances. In a politically centralized country like France, the regional variations were slight, whereas Italy presents characteristic local models of expression. Regardless of country, however, the *cultural* factors were of prime importance.

Italy

Towards the end of the sixteenth century, the development of Italian architecture became centered on Rome. The main force behind this process was the Counter-Reformation which brought forth a centralization of ideas and artistic potential. As a result, a vigorous Roman Baroque architecture evolved, which extended its sphere of influence to the whole Catholic world, and even beyond. Although Roman Baroque architecture pro-

duced its main works after 1630, many of the basic intentions had been manifest quite a lot earlier. In general, the aim was to create an environment having a stronger emotional and persuasive impact, and to make every single building appear as an expression of a universal system of values. We have seen, thus, how churches and palaces started to interact with their urban environment, mainly because of the introduction of a longitudinal axis that "opened" the traditional self-sufficient architectural form. The inner disposition of the buildings also became a function of the main axis. The churches, however, constituting the principal foci of the meaningful system, also needed a dominant vertical axis around which spatial extension was organized.

These general intentions are already apparent in the works of *Giacomo della Porta* (1533-1602). Della Porta is often considered an architect of secondary importance. This may be due to the fact that he mostly finished the works of others or left his own buildings to be completed by his successors. We have, however, demonstrated that he had a real inventive power, making essential contributions to the development of the Baroque church and palace.[2] A decisive clarification of ends and means characterizes the designs of *Carlo Maderno* (1556-1629). The reputation of Maderno has been somewhat damaged by the unfortunate fate of the façade of St. Peter's. In general, however, his works have a convincing strength and subtlety of detail. This is particularly evident in his façade for S. Susanna in Rome (1597-1603), which is usually considered the first full-grown example of Baroque architecture. Here the general intentions of Della Porta are developed towards an increased plasticity, for the purpose of strengthening the emphasis on the central axis. Thus we find a progression from pilaster to half-column, three-quarter column and full column towards the middle of the façade. In his secular works, such as the Palazzo Mattei and the Palazzo Barberini, Maderno solved corresponding problems by means of new ingenious spatial dispositions. "By the time Maderno died, he had directed Roman architecture into entirely new channels. He had authoritatively rejected the facile academic Mannerism which had belonged to his first impressions in Rome, and, although not a revolutionary like Borromini, he left behind, largely guided by Michelangelo, monumental work of such solidity, seriousness and substance that it was equally respected by the great antipodes Bernini and Borromini."[3]

In general, however, Early Baroque architecture was characterized by a relatively superficial approach to the problem of architectural form. To realize the intended persuasive impression, the articulating elements were multiplied and combined in complex ways, so that a certain overloaded effect often resulted. A typical example is furnished by Martino Longhi's façade for SS. Vincenzo ed Anastasio in Rome (1644), where an unsurpassed condensation towards the middle of the façade is achieved by means of triple columns and interlocking aediculae which gradually step forward to emphasize the central axis.[4] The transition from the "Early Ba-

263. Carlo Maderno, Rome,
S. Susanna, façade, axonometric
drawing (D.A.U.).
264. Rome, S. Susanna, façade.

roque" to the "High Baroque" is marked by a deeper penetration into the problems. That is, the aims of spatial integration and persuasive expression were satisfied through a transformation of the basic form rather than by applied decoration. Maderno initiated this research, but the decisive results are to be found in the works of Bernini, Borromini and Cortona.

The new approach is evident already in the first architectural work of *Gianlorenzo Bernini* (1598-1680), the *Baldacchino* in St. Peter's (1624-33). The four twisted bronze columns repeat the shape of the Early Christian columns, which had served in the *pergola* of Old St. Peter's. They have, however, grown to giant size "expressing symbolically the change from the simplicity of the early Christians to the splendour of the counter-reformatory Church, implying the victory of Christianity over the pagan world."[5] The twisted shape also resolves an important formal problem. Straight columns would have looked like diminished versions of the immense pilasters that constitute the main order of the church, and would not have given the necessary emphasis to its focus: the site of St. Peter's grave. The twisted column represents a dynamic and emphatic variation on a "normal" column, and the baldachin thus manages to dominate and centralize the grand space by which it is surrounded. Above the columns, huge S-shaped scrolls rise to support the cross above the golden orb. We have reason to believe that the scrolls were designed by Borromini, who at the time served as an assistant to Bernini. At any rate the *Baldacchino* may be considered "il manifesto dell'architettura barocca."[6] Its rich and persuasive form stems from a transformation of the basic elements, rather than added decoration, and the result is a simple, integrated whole characterized by plastic continuity. The *Baldacchino* represents in equal measure a point of departure for the antipodes Bernini and Borromini. It has the grand simplicity and powerful impact of Bernini's later designs, but also the dynamism and synthetic character which mark the works of Borromini.

The more important buildings of both architects have been discussed above, but we should mention a few significant contributions. Among Bernini's works the *Scala Regia* in the Vatican (1663-66) has a prominent place. The narrow space available hardly allowed for the development of a monumental staircase, but by ingenious tricks of perspective and illumination, Bernini corrected the real dimensions of the space. The converging walls, thus, would have given an impression of excessive depth, had not Bernini placed rows of columns in front which converge *less* than the walls.[7] Bernini's works, in fact, aim at an *objectification* of phenomena that go beyond the measurable, "real" properties of the situation. He makes us participate in situations that seem to be natural and self-evident, but which have a significant irrational content. Architecturally the objectification is realized by the employment of apparently simple volumes, and by a regular, integrative articulation.

In the works of *Francesco Borromini* (1599-1667), on the other hand, the irrational, "synthetic" content is expressed by a correspondingly complex

form. Borromini, however, overcomes complexity as such by means of spatial and plastic continuity. He thereby unifies heterogeneous elements into synthetic wholes that represent new psychic and existential characters. This is particularly evident in two works that have not been mentioned so far: the unfinished campanile and dome of S. Andrea delle Fratte (1653) and the Cappella Spada in S. Girolamo della Carità (1662). In S. Andrea delle Fratte, Borromini transformed the traditional static and enclosed drum into a dynamic, radiating organism. The convex bays in the middle indicate the expansive movement of interior space that interacts with exterior space to create a strong radiation along the diagonal axes. By adding a freestanding campanile, Borromini moreover realized an urban focus that, without losing its identity, changes according to our position.[8] The dome and campanile of S. Andrea delle Fratte thus represent an eminently Baroque focus that participates in an extended "field" of spatial relations. The Spada chapel illustrates better than any other work how Borromini made *space* the protagonist of architecture. Instead of focusing attention upon a plastically modelled altar, he reduced plasticity to a minimum by covering the walls with continuous inlaid marble decoration. The decoration is not "applied" but constitutes a space that is extremely simple and at the same time highly irrational. Borromini, thus, also aimed at a certain "objectification." While Bernini made the supernatural real, through its appearance in a simpler rational space, Borromini gave structure to irrational supernatural space, so that it became imaginable and integrated in man's existential space.

The ideas of Borromini had a certain following. Some architects adopted his formal means without understanding the revolutionary content of his works. A typical example is *Giovanni Antonio de Rossi* (1616-95) who, before anyone else, employed Borrominian methods of articulation. His masterpiece is the well-balanced and formally integrated Palazzo d'Aste-Bonaparte (1658-65), where the corner solution and the window pediments clearly derive from Borromini. A more original and truly inventive follower of Borromini was *Guarino Guarini* (1624-83), who continued Borromini's research into the creation of new synthetic "characters," as well as the possibility of using space as the constituent element in architecture. The articulation and decoration of Guarini are highly personal and the content expessed, however profound, is rarely directly comprehensible. As a typical example, we may mention the complex detailing of the *Collegio dei Nobili* in Turin (1679). This aspect of his work, therefore, had little following. As we have already seen, however, his handling of space opened up new fundamental possibilities. Basically, Guarini concretized his complex and highly irrational contents by ingenious but rational systems of spatial extension. Like Bernini and Borromini, thus, his basic aim was an objectification of the irrational, but whereas Maderno, Bernini and Borromini were representatives of a *Roman* Baroque architecture, Guarini's works do not belong to any par-

267. *Gianlorenzo Bernini, Rome,
Vatican, Scala Regia.*

ticular place or region. In spite of his personal style, Guarini therefore expressed the universality of the Counter-Reformatory church.

Roman Baroque architecture always retained a characteristic identity through all personal variations. As a primary property of the Roman character, we may mention the emphasis on mass and plasticity. It is present even in Borromini's works, as his undulating walls ought to be understood as abstract expressions of the dramatic interaction of interior and exterior forces which constitute Roman plasticity and dynamism. In the works of *Carlo Rainaldi* (1611-91) the same aim is evident, but in spite of his inventiveness, Rainaldi does not arrive at a true Baroque synthesis of mass, space and surface.[9] His principal means of articulation are columns that are rhetorically "applied" in an Early Baroque manner, rather than plastically integrated. A true plastic integration, however, characterizes the works of *Pietro da Cortona* (1596-1669). Instead of taking spatial cells or wall membranes as his point of departure, Cortona composes with continuous series of plastic members, whose variations in density constitute a space that seems eminently alive. This is already evident in his first building, the Villa Sacchetti (1625-30).[10] A complex interaction of spaces that foreshadows his later works is constituted by groups and rows of pilasters and columns that create a rich, vibrating play of light and shadow. In general, the Villa Sacchetti possesses a singularly convincing equilibrium between mass and space. The same holds true for his last masterpiece, the dome for S. Carlo al Corso (1668-72). Here, the drum is constituted of clusters of muscular columns and pilasters that carry a strongly projecting entablature and a plastically articulated attic. Vigorous ribs transform the dome into an active, dynamic organism. Cortona, thus, may be considered a Baroque representative of classical, anthropomorphic architecture, making the traditional "objective" characters take part in a process of interaction and transformation.[11]

In spite of the central importance of Rome in seventeenth-century Italian architecture, some valid regional styles also appeared. We have already mentioned the important contributions of *Francesco Maria Ricchino* (1584-1658) who continued the local Milanese tradition of Pellegrino Tibaldi and Lorenzo Binago. In Turin we find the center of a particularly rich Piedmontese architecture, which was initiated by *Ascanio Vitozzi* (1539-1619) and continued by *Carlo* (1560-1641) and *Amedeo* (1610-83) *di Castellamonte*. This first phase of Piedmontese Baroque architecture unites influences from Rome and Paris. Whereas the individual buildings have an unmistakable "Italian" character, the urban environment is stamped by French rationalism.

A pronounced local character is found in Venice, where the traditional picturesque and decorative approach was given a Baroque interpretation by *Baldassare Longhena* (1598-1682). His Palazzo Pesaro (1663) shows a rich but controlled interplay of mass and space, light and shadow, and has a true Baroque plasticity, in spite of the somewhat conventional composi-

272. Pietro da Cortona, Rome,
Villa Sacchetti (contemporary
engraving).

273. Pietro da Cortona, Rome,
S. Carlo al Corso, exterior, apse
and dome.

274. Baldassare Longhena, Venice,
Palazzo Pesaro.

275. Carlo Fontana, Rome,
S. Marcello al Corso, façade.

276. Salomon de Brosse, Paris,
St. Gervais, façade.

277. François Mansart, Paris,
Church of the Minimes (engraving
by Marot).

tion. The Baroque architecture of southern Italy mainly belongs to the eighteenth century. We should, however, mention the Neapolitan *Cosimo Fanzago* (1591-1678), Baroque in versatility but without real creative talent. Towards the end of the century, Roman architecture was dominated by the mediocre, classically-minded *Carlo Fontana* (1638-1714). In general, Italian seventeenth-century architecture was determined by the church as the leading building task. Except in Turin, the environment, therefore, does not possess a systematically organized horizontal extension. It is dominated rather by the vertical axes of the churches, whose interaction with the urban environment, i.e. "society," is expressed by a "dynamic" and persuasive plastic form.

France

In France the process of centralization was stronger than in Italy. A certain regional activity existed up until the death of Mazarin (1661), but the artistic potential had been centered on Paris since the beginning of the century. French seventeenth-century architecture, therefore, has an unequivocal character and development. The driving force was the idea of absolute monarchy by divine right, and the result was a new kind of state architecture.[12] It unified the poles of reason and transcendence. We have already analyzed the conception of space that concretized these intentions, and have also pointed out how regional and Gothic traditions were absorbed by the new architecture, which, in general, employed a formal language imported from Italy.[13] The leading building type was the palace, which formed the focus of an infinitely extended space. Extension presupposes that the constituent elements have a certain uniformity, and, in fact, French seventeenth-century architecture does not present the plastic modelling and emphasis that characterize contemporary Italian buildings. It is therefore often regarded as less "Baroque" and more "classical." Such a judgement, however, stems from a superficial definition of the categories in question. "Baroque architecture" only becomes a useful concept if it denotes concretizations of a certain kind of existential space, rather than particular formal traits.

The typical French approach is evident already in the works of *Salomon de Brosse* (1571-1626). His façade for St. Gervais in Paris (1616)[14] shows a "correct" superposition of the three classical orders. Vertically as well as horizontally, the composition is based on regular repetition, although the façade as a whole gives emphasis to the longitudinal axis of the building. A similar solution was used by De Brosse and his followers in secular buildings as well: we may for instance recall the central *ressaut* of François Mansart's Château de Maisons.[15] The motif unifies in a simple formula the basic canons of classical architecture, Gothic verticalism and Baroque movement in depth, and thus became a token of French seventeenth-century architecture. The secular works of De Brosse still show Mannerist

278. *Louis Le Vau, Paris, Collège des Quatre Nations (Institut de France).*

279. *Paris, Collège des Quatre Nations (Institut de France), perspective view (engraving by Perelle).*

traits, such as interlocking rustication and orders, but the tensions and contradictions typical of Mannerism have been substituted by regularly extended rhythms. De Brosse, thus, defined the basic ends and means of the century.

François Mansart (1598-1666) belongs to the generation of Bernini, Borromini and Cortona, and played an analogous role in making architecture a flexible and subtle tool for expressing the contents of the epoch. His works are characterized by great inventive power, but also by a restraint that makes the radical traits less evident. Although his articulation is highly original, a "correct" use of the orders creates a general classic character. Mansart, thus, manages to objectify the dynamism and irrational variations inherent in Baroque architecture by the employment of a rational, well-known vocabulary of forms. Few architects in history have attained a similar equilibrium of the general and the particular, the objective and the personal. In the façade for the church of the *Minimes* in Paris (1657) the ability of Mansart is clearly evident.[16] The problem of giving emphasis to the longitudinal axis and at the same time making the building part of the street in front has been solved in a way that reminds us of Borromini's S. Agnese in Piazza Navona. Within the continuous wall system, however, Mansart gives clear definition to each volume, as he had already done in his Château de Berny (1624). Verticality and horizontal extension are thus combined to form a well-balanced whole. The dome placed over the entrance to the church also terminates the axis of the Place des Vosges, so that a highly original integration of building and urban environment is achieved.

In the works of *Louis Le Vau* (1612-70), we find a different approach to similar problems. The difference becomes evident when we compare the Minimes with Le Vau's Collège des Quatre Nations (Institut de France) of 1600. In both cases, a dome marks the termination of an urban axis, whereas outstretched wings create lateral extensions. In Le Vau's building, however, the subtle tensions of Mansart have been substituted by a Baroque rhetoric based on the contrast between convex and concave volumes, and colossal and normal orders. A general continuity is maintained by means of a uniform repetition of openings.[17] In spite of his interest in grand relationships, Le Vau made an essential contribution to the development of the commodious and practical dwelling. He showed a particular ability for solving functional plans and seems to have been "temperamentally well suited to the demands of his patrons, whereas Mansart threw away commissions owing to his obstinacy and arrogance."[18] The problem of the Louvre, however, grew beyond the capacity of Le Vau.

The intervention of Bernini has already been discussed but we ought to say a few words about the final solution. The east front of the Louvre is usually considered to be the culmination of French classical architecture. Over a closed ground-floor rises a splendid row of coupled columns. The typically French repetitive extension is articulated by subtle variations.

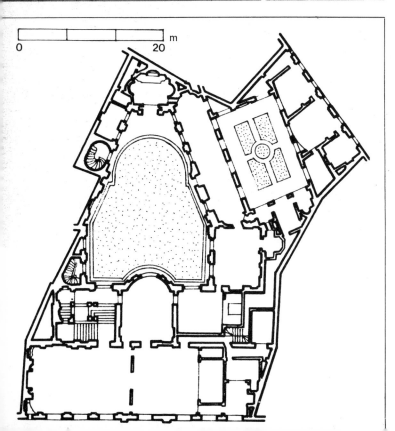

280. François d'Orbay, Paris,
Louvre, east façade.
281. Paris, Louvre, east façade.

282. Antoine Le Pautre, Paris,
Hôtel de Beauvais, plan of first
floor (from Blunt).

The wall consists of five sections which have a different characterization. The corners are defined as solid pavilions by a unification of wall and order. The columns, thus, have become pilasters, and only the "open" center is marked by pairs of pilaster and column. The long walls between the corners and the central *ressaut* are transparent colonnades that simultaneously remind us of a Roman temple and a Gothic "diaphanous" structure. In the central *ressaut* mass and skeleton structure are combined to create an active but restrained expression of interaction between interior and exterior. Rarely has the dialectic of order and variation been demonstrated in a more masterly way. Who, then, was the creator of this magnificent design? The general layout obviously goes back to a project by Le Vau from 1664, and, in fact, the characterization of the five wall sections corresponds to the typical disposition of his other buildings, and in his work we also find the coupled order (Hôtel de Lionne, 1662). The simple classical grandeur of the final solution (1667-68) has been proved to be due to his pupil and collaborator, *François d'Orbay* (1631-97).[19]

Whereas D'Orbay gave French architecture a more classical direction, Le Vau's pupil *Antoine le Pautre* (1621-91) developed the Baroque aspects of his work. Le Pautre did not build much, but his Hôtel de Beauvais in Paris (1654-56) demonstrates a great ability to exploit a difficult building site. The transition from the entrance to the courtyard is emphasized by lateral walls, articulated by a giant order, that converge at an aedicula at the far end. At the same time, however, the space is circumscribed by a continuous, strongly projecting cornice. Virtually no other space in French seventeenth-century architecture has a similar plasticity and dynamism. Most famous of Le Pautre's works is the project for a château, published in his *les Oeuvres d'Architecture* (1652).[20] The general disposition is derived from the Luxembourg palace with corner apartments and a central vestibule, and the wall articulation follows the usual scheme of Le Vau with a giant order on the wings. The desire for plastic and spatial systematization, however, surpasses anything conceived previously. The grand circular vestibule that is crowned by a "drum-without-dome" defines the center of a system of radiating directions, among which the main axis has prime importance. Along the transverse axis one rises up to the first floor through a series of varied spaces. The use of *dégagements* is very progressive, but as a whole the plan has a somewhat theoretical character. The whole complex bi-axial organism is unified by a continuous entablature. We may assume that Bernini knew the publications of Le Pautre and that the château project influenced his first design for the Louvre.

The last decades of the seventeenth century were dominated by *Jules Hardouin-Mansart* (1646-1708). He is often considered a somewhat dry and uninspired designer; we have shown, however, that his uniformly extended structures were the result of deliberate intentions, and we have also pointed out his ability to solve more particular problems, such as the Place des Victoires or the Dôme des Invalides. "He served the needs of his

time perfectly, and applied to them vast talents: an exceptional sense of grandeur, great skill in directing a team of craftsmen and, when it was called for, considerable mastery of the strictly practical side of the architect's profession."[21] His clear and assured style is particularly evident in the chapel at Versailles (1689-1710). The chapel had to consist of two stories, the ground-floor for the courtiers and the public, and the upper-floor for the King, in direct communication with his apartment. Hardouin-Mansart solved the problem in a manner that recalls the Louvre façade, not only on account of the clarity of the design, but equally because of the relation between massive base and "transparent" main story. The King, so to say, rises with full self-assurance over his followers, a content that is emphasized by the "Gothic" proportions of the space. With the Louvre façade and the chapel at Versailles, French classical architecture reached a culmination point. The two works give a consummate concretization of the rational and transcendental *esprit de système* of seventeenth-century France.

During the first half of the century, French ecclesiastical architecture still had a creative impulse, as shown by the works of François Mansart, and space was not only experienced as an abstract extension, but, in the Italian way, as a concrete phenomenon. As state architecture came to dominate the scene, with the palace as the leading construction, churches were thrown into the background. Domes tended to disappear, and the ideal form was a neutral hall which no longer acted as a primary focus.[22] The abstract properties of space were emphasized, in particular problems of proportion, and architecture tended to follow the laws of nature and reason rather than imagination and individual circumstances. The approach was codified by the leader of the Academy, *François Blondel* (1617-86), who wanted to establish a set of rules with absolute validity. In his *Cours d'Architecture* (1675), he said: "...proportion is what determines beauty and elegance in architecture, and this must be made into a constant, stable principle by means of Mathematics." Fortunately the doctrine of Blondel was never applied with full vigour, but it initiated an "academic" approach to architecture that has been retained until the twentieth century.

Spain

Spain experienced its peak of imperial power in the sixteenth century under Philip II. Under Philip III, who ruled from 1598 to 1621, greatness turned into decline. The country was threatened by military and economic collapse, and the wretched Spanish world found its expression in Cervantes' *Don Quixote* (1605). The conditions, therefore, were not favourable for the development of a true Baroque architecture. The great intentions of Philip II's Escorial were abandoned and Spanish architecture was reduced to secondary importance.[23]

The Escorial was planned by *Juan Bautista de Toledo* in 1562 and was mainly executed by *Juan de Herrera* (1530-97) between 1572 and 1584. It represents a great synthesis of building types, since it was to provide Philip with a palace for his court, a monastery to which he could retire, a great church, and a tomb. It thus symbolized the particular character of the Spanish state. The large, symmetrical rectangle has many ancestors, going as far back as Diocletian's palace in Split, and it became a model for the great *Fürstabteien* of the eighteenth century in Central Europe. In 1585 Herrera planned the Cathedral of Valladolid on an interesting bi-axial layout, giving emphasis to movement in depth as well as centralization. The concept had a certain following, as for instance in the Cathedral of Mexico City and the interesting Pilar Church in Saragossa (1680). Herrera's successor, *Juan Gómez de Mora* (1580-1648), however, returned to a more conventional scheme when he planned the Jesuit Clerecía in Salamanca in 1617. The disposition follows Il Gesù, without having the rhythmical richness and spatial unity of the Roman church. More interesting is the Cathedral of Madrid, S. Isidro, built by *Francisco Bautista* (1594-1678) after 1629. Here the nave shows an alternation of wide and narrow bays, a motif that is repeated in the ends of the transept. The articulation has a new richness that makes the wall increasingly become a continuous surface ornament. The idea may be a Moresque inspiration, and it initiated an important development in Spanish Baroque architecture. The development of the longitudinal church culminated with S. Maria Magdalena in Granada by *Juan Luís Ortega* (1628-77), built after 1677. Here a bi-axial nave is joined to a dominant, tall dome, a solution that is related to contemporaneous Roman churches. Among the centralized structures in Spain, we may mention the Desamparados church in Valencia by *Diego Martínez Ponce de Urrana*, built 1652-67. A longitudinal oval is inscribed in a rectangle, prefiguring the double spatial delimitation typical of the eighteenth century. The space ends with a *camarín*, namely a space above the altar for the display of the sacrament.[24] In general, Spanish seventeenth-century architecture tended increasingly towards a decorative approach, which represented a variation on the Baroque theme of persuasion. It is therefore natural that it reached a climax in the buildings for the missions in America. Even illiterate people of a foreign civilization could "understand" the language of exuberant ornament, colors, and images. We find, thus, a typically "Baroque" bias but the individual buildings do not represent any significant contribution to the history of architecture.

England

Up until the beginning of the seventeenth century, English architecture had lived its own life. In spite of the general cultural contact with the continent during the reign of Queen Elizabeth, architecture remained isolated. During the second decade of the century, the situation suddenly changed, due to the fundamental contribution of a single architect: *Inigo Jones* (1573-1652). Jones had visited Venice between 1597 and 1603, and in 1613-14 he again spent a year and a half in Italy. In the meantime (1609), he had also visited Paris. Jones' formation, thus, took place before the real development of Roman and French Baroque, and he found his source of inspiration in the theoretical approach and works of Palladio. From then on, Palladio was always present, in one way or another, in English architecture. It is significant that Palladio was the only architect to create *a complete architectural system without Baroque rhetoric.* His combination of versatility and self-restraint fitted the character of English society and the English psyche particularly well. In seventeenth-century England, in fact, we find neither a dominant Church nor an absolute monarchy. Rather, religion and aristocracy appeared as factors in a more complex totality, which also included the burgher, the merchant, and the free thinker. The resulting pluralism, however, did not prevent England from possessing a powerful "system" of its own kind. Although the country experienced civil war and the decapitation of its King, we may still talk of a more democratic society than in the other European countries. Inigo Jones built for the court, but his "Palladian" style makes the desire for a corresponding "democratic" architecture manifest. The aim was to create an architecture possessing a neutral universality. "Jones saw certain things clearly—more clearly than his Italian and French contemporaries with their immensely richer and more sophisticated backgrounds could do. He saw that antiquity offered, in the five orders and in their attachment to specific forms of spatial arrangement, a language of timeless validity. His was not the spirit of revolution, but such was the force of his example that, sustained through two generations of eclectic experiment and Baroque adventure, it showed the way, in a new age, to a new enlightenment."[25]

The first work that demonstrates the approach of Jones is the Queen's House at Greenwich (1616-35). Originally the building consisted of two wings linked by a bridge at first-floor level, together forming a square. The slightly projecting center of the entrance wing indicates the great cubical hall, which runs up through both stories. The ground-floor is rusticated, and originally had smaller windows. The higher piano nobile has a simple Ionic character, particularly evident in the loggia on the garden side. The flat roof contributes to the Italianate impression. The tall windows and the horizontally elongated proportion of the block, however, are of Nordic origin, and create a subdued play of tensions that also comprises a certain emphasis on the main axis.[26] In 1617 Jones made a design for a new Star Chamber, employing a giant order over a rusticated base. The interior, articulated by two tiers of half-columns, should have resembled a Roman basilica. The same theme is monumentalized in the Banqueting House (1619-22) which is the most important surviving work by Jones. The bi-axial, two-story interior is articulated by Ionic half-columns below and Composite pilasters above, and is circumscribed by a cantilevered gallery. Originally an apse gave direction to the space, which has the static propor-

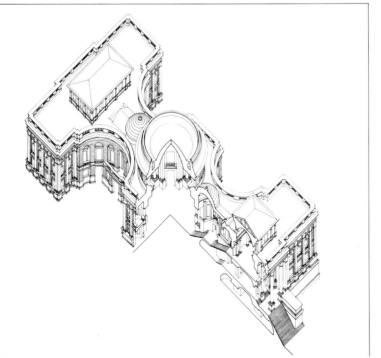

LVDOVICO MAGNO.

287. Juan Bautista de Toledo, Juan
de Herrera, Madrid, El Escorial.
288. Juan Gómez de Mora,
Salamanca, Jesuit Clerecía and
Cathedral.

289. Francisco Bautista, Madrid,
S. Isidro, interior.

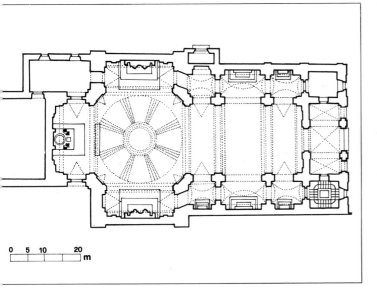

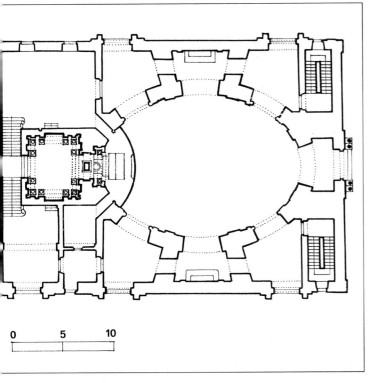

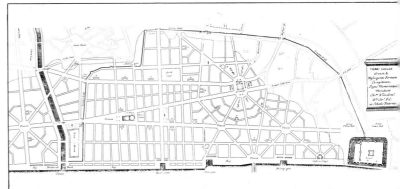

tion of a double cube. The orders of the interior correspond to those of the beautifully detailed exterior. Here, however, we find a similar treatment of the two tiers. Coupled pilasters mark the corners, and the three middle bays are emphasized by columns. The harmonious articulation appears on a rusticated surface, a Mannerist motif that has lost any sense of conflict. In general, the Banqueting House seems to symbolize the reconciliation of opposites and the ideal of peaceful democratic collaboration. A similar character is found in Lindsay House at Lincoln's Inn Fields (1638-40), probably designed by Jones, where a colossal order rises over a low rusticated ground-floor. Jones' plan for Covent Garden (1631) introduced the idea of the *place* in London. The space was unified by arcades and centered on the church of St. Paul's which was built as a Tuscan temple. "It is an extraordinary performance, ...an archaelogical essay... prophetic of the theory and practise of neoclassicism..."[27] The great project for the Whitehall Palace (1638), which would have been Jones' *magnum opus*, was stopped by the Civil War (1642-49). The design shows a large rectangle, somewhat repeating the layout of the Escorial and more than twice its size. The articulation indicated in Jones' sketches does not detract from the monotonous gigantism that appears as a caricature of English values. "Had Charles I lived to build it, the new Whitehall would have been a grave and fitting backcloth for the bloodier revolution which it would most certainly have helped to precipitate."[28]

English architecture of the seventeenth century was split into two distinct phases by the Civil War. As Inigo Jones dominated the first, *Christopher Wren* (1632-1723) was the protagonist of the second. Wren started as an astronomer and mathematician, and became a member of the Royal Society when it was founded in 1662. As an architect, he must be considered a learned dilettante, since his only education outside England consisted of a trip to Paris in 1665, where he met Bernini. In a letter he wrote: "I have busied myself in surveying the most esteem'd Fabricks of Paris, and the Country round. The Louvre for a while was my daily Object, where no less than a thousand hands are constantly employ'd in the Works... Mons. Abbé Charles introduc'd me to the Acquaintance of Bernini, who shew'd me the designs of the Louvre... Bernini's design of the Louvre I would have given my skin for..."[29] After a few tentative attempts, Wren's golden opportunity came after the Great Fire of London in September 1666. In a few days, more than thirteen thousand houses and eighty-seven churches were destroyed by the fire, as well as the great Cathedral of St. Paul's. About two hundred thousand people became homeless. Shortly afterwards Wren presented a plan for the New City to King Charles II. The solution shows a Baroque system of piazze and radiating streets, with the Royal Exchange serving as the main focus. The new Cathedral of St. Paul's also had a prominent position between the streets leading from Ludgate in the west to the Tower and the Exchange. Many of the secondary streets were centered on parish churches.

XXIII. Stockholm, Tessin Palace, garden.

XXIV. Prague, Czernin Palace,
detail of façade.

297. London, St. Paul's Cathedral.
298. Christopher Wren, London,
St. Stephen Walbrook, plan
(D.A.U.).

299. London, St. Stephen
Walbrook, interior.
300. Christopher Wren, Greenwich,
Royal Naval Hospital.

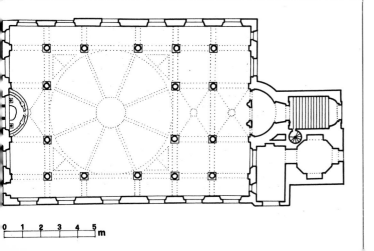

0 1 2 3 4 5 m

The great plan, however, was not carried out, as it took too little account of the ownership of land. Instead, Wren was commissioned to rebuild the Cathedral and the city churches. All in all, he built fifty-one churches, mostly designed in 1670 and shortly afterwards, but only a few of them were really designed in detail by Wren himself. Usually they are rectangular in plan, and represent reductions of traditional basilican schemes, forming halls with or without aisles. Particular attention is given to the steeples, which should rise "in good proportion above the neighboring houses... may be of sufficient Ornament to the Town."[30] They show Wren's great inventive power, and combine classical, Gothic, and Baroque traits into highly efficient urban foci. But they also demonstrate a certain eclecticism of approach, and often seem compiled rather than composed. Among the city churches, St. Stephen Walbrook (1672-87) represents an important and highly original achievement. Into a regularly subdivided rectangle has been placed a dome that rests on eight arches carried by columns. Four of these arches also indicate a Latin cross. The result is an ingeniously simple synthesis of longitudinal, central, and cross-shaped plans, an "architectural equivalent of the Anglican compromise between the austerities of Calvinism and the splendors of Baroque Rome."[31]

When planning the new Cathedral of St. Paul's, Wren aimed at a similar synthesis, only on a much larger scale. In 1673 he presented his project in the form of a *great model*. The centralized main space is clearly derived from Michelangelo's project for St. Peter's, but smaller domed spaces on the diagonals open onto the main center. A "Baroque" desire for spatial integration, thus, is present. But while Michelangelo's plan is centripetally enclosed, Wren makes his spatial group interact with the surroundings by means of concave external walls. A domed vestibule and a classical portico introduce a longitudinal axis. The articulation of the exterior is also derived from St. Peter's, as is the general relationship between the main building and the dome. Unfortunately the clergy did not find the magnificent project "enough of cathedral-fashion." Wren, thus, had to remake the project. The final solution (1675) is a rather awkward combination of longitudinal basilica and domed center. The two schemes do not form any convincing whole; particularly unfortunate is the solution of the diagonal axes, where the uniform ring of arches from St. Stephen Walbrook is superimposed on a structure it does not relate to. The articulation of the exterior is also weaker than in the great model, as its colossal order has been substituted for two tiers of small pilasters. A certain monotonous and petty character result.[32] The main façade gains because of the introduction of columns, and the towers are well integrated with the central part by means of a "Baroque" interpenetration. Vertically, however, the design falls apart, as the towers are topped by entirely "foreign" superstructures of a loosely Borrominian character. The dome, on the other hand, has a regularity that makes it a rather banal expression of the ideals of English architecture. Its "external effect has never, in the opinion of Englishmen

(and even some foreigners), been equalled."[33] In addition to his ecclesiastical works, Wren also designed several large public buildings. The Royal Hospital in Chelsea (1682-89) introduces a great U-shaped Baroque layout, but the articulation continues the simple classicism of Inigo Jones. In 1683 Wren made a plan somewhat similar to Versailles for Winchester Palace, and in Hampton Court (1689) he applied a simple repetitive articulation of an approximately Palladian character to a large, extended organism. His most interesting design, however, was for the Royal Naval Hospital at Greenwich (1695). After a preliminary project, Wren arrived at a solution where the Queen's House by Inigo Jones is used to terminate an axis defined by a wide "avenue" between colonnades and a courtyard opening on the river Thames. The transition between the two spaces is marked by tall domes over the chapel and the hall. The design is a magnificent variation of Baroque themes, and shows a mature handling of the relation between mass and space. A strong sense of unity is achieved by the use of coupled columns throughout, even in the domes which have a certain affinity to Hardouin-Mansart's Invalides. The Hospital in Greenwich was completed by Vanbrugh and Hawksmoor, but the general layout is Wren's and it must be considered his most successful work.

Two other architects who were active during the second half of the seventeenth century have to be mentioned, because they contributed decisively to the development of secular architecture in England. *Roger Pratt* (1620-84) had spent the years of the Civil War in France and imported the *appartement double* and the cour d'honneur to England. In Coleshill (1650),[34] he arranged a splendid staircase and a saloon symmetrically behind each other on the main axis, and in Clarendon House in Piccadilly (1664-67) he combined a French U-layout with a simple "Palladian" articulation, creating a type that was imitated far and wide. *Hugh May* (1622-84) stayed in Holland during the Commonwealth, and brought Dutch classicism to England. His only surviving building, Eltham Lodge in London (1663-64), repeats the "double" plan of Coleshill, but the three central bays are framed by giant pilasters, following the example of Jacob van Campen and Pieter Post.

The Netherlands

During the seventeenth century, the Netherlands was the most prosperous country in Europe. After the foundation of the seven united provinces in 1579, trade and industry flourished and the cities grew in importance and population. The Netherlands had always been a country of cities with a relatively decentralized form of government. Even after 1579 we do not find an absolute monarch, but rather military leaders who did not have any real civilian authority or cultural importance. Conditions, therefore, did not favor the development of any truly Baroque architecture. The burgher class favored a milder form of Calvinism, which brought about a general

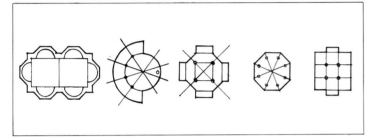

303. Pieter Noorwitz, The Hague,
Nieuwe Kerk.

simplicity of taste. No wonder, then, that Dutch architecture also adopted a sort of Palladian classicism, more Puritan in character than the related movement in England.

By 1600 Amsterdam had become the commercial center of the country.[35] It was a flourishing city of fifty thousand inhabitants, ably directed by a Council composed largely of merchants. Towards the end of the sixteenth century, the Council commissioned *Hendrik Staets* to make a plan for the extension of the town. He designed the famous "plan of the three canals" that forms concentric rings around the old urban core. Sites for local churches and market places were reserved. The plan was carried out by *Daniel Stalpaert* (1615-76) who made a zoning plan allocating the frontages along the three monumental canals to large business houses and town houses for merchants, and the building blocks formed by the radial canals to lower middle-class and artisan dwellings. In the areas between the three concentric canals, the plot sizes averaged twenty-six feet frontage and one hundred and eighty feet depth. A maximum site coverage of fifty-six percent was secured. Other prescriptions contributed to give Amsterdam one of the most integrated cityscapes in existence.

The civic pride of the city was grandly expressed in the new Town Hall by *Jacob van Campen* (1595-1657), which was started in 1648, the year of the peace of Westphalia when the independence of the Netherlands was officially recognized. The Town Hall of Amsterdam, thus, has considerable symbolic importance and the great Hall may be understood as the "Cathedral" of the Dutch republic. The plan of the large rectangular building shows a pronounced desire for systematization and the façades are articulated by a uniform system of pilasters and openings which is repeated without variation in both stories. The result is a rather austere building that unites self-assurance and sobriety. More charming is the small Mauritshuis in The Hague (1633), built by Van Campen for Prince Johan Maurits van Nassau. The simple, almost square volume is articulated by a colossal order of Ionic pilasters, which is used to give a different characterization to the façades. The entrance-wall, thus, has a wider bay in the middle to define the main axis, and the outer bays are characterized as rudimentary wings by means of a break in the entablature. The "garden" wall, which here faces the water, has a tri-partite *ressaut* in the middle. The lateral façades show a uniform repetition. The Mauritshuis contains therefore all the usual elements of the seventeenth century palace, but they are indicated rather than emphasized. The controlled and subtle result is usually called "Palladian"; it would, however, be more appropriate to call it "Dutch." The classicism of Van Campen was continued by his pupil and collaborator, *Pieter Post* (1608-69), whose main work is the Town Hall in Maastricht (1659-64). A related approach is also found in the works of *Philip Vingboons* (1614-78), whose Trippenhuis in Amsterdam (1660-62) gives a certain monumental note to the theme of the Mauritshuis.

The development of the Protestant church is closely connected with the

304. *Nicodemus Tessin the Younger, Stockholm, Royal Palace, forecourt.*
305. *Stockholm, Tessin Palace, plan.*

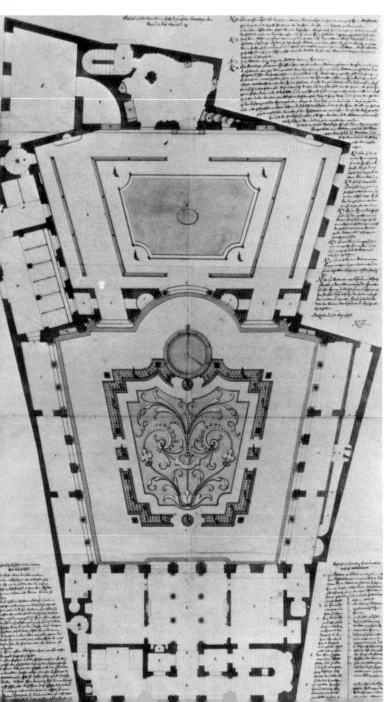

Netherlands. The new churches of Amsterdam from the beginning of the seventeenth century are rather conventional pseudo-basilicas; we may, for instance, mention the Zuiderkerk (1606-14) and the Westerkerk (1620-38) by *Hendrik de Keyser* (1565-1621). The Norderkerk, however, by Staets shows a more original approach (1620-23). The plan is a Greek cross with cut-off inside corners to create a better spatial integration. Within this space, the seats are diagonally oriented. The detailing is Mannerist with Gothic reminiscences. In 1639 *Arent van s'Gravesande* (d. 1662) started building the octagonal Marekerk in Leyden. The church is classical in character and is covered by a dome. Another "basic" type of plan was used by Van Campen in the Nieuwe Kerk in Haarlem (1645): a square with an inscribed Greek cross. More unusual is the Nieuwe Kerk in The Hague (1649) by *Pieter Noorwits* (d. 1669) and B. van Bassen, which consists of two squares with apses added all around, giving the basically simple building quite a rich and complex character. A regular succession of pilasters makes the wall appear as a continuous "shell." The bi-axial organism is centralized by a steep roof which embraces both the squares of the plan and a centrally placed steeple. The interior is also centralized, as the pulpit is placed on the shorter axis. Finally, we should mention the Nieuwe Lutherse Kerk in Amsterdam (1668) by *Adriaen Dortsman* (1625-82). Here the plan is based on the circle. A main domed area is surrounded by an ambulatory along half of its periphery, creating a somewhat theater-like space. The articulation shows Doric (Tuscan) columns in the interior and pilasters outside. It is apparent then that the Dutch Protestant churches tend towards centralized plans, and it is highly significant that the shapes employed are the basic geometrical elements: square, octagon, Greek cross, double square, and circle. It is as though the architects wanted to present a "catalogue" of possible solutions within the limits of the same general type: a static, centralized space that satisfies the desire for self-evident clarity and regularity. A Calvinist ideal is thereby expressed; already in 1564 the Huguenots built three centralized "temples" in Lyon (Fleur-de-lis, Paradis, Terreaux),[36] which presented the characteristic traits of later Protestant churches. Later, Calvinism became the religion of the commercial city-states where its hard, clear and effective discipline well fitted the general character of the society. The small Calvinist centers needed common defense. A Calvinist International was therefore established. The Synod of Dordt (1617) was its equivalent to the Catholic Council of Trent. In spite of its "anti-Baroque" character, Calvinist architecture, thus, is also united by a Baroque *esprit de système*.

Scandinavia

Although the Scandinavian countries accepted Protestantism, they retained an absolute monarchy. Seventeenth-century society in Scandinavia, therefore, lacked the unequivocal direction we have found in

other European countries. On the one hand, a centralization existed that brought the nobility to the capital cities, Copenhagen and Stockholm; on the other hand, a development of trade and industry that, on a smaller scale, resembled that of the Netherlands became evident. In architecture, thus, there was a multitude of influences: French, Dutch, and even Italian. It is not possible to talk about a specific Scandinavian architecture but there are several important individual buildings that ought to be mentioned.[37]

In Denmark building activity flourished under King Christian IV (1577-1648) who wanted to transform Copenhagen into a true capital city. From 1626, its area was doubled, and already before that, many splendid buildings were erected in an original Mannerist style. We may mention the pleasure palace Rosenborg (1606-17) and the Exchange (1619-30), for which the King himself designed the plans. He planned an octagonal square as the focus for the new town, but it was not carried out, as the unfortunate role played by the King in the Thirty Years' War put a stop to building activity, and during the reign of his successor very little of interest took place. Only in 1672 was the first Baroque palace, Charlottenborg, built in Copenhagen, placed between a kind of place royale, Kongens Nytorv, with the statue of Christian V, and a garden.

Sweden, however, rose to full power during the seventeenth century, and experienced an age of great artistic achievement. During the first three decades, architecture followed the approach of Danish Mannerism. A change is marked by the appointment of the Frenchman, Simon de la Vallée, as Royal architect in 1639. He educated his own son, *Jean de la Vallée* and *Nicodemus Tessin the Elder* (1615-81), who were both to have a decisive importance for the development of a Baroque architecture in Sweden.

Back from Italy in 1650, Jean de la Vallée built the Oxienstierna Palace in Stockholm as a Roman palazzo. In 1656 he tackled the problem of the Protestant church with the large St. Katarina. The plan is an interesting synthesis of square and Greek cross. The same year he built the Bonde Palace, introducing the cour d'honneur to Sweden. The complex building is unified by continuous rustication, but the single volumes are defined by tall roofs.[38] The corps de logis and its corner pavilions are articulated by a giant order of rusticated pilasters. The palace, thus, represents a further development of the style of De Brosse. In 1659, De la Vallée took over the construction of the Riddarhuset (House of Nobility), which had been planned by the Dutch architect Justus Vingboons in 1653. Vingboons is responsible for the introduction of a "Dutch" colossal order of pilasters, a theme that he had already employed in the palace of the Dutch merchant, Louis de Geer, in 1646, a building that repeated the basic disposition of the Mauritshuis. De la Vallée wanted to give the Riddarhuset a cour d'honneur, but the projecting wings were never executed.

Nicodemus Tessin the Elder became Royal architect in 1649, and built

several important structures that show a curious mixture of French and Italian traits. His cathedral in Kalmar (1660) is an elongated bi-axial organism with four towers to emphasize the center. The style of the articulation comes close to Roman Cinquecento architecture. In the Caroline Mausoleum, in Stockholm (1672), Tessin approaches French classicism, but a true Baroque integration is achieved by means of convex corners that continue into the dome. The solution is remarkable, and gives the building a place of honor in Scandinavian seventeenth-century architecture. Tessin's *magnum opus*, the large country palace of Drottningholm (1662), has a double corps de logis with corner *ressauts* and added pavilions. The articulation is simple and strong, showing a colossal order of pilasters over a rusticated ground-floor. All in all, the building has a somewhat conservative character.[39]

It was Tessin's son, *Nicodemus Tessin the Younger* (1654-1728), who gave Swedish seventeenth-century architecture its major works. An architect of exceptional talent, he was educated in Rome (1673-78 and 1687-88), where he frequented Bernini and Carlo Fontana. In 1678-80 and 1687 he also visited France, and studied the works of Le Nôtre.[40] A first result of his travels was the splendid garden at Drottningholm. As the Royal architect of the young and dynamic Charles XII, Tessin got many commissions, culminating with the rebuilding of the Royal Palace in Stockholm, which was started soon after his return to Sweden in 1688. Because of his interest in religion, the King first of all wanted a new palace chapel (1689), but in 1690 he also decided to build a new wing towards the north. Tessin's project[41] shows a large Roman palazzo on a base of "natural rocks" and rustication. The derivation from Bernini's Montecitorio Palace is evident. In 1697 the old palace burned down, and soon afterwards Tessin had the plans for a new grandiose building ready. A few years earlier (1694) he had designed a project for a new Royal Palace in Copenhagen, employing a U-plan with a large cour d'honneur. Its character, however, was to be entirely Roman, reflecting inspiration from Bernini's Palazzo Chigi-Odescalchi. The young King Charles XII of Sweden wanted a still more magnificent building, and Tessin developed a large square courtyard-palace incorporating the northern wing that he had designed several years before. The appearance of the building is that of a unified block, which makes us think of Bernini's final project for the Louvre. To the west, however, Tessin added low curved stables forming an *avant-cour*, and to the east he defined a spacious garden-terrace by means of projecting wings. The solution, thus, represents a combination of Italian and French types. The large courtyard was intended as a place royale, where Tessin proposed to erect an equestrian statue of Charles XI. The palace would thereby have received a focus that is lacking today. The wall-articulation is Roman in character, but the general proportions create an effect of extension. The façade on the cour d'honneur has a certain affinity to the Palazzo Barberini, whereas the centers of the other elevations are em-

phasized by colossal pilasters or columns. The Royal Palace in Stockholm without doubt is the most unified of the great palaces of the European Seicento, and represents a worthy conclusion to an epoch in architectural history.[42]

In connection with the Royal Palace, Tessin planned a grandiose monumental center for Stockholm, with a new cathedral across the river on the transverse axis of the palace, as well as other public buildings (1704-13). The monumental projects of Tessin are distinguished by classical regularity, and do not exhibit any true Baroque plasticity or spatial dynamism. In his own city house, the Tessin Palace, however, he took the liberty of a free experimentation (1692-1700). The house is situated in front of the Royal Palace on a narrow, irregular site. The corps de logis overlooks the street in the Italian manner, and the façade has a Roman character. Two projecting walls, however, indicate a kind of cour d'honneur.[43] Behind the corps de logis, we find a splendid garden which is accompanied on both sides by shallow diverging wings. At about half-way the space narrows and here two freestanding architectural elements are placed which define a semicircular exedra containing a fountain. The exedra creates an efficient spatial interpenetration of the two parts of the garden, and the whole composition ends with a tall niche, which, due to a trick of foreshortening, appears like a deep colonnade. The garden, thus, combines intimacy and a seemingly infinite movement in depth. In the entire secular architecture of the seventeenth century, it would be difficult to find a more fascinating and truly Baroque space. In a highly original manner, it unifies Roman and French ideas, and gives testimony to the great talent of its creator. With Tessin, Scandinavian architecture reached a European level, perhaps for the only time in history.

Central Europe

The Thirty Years' War (1618-48) indicates the confused situation of the Germanic countries during the seventeenth century. Before the war started, however, we find a multitude of building initiatives, mainly in connection with the movements of Reformation and Counter-Reformation. During the last decades of the century building slowly resumed its monumentum, but the fully developed German Baroque belongs to the eighteenth century.[44]

The architecture of the Counter-Reformation was introduced in Germany with the Jesuit church of St. Michael in Munich, built after 1583 by an unknown master. The wide nave is clearly related to Il Gesù, but the system is transformed in a significant way by adaptation to the local tradition of *Wandpfeiler* construction. "Wall-pillars" are Late Gothic buttresses, placed inside rather than on the exterior of the building. In the Church of St. Michael a large barrel-vault, spanning twenty meters, rests directly on such pillars. Between them tall niches penetrate into the vault. The out-

side wall is therefore reduced to a structurally neutral surface. A reminiscence of classical articulation is present in the continuous architrave which forms a gallery between the wall-pillars. In general, an integration of space and structure is achieved, which surpasses the possibilities of the Roman basilica.

The new approach initiated in St. Michael was further developed by *Hans Alberthal* (c. 1575-1657), who built three wall-pillar churches for the Jesuits: Dillingen (1610-17), Eichstätt (1617-20) and Innsbruck (1619-21).[45] In these buildings, the horizontal gallery has been omitted, so that a most impressive spatial integration results. The Thirty Years' War interrupted the original initiative of Hans Alberthal, however, and it was continued by the Vorarlberg builders fifty years later, and had decisive importance for the development of the great sacred architecture of the Late Baroque in Central Europe.[46]

It is hardly possible to talk about a secular Baroque architecture in Germany before the Thirty Years' War. German writers often praise the Town hall in Augsburg (1614-20) as the first Baroque building north of the Alps. It was built by *Elias Holl* (1573-1646) for this important trading center. The building is a curious combination of a tall, medieval burgher's house and an Italian palazzo, built in a style that shows a mixture of Roman and Palladian elements. In spite of the awkward articulation, the general effect is quite impressive, and the building functions well as a *Stadtkrone*.

In Bohemia the war had already ended in 1620 with the Catholic victory at the White Mountain. In 1621, Wallenstein started the construction of a large city-palace in Prague, with the Italian Andrea Spezza as his architect. The most interesting feature of the building is the wall articulation of the large Hall, where the entablature is interrupted to make the vertical members appear as separate units, forming together with the vault a large baldachin. Another Italian, *Carlo Lurago* (1618-84), played an important role in Bohemia around the middle of the century. His Klementium (Jesuit College) in Prague is still Mannerist in character (1654-58), but towards the end of his career he realized a full-grown Baroque architecture, above all in the splendid nave of the Cathedral in Passau (1668). The space is conceived as a succession of transverse oval saucer domes on pendentives, and has a sumptuous stucco decoration by Giovanni Battista Carlone. In Prague, the construction of palaces was continued by *Francesco Caratti* (d. 1679), who probably designed the Nostitz palace with the first true colossal order in the city (1660). Later Caratti built the immense Czernin palace (1669-89), where a Palladian type of giant order is repeated *ad infinitum* to create an effect of Baroque rhetoric. With the arrival in Prague of the French architect, *Jean-Baptiste Mathey* (1630-95), Bohemian architecture achieved a more refined character.[47] His Troja garden palace (1679-97) employs the French pavilion system, and is unified by a continuous order of colossal pilasters. The main work of Mathey is the St. Francis Church

313. *Domenico Martinelli, Vienna,*
Liechtenstein Palace.

314. *Andreas Schlüter, Berlin,*
Royal Palace and square
(contemporary engraving).
315. *Andreas Schlüter, Berlin,*
Kamecke House.

(Kreuzherren Kirche), built 1679-88. The plan is a combination of longitudinal oval and elongated Greek cross, and the exterior shows a very sensitive articulation. The basic elements are Roman (such as the giant aedicula of the façade and the dome) but the refined surface detailing reminds one of French classicism.

In Vienna, building activity started somewhat later, and only received a real momentum after the defeat of the Turks in 1683. The first work of any importance is the new façade for the Jesuit church "am Hof" built in 1662 by *Carlo Antonio Carlone* (d. 1708). By means of projecting wings, the church is integrated with the adjoining palaces and interacts spatially with the square in front. The solution is related to François Mansart's Minimes church. About the same time, Filiberto Lucchese built the Leopold range of the Hofburg, employing a restrained Mannerist wall articulation (1661-68). A true Baroque approach is introduced by *Domenico Martinelli* (1650-1718), who settled in Vienna in 1690.[48] His most important works are the two Liechtenstein palaces, the city-palace initiated in 1692 and the garden palace from 1696. The city-palace is the first full-grown Baroque building in Vienna. It appears as a monumentalized version of Bernini's Chigi-Odelscalchi palace, and gives testimony to a considerable architectural talent. The garden palace has a splendid vestibule that runs through the entire depth of the building. Symmetrically disposed staircases add to the spatially advanced solution. The exterior articulation follows the best Roman tradition with a giant order of pilasters over a rusticated groundfloor. Martinelli's talent was confirmed by his palace at Austerlitz (Slavkov), built shortly after 1700, where he introduced the cour d'honneur.[49] Italian architects also dominated building activity in southern Germany. The most important personality is *Agostino Barelli* (1627-99), who designed the large Theatine church in Munich (1663), using S. Andrea della Valle in Rome as a model. Twin towers were added to the façade, creating an impressive ensemble.[50] The interior has a somewhat "classical" character, due to an articulation by fluted half-columns. At any rate, the space is less interesting than the contemporary nave in Passau. Barelli also initiated the palace of Nymphenburg (1664), which was continued by *Enrico Zuccalli* (1642-1724),[51] who also designed the large palace at Schleissheim (1692). Almost all the works mentioned above are due to Italian architects, who dominated the scene in Central Europe after the Thirty Years' War. Most of them were secondary figures from northern Italy (or the Italian part of Switzerland), and their works rarely attain any true, creative originality. They contributed, however, in a decisive way to the general diffusion of the ideas of the epoch, and together with a crowd of Italian masons and stucco workers laid the foundation for the great Late Baroque architecture of the eighteenth century.

Before we conclude, we should, however, mention one German architect who spiritually belongs to the seventeenth century: *Andreas Schlüter* (1664-1714). Originally a sculptor, he was commissioned to design the

Royal Palace of Berlin in 1698.[52] The palace was intended as part of a larger urban scheme, with a cathedral defining the main axis, and the palace the transverse one. The conservative courtyard layout was determined by the old Schloss, and the general character is clearly influenced by Bernini's project for the Louvre. Schlüter added, however, plastic accents and varied motifs, creating a pronounced rhetorical effect. The palace was pulled down after the Second World War, to erase the memory of the beginnings of German absolutism.

Conclusion

The Baroque is traditionally considered the last of the great universal "styles" of European art. This seems very natural when we remember the strong desire of the epoch to conceive the world in terms of an integrated *system*. But we have also seen that the seventeenth century offered a multitude of *different* systems, of a religious, philosophical, or political kind. How, then, is it possible to maintain a unitary concept of "Baroque"? In fact, many scholars stress the diversity of seventeenth-century art, although some point out the evident and strong common traits of the epoch.[53] In our exposition we have tried to show that all the Baroque systems, in fact, have basic properties in common. These properties do not primarily derive from particular contents, but from more general concepts. To describe these, we have used two types of concepts: psychic and spatial. All the Baroque systems, thus, operated through psychic *persuasion, participation,* and *transportation,* and were concretized in terms of spatial *centralization, integration,* and *extension.* Regardless of the various concrete types of participation resulting from the different initial choice, Baroque existence, therefore, had a common basic structure, and we may with justification talk about an existential space that distinguishes the epoch, just as we may point out fundamental analogies between its great philosophical systems.[54] We should also remember the new scientific concepts which were assimilated by all the existential systems, in particular the ideas of *infinity* and *movement.* "The whole of the art of the Baroque is full of the echo of the infinite spaces and the interrelatedness of all being. The work of art in its totality becomes the symbol of the universe, as a uniform organism alive in all its parts. Each of these parts points, like the heavenly bodies, to an infinite, unbroken continuity; each part contains the law governing the whole, in each the same power, the same spirit is at work."[55]

Baroque architecture concretizes the existential structure of the epoch on all environmental levels. According to the system in question, particular emphasis may be given to one or more of the levels. In France, thus, *landscape* became the principal level, and we may consider Le Nôtre the real protagonist of French seventeenth-century architecture. The city reflected the influence of landscape design, and thereby received a new dimension. In Italy the *building* remained the constituent environmental element, and in particular the church. In both cases, however, the problem of spatial articulation was essential. French architects developed a rational system of spatial organization based on *rond-points* and *places* and connecting, straight paths.[56] Italian architects (especially Borromini and Guarini) treated space as a kind of "negative" building, as a plastic "body" that can be modelled and that interacts with the surrounding spaces. Italian Baroque architecture, therefore, has a more direct sensual impact than the "intelligent" French layouts. In France the foci are usually spaces, while the Italian foci are plastic "things." Furthermore the particular dynamism of Italian architecture stems from the interaction of space and mass, while French architecture is better characterized as pure spatial extension. We have already interpreted these basic traits as expressions of the existential systems of the two countries. In other European countries the idea of system was less strongly developed, so that we do not find fully integrated architectural systems. This is particularly evident in the Netherlands which maintained an outdated regional self-government.[57]

Essentially, Baroque architecture was a concretization of centralized authoritarian systems. In spite of this fact, we may talk about the actuality of Baroque architecture. As a set of particular phenomena, the Baroque certainly belongs to the past. In addition to the history of events, however, it is necessary to introduce a history of ideas or existential *possibilities.* In this history Baroque architecture occupies an important place, as a system of forms that significantly extends the existential space of man, offering him an "open" world related to centers of meaning.[58] This general model may receive ever new and particular contents, and may therefore help us to make a new pluralistic world operant.

NOTES

CHAPTER ONE

[1]E. Cassirer, *The Philosophy of the Enlightenment* (1932), Boston, 1955, p. 39.

[2]Alberti thus says: "It is manifest that nature delights principally in round Figures..." (*Ten Books on Architecture*, VII/iv, London, 1755, p. 138).

[3]Pico della Mirandola, *Oration on the Dignity of Man* (1486). English translation by Elizabeth Livermore Forbes in *The Renaissance Philosophy of Man* (ed. E. Cassirer, P.O. Kristeller, J.H. Randell Jr.), Chicago, 1948.

[4]Goethe calls the heliocentric world of Copernicus "die grösste, erhabenste, folgenreichste Entdeckung, die je der Mensch gemacht hat, wichtiger als die ganze Bibel" (Letter to von Müller 1832).

[5]René Descartes, *Discourse on Method*. English translation by F.E. Sutcliffe. Harmondsworth, 1968, p. 54.

[6]F.E. Sutcliffe, *Introduction to Descartes: Discourse on Method*, p. 19.

[7]See D'Alembert's "Discours préliminaire" to the French *Encyclopédie* (1751), where he distinguished the interest in the system as such from the *esprit systématique* of his own century.

[8]Today pluralism has entered a new phase, thanks to the new means of communication.

[9]Giordano Bruno, *De l'infinito universo e mondi*, Dialoghi I, III (1584).

[10]Thus Galileo says: "Non sono io che voglia che il Cielo come corpo nobilissimo, abbia ancora forma nobilissima, quale è la sferica perfetta, ma l'istesso Aristostele... ed io quanto a me, non avendo mai lette le croniche e le nobiltà particolari delle figure, non so quale di esse sieno più o men nobili, più o men perfette; ma credo che tutte siano antiche e nobili a un modo, o per dir meglio, che quanto a loro non sieno nè nobili e perfette, nè ignobili ed imperfette," in *Opere*, Florence, 1842-56, vol. IV, p. 293.

[11]There are a few important exceptions, such as the treatises of Blondel, Perrault and Guarini, but we may notice that these authors were not professionals in the ordinary sense of the word.

[12]F.E. Sutcliffe, op. cit., p. 14.

[13]*Canons and Decrees of the Council of Trent*. Session XXV, Tit. 2, quoted from A. Blunt, *Artistic Theory in Italy 1450-1600*, Oxford, 1956, p. 108.

[14]Albert Schweitzer has in fact demonstrated how the works of Bach are based on the use of "naturalistic" and "literary" images, whereby they possess the two basic Baroque characteristics: systematic structure based on an "axiomatic" theme, and persuasive expression. See A. Schweitzer, *J.S. Bach*, Leipzig, 1908.

[15]The Royal French Academy of Painting and Sculpture was founded in 1648, and the Academy of Architecture in 1671.

[16]The attitude is already evident in the works of Bramante's pupils Raphael and Peruzzi.

[17]With the exception of Palladio, who certainly created a very clear and comprehensive "architectural system." We will later return to his achievement and its relation to the architecture of the seventeenth century.

[18]A good account is given by S. Giedion, "Sixtus V (1585-90) and the planning of the Baroque Rome," in *Space, Time and Architecture*, fifth edition, Cambridge, Mass., 1667, pp. 75 ff. See also: G. Giovannoni, "Roma dal Rinascimento al 1870," in *Topografia e Urbanistica di Roma* (Storia di Roma, volume XXII, Rome, 1958).

[19]Giedion, op. cit., p. 93, translated from *Della Trasportazione dell'Obelisco Vaticano et delle Fabriche Di Nostro Signore Papa Sisto V, fatto dal Cav. Domenico Fontana, Architetto di Sua Sanità* (Rome, 1590).

[20]The central street, the *Corso*, follows the ancient *Via Lata*, whereas the one to the right, *Via di Ripetta*, was carried through under Pope Leo X (1513-20), and Pope Paul III (1534-49).

[21]Giovannoni, op. cit., p. 407.

[22]Descartes, op. cit., Discourse 2.

[23]The first obelisk was erected to define the primary place of the city, the Piazza S. Pietro. Domenico Fontana solved the difficult technical problem, and on 10 September 1586, the large monolith was *in opera*.

[24]G.C. Argan, *L'Europa delle Capitali 1600-1700*, Geneva, 1964, p. 45.

[25]The word "monument" is used here in its original sense, that is, something which makes us remember.

[26]Argan, op. cit., p. 57.

[27]P. Lavedan, *French Architecture*, Harmondsworth, 1956, p. 239.

[28]L.B. Alberti, *Ten Books on Architecture*, English edition, London, 1755. Reprint, London, 1955, p. 136.

[29]A. Palladio, *I quattro libri dell'Architettura*, Venice, 1570. English edition by Isaac Ware, London, 1738.

[30]An exception is Pietro Cataneo who maintains that the principal church in a city should be cruciform, because the cross is the symbol of redemption. P. Cataneo, *I Quattro Primi Libri di Architettura*, Venice, 1554.

[31]See S. Sinding-Larsen, "Some functional and iconographical aspects of the centralized church in the Italian Renaissance," in *Acta ad archaeologicam et artium historiam pertinentia*, vol. II, Rome, 1965, pp. 203 ff.

[32]See C. Norberg-Schulz, "Le Ultime Intenzioni di Alberti," in *Acta ad archaeologicam et artium historiam pertinentia*, vol. I, Oslo-Rome, 1962, pp. 131 ff.

[33]Sinding-Larsen, op. cit., p. 240.

[34]See W. Lotz, "Die ovalen Kirchenräume des Cinquecento," *Römisches Jahrbuch für Kunstgeschichte*. Bk. 7.

[35]C. Borromeo, *Instructiones Fabricae et Supellectilis Ecclesiasticae* (1577). Translation by Sinding-Larsen, op. cit., p. 205.

[36]The church was begun in 1568 by Vignola and finished in 1576 by Giacomo Della Porta who designed the façade and the dome. About the same time Palladio recognized the basilica as the model of the contemporary church, saying: "Mai noi... edifichiamo li Templj che si assimigliano molto alle Basiliche..." (op. cit., IV, 5).

[37]See C. Galassi Paluzzi, *Storia segreta dello stile dei Gesuiti*. Rome, 1951. "Era stato così posto in luce che le costituzioni dell'Ordine in merito alla costruzione di chiese, collegi, convitti ecc., non prescrivevano nessuna legge, nè prevedevano regolamenti circa lo stile architettonico, o le piante, o la decorazione pittorica o scultorea" (p. 39).

[38]A. Blunt, op. cit., pp. 127 ff.

[39]Argan, op. cit., p. 106.

[40]Basically the church is an extension of the *public* space of the city, although with a particular sacred qualification, as the private "house of God."

[41]Its roots, of course, are found in Roman Antiquary. The villa, therefore, represents a conscious attempt at a "Renaissance." Alberti quotes Martial:

> You tell me, Friend, you much desire to know,
> What in my Villa I can find to do?
> I eat, drink, sing, play, bathe, sleep, eat again,
> Or read, or wanton in the Muses Train.

Alberti, op. cit. IX, ii.

[42]The examples are legion. We just wish to recall Giuliano da Sangallo's Poggio a Caiano for Lorenzo il Magnifico (1480).

[43]I.e., Palazzo Pitti in Florence by Brunelleschi (?), c. 1455, and Palazzo Piccolomini in Pienza

by Bernardo Rossellino (c. 1460). The real villa suburbana was developed during the sixteenth century.

[44]Alberti, op. cit., V, xviii.

[45]Alberti, op. cit., IX, ii.

[46]S. Serlio, *Tutte l'Opere d'Architettura*, IV.

[47]A. Palladio, op. cit., II/12.

[48]This contrast in scale and texture is well illustrated in Ferrara, where the medieval town was extended by Biagio Rossetti after 1492. Rossetti introduced a system of regularly spaced palaces. See B. Zevi, *Biagio Rossetti*. Turin, 1960.

[49]Alberti, op. cit., IX, ii.

[50]The Viennese city-palace, thus, is typologically a derivation of the Italian palazzo rather than the French hôtel, which represents a different relation between the building and its environment.

[51]This problem has been brought forth with great emphasis by Robert Venturi in his fundamental study *Complexity and Contradiction in Architecture*, New York, 1966.

[52]L.C. Sturm, *Vollständige Anweisung alle Arten von regulären Prachtgebäuden nach gewissen Regeln zu Erfinden*, Augsburg, 1716, ch. 2.

[53]A.C. Daviler, *Cours d'Architecture qui comprend les ordres de Vignole*, Paris, 1691. Préface.

[54]Le Corbusier, *Vers une Architecture*, Paris, 1923, English edition, London, 1927, pp. 126, 188, 191.

[55]Vitruvius, *De Architectura*, I, ii, 5. English edition, London, 1931, p. 29.

[56]See E. Forssman, *Dorisch, Ionisch, Korintisch. Studien über den Gebrauch der Säulenordnungen in der Architektur des 16.-18. Jahrhunderts*, Stockholm, 1961.

[57]Serlio, op. cit., IV, preface.

[58]Serlio, op. cit., IV.

[59]M. de Chantelou: *Journal du voyage du Cav. Bernin en France*, Paris, 1855 (20 October 1665.)

[60]M. Heidegger, *Sein und Zeit* (1927), 11th ed. Tübingen 1967, p. 104.

[61]See C. Norberg-Schulz, *Existence, Space and Architecture*, London, 1970.

[62]See C. Norberg-Schulz, op. cit. We may also refer to Susanne K. Langer who says: "A culture is made up factually of the activities of human beings; it is a system of interlocking and intersecting actions, a continuous functional pattern... The architect creates its image; a physically present human environment that expresses the characteristic rhythmic functional patterns which constitute a culture." (*Feeling and Form*, New York, 1953, p. 96.)

CHAPTER TWO

[1]For a comprehensive survey, see E.A. Gutkind, *International History of City Development*, New York, 1964.

[2]The villa of the Pope, Villa Montalto, was integrated in this "star," having its main entrance on the piazza in front of the apse of S. Maria Maggiore, from which a trident led through to the garden. It was built by Domenico Fontana in 1570 while Sixtus V was still a Cardinal. The villa was destroyed in the nineteenth century. The connection between S. Maria Maggiore and S. Lorenzo fuori le Mura has also disappeared because of the construction of the railway station. A street leading from S. Trinità dei Monti to the Piazza del Popolo was never built. It would have added a fourth member to the radiating streets of the piazza.

[3]For instance, the busy Piazza Colonna which breaks the longitudinal movement of the Corso. It was laid out already at the time of Sixtus V. See S. Giedion, op. cit., p. 99.

[4]A considerable number were built by Giacomo della Porta who had become "Architetto delle

fontane di Roma" already before the pontificate of Sixtus V: Piazza Colonna (1574), Piazza Navona (lateral fountains 1574-76), Piazza della Rotonda (1575), Piazza Mattei (1581-84), Piazza Madonna dei Monti (1588-89), Piazza Campitelli (1589), Piazza d'Aracoeli (1589), Piazza della Chiesa Nuova (1590), Via del Progresso (1591), Piazza del Quirinale (1593). See C. D'Onofrio, *Le Fontane di Roma*, Rome, 1957.

[5]Fontana's Palazzo del Laterano (1586), for instance, is generally characterized as a "dull" building. The plan, however, shows a systematic disposition hardly found in any other Roman palace of the period.

[6]Fontana, op. cit.

[7]See H. Siebenhüner, *Das Kapitol in Rom*, Munich, 1954. Also, J.S. Ackerman, *The Architecture of Michelangelo*, London, 1961.

[8]At the time of its erection (1539) many believed the statue to represent Constantine, the first Christian emperor.

[9]See C. de Tolnay, "Michelangelo architetto," in *Il Cinquecento*, Florence, 1955.

[10]The third palace, imitating the Palazzo dei Conservatori, was finished by G. Rainaldi in 1654.

[11]See Ackerman, op. cit., II, pp. 76 ff.

[12]The distinction made by Hans Rose who defines the trident leading away from a point as "Italian" and the opposite figure as "French," stems from a misunderstanding. Baroque radiation naturally can be "read" both ways, although it may in certain cases be *used* for concentration or radiation alone. See *Spätbarock*, Munich, 1922, p. 79.

[13]P. Portoghesi points out that this effect is strengthened by the fact that the axes of the churches converge towards the piazza. See *Roma Barocca*, Rome, 1966, p. 277.

[14]See R. Wittkower, "Carlo Rainaldi and the Roman Architecture of the Full Baroque," *The Art Bulletin*, Vol. XIX, No. 2, June 1937.

[15]The project by Rainaldi shows a portico crowned by an attic, which was later omitted by Bernini who joined in as supervisor in 1674. See Portoghesi, op. cit., p. 277.

[16]In 1878, Porta del Popolo was extended with two lateral gateways because of the increased traffic.

[17]The commission goes back to 1794 and the final plan was ready in 1812.

[18]For the history of Piazza Navona, see P. Romano and P. Partini, *Piazza Navona nella storia e nell'arte*, Rome, 1944.

[19]The history of S. Agnese in Agone goes back to 1123 when a church was dedicated to the virgin saint. In 1652, Carlo Rainaldi was asked to build a new church on the spot. When the foundations had been laid, Borromini took over (1653) and changed the project considerably. First of all, he gave the centralized structure a new concave façade and he also heightened the cupola, putting the dome on a high drum. But Borromini was put aside before the church was finished, and a group of collaborating architects took over (1657). G.M. Baratta designed the bell towers and Carlo Rainaldi the lantern. See E. Hempel, *Francesco Borromini*, Vienna, 1924, pp. 138 ff.

[20]See D'Onofrio, op. cit., pp. 201 ff.; also R. Wittkower, *Bernini*, London, 1955, pp. 34 ff.

[21]Portoghesi, op. cit., p. 229. For a comprehensive study on S. Maria della Pace, see P. Portoghesi, "S. Maria della Pace, di Pietro da Cortona," *L'architettura*, VII, pp. 840 ff.

[22]S. Maria della Pace also shows several characteristic details which were to be absorbed by Late Baroque architecture such as the soft swelling triglyphs of the parapet on both sides of the church.

[23]The project is known to us from a drawing published by Portoghesi (*Roma Barocca*, p. 193).

[24]For a complete history of the project see H. Brauer and R. Wittkower, *Die Zeichnungen des Gianlorenzo Bernini*, Vienna, 1931. Also C. Thoenes, "Studien zur Geschichte des Petersplatzes," *Zeitschrift für Kunstgeschichte*, 1963.

[25] The oval is based on two intersecting circles running through each other's centers, a solution already found in Serlio, op. cit., I, p. 14. Measure inside: 196x 142 m.

[26] Codice Chigiana H. II, 22.

[27] See R. Wittkower, "Il terzo braccio del Bernini in Piazza San Pietro," in *Bollettino d'Arte*, 1949, pp. 129 ff.

[28] The trapezoid shape of the piazza retta was suggested by the existing Vatican palace. Bernini, thus, took advantage of a given condition, just as Michelangelo had done a hundred years earlier when he planned the Capitoline Square.

[29] We may in this connection mention the interesting interpretation of the colonnade as consisting of a series of honorary columns: the world is "filtered" into the square through rows of saints. See Maurizio and Marcello Fagiolo dell'Arco, *Bernini*, Rome, 1967, p. 153.

[30] Argan, op. cit., p. 45.

[31] See H. Hibbard, *The Architecture of the Palazzo Borghese*, Rome, 1962, pp. 75 ff.

[32] See C. Elling, *Function and Form of the Roman Belvedere*, Copenhagen, 1950, p. 44.

[33] We ought to mention that the population of Rome during the seventeenth century only amounted to slightly more than 100,000 persons.

[34] We have already mentioned that at the time of its erection, the statue of Marcus Aurelius was believed to represent Constantine. Pierre Lavedan forgets the Capitoline Square and explains the place royale as a unification of the Italian Renaissance square (e.g. Vigevano) and the statue of a ruler (e.g. the statue of the Grand Duke Ferdinando of Tuscany in Leghorn). See P. Lavedan, *Les Villes Françaises*, Paris, 1960, p. 128.

[35] The statue was commissioned by Henry's wife, Maria de'Medici, in 1604 and finally put up in 1614 after the death of the King.

[36] The development of the Ile St. Louis, the transverse axis between the Collège des Quatre Nations (1662) and the Louvre, and the different projects for symmetrical squares in and along the islands from the eighteenth century (published by Patte in 1765) may be mentioned in this connection.

[37] The base of the triangle was torn down in 1874 and the houses have been much altered.

[38] The Place Royale was built between 1605 and 1612. It forms a square of 140x140 meters. The name was changed after the French Revolution.

[39] Covent Garden by Inigo Jones (1631-35) is clearly derived from the Place Royale in Paris.

[40] The project was made by Claude Chastillon and Jacques Alleaume, who together with Louis Métézeau and Baptiste du Cerceau served as architects to the King. It is generally assumed, however, that the King himself was the real planner, just as Sixtus V had been in Rome. See A. Blunt, *Art and Architecture in France 1500-1700*, Harmondsworth, 1957, p. 94.

[41] P. Lavedan, *French Architecture*, Harmondsworth, 1956, p. 239.

[42] See Lavedan, *Les Villes Françaises*, p. 120.

[43] Also in other fields the period is characterized by rich and varied activities; in religion, St. François de Sales, St. Vincent de Paul, Cornelis Jansen; in philosophy, Descartes, and in literature, Corneille.

[44] The word *boulevard*, in fact, originally meant the flat top of a rampart.

[45] As the scheme had to be adapted to the concrete urban circumstances, the symmetry is not exact. Four groups of Tuscan columns were placed at the street corners to illuminate the square. They have since disappeared, and other alterations have deprived the space of much of its architectural coherence. The diameter of the Place des Victoires is 78 meters, while the façades are a little more than 15 meters high. The relation thus is 1:5, in accordance with the rule of Alberti. Under the statue of Louis XIV there were four figures in chains: Germany, Piedmont, Spain and Holland. For the general history of the project see P. Bourget and G. Cattaui, *Jules Hardouin Mansart*, Paris, 1956, p. 99 ff.

[46] The general effect is today disturbed by the tall Vendôme column put up by Napoleon in 1810 after the destruction of the statue during the Revolution, and by the new streets to the north and south. The square measures 124X140 meters.

[47] In the case of the Piazza del Popolo and the Piazza Navona, we should say that the space is *related* to buildings.

[48] Two of these gates are still preserved, the Porte St. Denis by François Blondel (1672) and the Porte St. Martin by Pierre Bullet (1679). Both are decorated with reliefs representing the victories of Louis XIV.

[49] An analogous phenomenon was experienced in Salzburg about the same time, and later in Vienna.

[50] The piazza was carried out from 1605 onwards. The arcades were paid for by the Duke himself, and given to those who built behind, who were obliged to follow the established scheme. For the urbanistic history of Turin see the magnificent three-volume *opus* by A. Cavallari-Murat, *Forma Urbana ed Architettura nella Torino Barocca*, Turin, 1968. We may add that Turin had 20,000 inhabitants in 1620 and 40,000 in 1700.

[51] The square was planned in 1637 and construction started in 1644 under the direction of Carlo's son Amedeo di Castellamonte (1610-83). It measures 170x76.7 meters.

[52] The Roman solution, however, is posterior to the churches of Carlo di Castellamonte.

[53] The tall dome belongs to the SS. Sindone Chapel, designed by Guarini in 1668, while the campanile was heightened by Juvarra in 1720. The group also comprises Guarini's Church of S. Lorenzo which is placed where the left wing of the Royal Palace meets the Piazza Castello.

[54] The solution, in general, stems from French prototypes, in particular the Palais du Luxembourg in Paris by Salomon de Brosse (1615). The tower which was built of wood and plaster was destroyed by fire in 1811, and the screen has since been demolished.

[55] The Porta di Po was demolished during the Napoleonic period together with the fortifications of Turin.

[56] The gardens were planned by Le Nôtre in 1697-98.

[57] In spite of this late date, the architect B. Alfieri kept surprisingly close to the spirit of Vitozzi and Castellamonte. See Cavallari-Murat, op. cit., p. 1282.

[58] Cavallari-Murat, op. cit., p. 1050; op. cit., p. 1036.

[59] The church was initiated soon after the arrival of Vitozzi in Turin in 1584. In 1596 he made a decisive contribution to the planning of the great pilgrimage church of Vicoforte near Mondovì.

[60] See A. Castellamonte, *La Venaria Reale palazzo di piacere e di caccia ideato dall'altezza reale Carlo Emanuele II*, Turin, 1674.

[61] The literature on Versailles is very rich. For a general introduction see B. Teyssèdre, *L'Art au siècle de Louis XIV*, Paris, 1967.

[62] Bourget and Cattaui, op. cit., pp. 113 ff.

[63] G.C. Argan, "Giardino e Parco," *Enciclopedia Universale dell'Arte*, VI, Florence, 1958, p. 159.

[64] "Man sucht also dreierlei: das Schmückende, das Wohnliche und das Natürliche, eine Trilogie der Bedürfnisse..." H. Rose: *Spätbarock*, p. 36.

[65] See M. Fagiolo dell'Arco, "Villa Aldobrandina Tuscolana," *Quaderni dell'Istituto di Storia dell'Architettura*, XI/62-66, Rome, 1964.

[66] See E. de Ganay: *André Le Nôtre*, Paris, 1962. H.M. Fox: *André Le Nôtre, Garden Architect to Kings*. London, 1962. For the phenomenology of the Baroque garden see the excellent presentation in Rose, *Spätbarock*.

[67] Thus we find the old motif of the "cardinal points" integrated in the scheme, symbolizing the "cosmic" character of the composition.

[68] See R. Blomfield, *Sébastien le Prestre de Vauban*, London, 1938.

CHAPTER THREE

¹The activity naturally gravitated towards Rome. Few of the leading architects active in Rome, however, were born there, a fact that illustrates the general "super-personal" character of the Baroque movement.

²With these terms we only introduce an expedient subdivision that makes it possible to structure a complex process. We do not intend historical entities of any kind.

³An important book is by Leonard Christoph Sturm, *Vollständige Anweisung aller Arten von Kirchen wohl anzugeben*, Augsburg, 1718.

⁴Whereas the architrave and the frieze are broken over each pilaster, the cornice runs through. Under the pendentives, however, it has a cut to eliminate the strongly projecting corners, and to achieve a certain vertical continuity between the crossing and the dome. The breaks in the architrave and frieze indicate the beginning of a tendency towards a more general vertical integration. Another peculiarity of the church is the introduction of a transverse axis in the nave, an idea that was to have considerable importance during the seventeenth century.

⁵Of particular interest are S. Maria in Valicella ("Chiesa Nuova") (1575) for the Oratorians, S. Carlo al Corso (1612), initiated after the canonization of St. Charles Borromeo and S. Ignazio (1626) for the Jesuits. All three are architecturally mediocre.

⁶A project for the church was made in 1689 by the Theatine, P. Francesco Grimaldi, from Naples. The plan that was used, however, probably stems from the intervention of Giacomo della Porta in the same year. Two bays of the nave were built before 1600. The later execution by Maderno was faithful to Della Porta's project. Only the dome clearly bears the personal stamp of Maderno. See H. Hibbard, "The Early History of Sant'Andrea della Valle," *Art Bulletin*, 1961, Vol. XLIII, pp. 289 ff.

⁷In the smaller church of S. Maria della Vittoria (1606) Maderno repeated the general system of S. Andrea della Valle.

⁸The dome was designed in 1723, but repeats the motif of the coupled columns, which also reflect the influence of Michelangelo's dome for St. Peter's.

⁹See R. Wittkower, *Carlo Rainaldi*, pp. 258 ff.

¹⁰Sinding-Larsen, op. cit., p. 205.

¹¹Le Corbusier, op. cit., pp. 158 ff.

¹²Argan, op. cit., p. 45.

¹³According to Förster, Bramante *did* include a nave in his final plan. As he cannot point to any definitive documentary evidence, the question must remain open. See O.H. Förster, *Bramante*, Vienna, 1956, pp. 240 ff., fig. 120.

¹⁴"La facciata maderniana (1612) sacrifica ogni regola o tradizione proporzionale alla necessità di non formare un impedimento ottico alla cupola: perciò è bassa e larga, perciò nell'ordine unico delle colonne si sovrappone un alto ottico, che raccorda alla cupola il piano frontale... Costretto a correggere Michelangiolo, il Maderno lo fa con discrezione ammirevole, ma anche con acuta intelligenza critica..." G.C. Argan, *L'architettura barocca in Italia*. Milan, 1960, p. 13.

¹⁵Bernini's proposal to separate the campanili from the façade proper by means of deep recesses would have been an ingenious solution. (The idea, in fact, was used by K.I. Dientzenhofer in St. Nicholas in Prague - Staré Mesto in 1732.) When Maderno planned his front, however, such a freedom in plastic modelling was inconceivable.

¹⁶The Palladian solution introducing a giant order to express the nave hardly influenced the design of Baroque basilica-façades (the giant order of S. Carlo al Corso in Rome must be characterized as very unfortunate indeed). Even during the eighteenth century, the two-story type was normal. A giant order is usually found in connection with smaller centralized organisms. The solution of St. Peter's with one main order plus an attic, however, had a certain following.

¹⁷The commission was taken over by Lemercier in 1646 when the building had reached the main entablature. See A. Braham, "Mansart Studies I: The Valde-Grâce," *Burlington Magazine*, 1963, p. 351 ff.

¹⁸The ideas of Mansart, however, did not lead to any creative development in France, although they may stem from De l'Orme's chapel in Anet (1549-52).

¹⁹Peruzzi already experimented with oval spaces, and Serlio published the plan for an oval church. Vignola also made an oval project for Il Gesù (before 1658). See W. Lotz, *Die Ovalen Kirchenräume des Cinquecento*.

²⁰The large oval dome was executed by Francesco Gallo after 1728.

²¹In general the solution is derived from Michelangelo's Cappella Sforza in S. Maria Maggiore (c. 1560). The history of the chapel given by G. Spagnesi in *Giovanni Antonio De Rossi*, Rome, 1964, pp. 101 ff., is incorrect. The preexisting chapel of Volterra and Maderno had a different plan.

²²R. Wittkower, *Art and Architecture in Italy 1600-1750*, Harmondsworth, 1958, p. 119.

²³See F. Borsi, *La Chiesa di S. Andrea al Quirinale*, Rome, 1966.

²⁴A kind of precedent exists in SS. Annunziata in Parma by Fornovo (1566) that is based on a transverse pseudo-oval, namely a rectangle plus two semicircles. See Lotz, op. cit., pp. 55 ff. Bernini's solution was probably suggested by the shallow building-site, but we should mention that he had used the transverse oval already in the chapel of the Propaganda Fide palace (1634, demolished c. 1654 by Borromini).

²⁵Wittkower, *Art and Architecture in Italy, 1600-1750*, p. 120.

²⁶The walls have been shortened recently to allow for a widening of the street in front.

²⁷The longitudinal oval appears in the chapel attached to the Louvre in his third project.

²⁸We may, for instance, mention the Trinity church in Kappel near Waldsassen by Georg Dientzenhofer (1685-9).

²⁹See P. Smith, "Mansart Studies III: The Church of the Visitation in the Rue St. Antoine," *Burlington Magazine*, 1964, pp. 202 ff.

³⁰In 1635 Mansart planned a smaller circular chapel for the Château de Blois, where the oval presbytery would have been joined to the main space in a similar way.

³¹The idea of using a simple aedicula for the façade of smaller centralized churches may be traced back to the "temple-front" of Alberti. Giacomo della Porta attempted an Early Baroque solution in S. Maria in Scala Coeli (1582), and Ricchino introduced a giant order in his façade for S. Pietro alla Rete in Milan (demolished 1623).

³²The church was finished only in 1747 and demolished in 1823.

³³It has been pointed out that even in some of the works of Brunelleschi a small domed presbytery has been added to the main space. The intention of using such spaces to introduce a longitudinal axis, however, stems from the sixteenth century. A domed presbytery, thus, was added to the octagonal church of S. Maria di Canepanova in Pavia (1499) after 1561. See F. Fagnani, *S. Maria di Canepanova*, Pavia, 1961. The earliest attempt at joining two primary domed spaces is to our knowledge Antonio da Sangallo's project for S. Maria di Monte Moro near Montefiascone (1526).

³⁴Particularly in the work of Johann Michael Fischer.

³⁵See Sinding-Larsen, op. cit.

³⁶R. Wittkower, "S. Maria della Salute: Scenographic Architecture and the Venetian baroque," *Journal of the Society of Architectural Historians*, XVI (1957). Also *Art and Architecture in Italy 1600-1750*, pp. 191 ff.

³⁷Wittkower, *Art and Architecture in Italy 1600-1750*, op. cit., p. 192.

³⁸Wittkower, op. cit., p. 194.

³⁹In general the handling of the spaces is additive. Behind the main altar, however, where the

church is added to the chapel of Libéral Bruant, an "incomplete" circular bay of transition indicates a spatial interpenetration. It is important to notice that this particular solution is used to define the longitudinal axis which is common to the church and the hôtel.

[40]The façade was added 1635-38 by G.B. Soria.

[41]Lemercier stayed in Rome from 1607 to 1614. Fischer von Erlach's Kollegienkirche in Salzburg (1694-1707) is also derived from S. Carlo ai Catinari.

[42]See E. Hubala, "Entwürfe Pietro da Cortonas für SS. Martina e Luca in Rom," *Zeitschrift für Kunstgeschichte*, XXV, 1962. P. Portoghesi, "SS. Luca e Martina di Pietro da Cortona," *L'architettura*, IX, 1963.

[43]The correspondence is general rather than exact. Until the nineteen-thirties, the church was built in among houses. The visible parts, however, were made according to the principles here outlined.

[44]A related, although less mature, approach is found in S. Maria di Loreto in Milan by Ricchino (demolished 1616), where a Greek cross is stretched in such a way that the nave becomes narrower and the transept wider. The dome, therefore, is a longitudinal oval.

[45]See F. Fasolo, *L'Opera di Hieronimo e Carlo Rainaldi*, Rome, 1960. Wittkower has traced the bi-axial organization back to Giovanni Magenta's S. Salvatore in Bologna (1605-23). G. Rainaldi built S. Lucia in the same city in 1623, that is, after the planning of S. Teresa.

[46]The bi-axial organization of S. Teresa had a certain following. We may mention S. Francesco di Paola by Torriani (1624-30) and S. Salvatore in Campo by Peparelli (1639), both in Rome. The scheme was also taken over by Carlo Rainaldi in Monteporzio (c. 1670) and in the Chiesa del Sudario, Rome (1687-89).

[47]See C. Norberg-Schulz, *Kilian Ignaz Dientzenhofer e il Barocco Boemo*, Rome, 1968, pp. 164 ff.

[48]G.C. Argan, "S. Maria in Campitelli a Roma," *L'architettura*, VI, 1960.

[49]S. Maria Maddalena was initiated by Carlo Fontana in 1668. The construction, however, did not proceed beyond the apse. In 1695, G.A. De Rossi took over and and gave the church its present plan. After the death of De Rossi, his pupil, G.C. Quadrio, completed the construction. The church was inaugurated on July 22, 1698. The façade was added 1734-35 by Giuseppe Sardi.

[50]See G. Spagnesi, *Giovanni Antonio De Rossi*, Rome, 1964, pp. 204 ff.

[51]P. Portoghesi, *Roma Barocca*, Rome, 1966, p. 155.

[52]Quoted by P. Portoghesi, *Borromini*, Rome, 1967, p. 375.

[53]P. Portoghesi, *Borromini nella Cultura Europea*, Rome, 1964, p. 32.

[54]Portoghesi, *Borromini nella Cultura Europea*, Plates B, C, D, E.

[55]Wittkower, *Art and Architecture in Italy 1600-1750*, op. cit., pp. 132 ff.

[56]This interpretation was given by Hans Sedlmayr, who showed that even the balustrade in front of the main altar is determined by the same structural principle. See *Die Architektur Borrominis*, Munich, 1930.

[57]See Portoghesi, *Borromini*, op. cit., pp. 50 ff.

[58]Portoghesi, op. cit., Plate XXXII.

[59]The frontally placed columns on the altar wall are due to a later intervention by Arcucci.

[60]F. Borromini, *Opus Architectonicum*, Rome, 1725, p. 11.

[61]Any space, of course, may be understood as a field of forces. Borromini, however, makes this fact "visible." See C. Norberg-Schulz, *Existence, Space and Architecture*. Also Portoghesi, *Borromini*, op. cit., p. 384.

[62]For the complex history of the Palazzo della Sapienza, see H. Thelen, "Der Palazzo della Sapienza in Rom," *Miscellanea Bibliothecae Hertzianae*, Munich, 1961. The courtyard system goes back to Guidetto Guidetti (1562), the exedra was introduced by his successor Pirro Ligorio,

while Della Porta carried out most of the construction between 1577 and 1602. Borromini's church was consecrated in 1660.

[63]F. Borromini, op. cit., p. 5.

[64]For the geometrical basis of the plan see Portoghesi, *Borromini nella Cultura Europea*, op. cit., Plates G, H, I.

[65]A vertical continuity similar to S. Ivo is found in the chapel in Lomec in Bohemia, built shortly before 1700, possibly by Giovanni Santini Aichel. In the Santuario della Visitazione al Vallinotto, Vittone repeated the plan of S. Ivo, giving it, however, a different vertical development.

[66]The commission goes back to 1647, but the chapel was built after 1660. We will return to the palace in the next chapter.

[67]Portoghesi (*Borromini*, p. 159) has worked out a fine reconstruction of Borromini's project showing an elegant system of interlacing ribs resting on a transparent clerestory.

[68]The following statement of Venturi therefore fits the works of Borromini particularly well: "Designing from the outside in, as well as from the inside out, creates necessary tensions, which help make architecture. Since the inside is different from the outside, the wall—the point of change—becomes an architectural event. Architecture occurs at the meeting of interior and exterior forces of use and space. These interior and environmental forces are both general and particular, generic and circumstantial." R. Venturi, *Complexity and Contradiction in Architecture*, New York, 1966, p. 88 ff. The concept of "field" (*campo*) has been introduced by Portoghesi in *Borromini*, p. 384.

[69]See C. Norberg-Schulz, *Existence, Space and Architecture*.

[70]The illustrations were published separately in 1686 under the title *Disegni d'architettura civile ed ecclesiastica*. A complete edition appeared in 1737, edited by B. Vittone.

[71]See E. Guidoni, "Modelli Guariniani," *Guarino Guarini e l'internazionalità del Barocco*, Accademia delle Scienze di Torino, 1970.

[72]Guidoni points out that the concept of cells was introduced in science by R. Hooke in his *Micrographia* (London, 1665). Guidoni, op. cit., p. 39.

[73]G. Guarini, *Placita Philosophica*, Paris, 1665, p. 755. Quoted after Guidoni, op. cit.

[74]The church is usually dated 1680. A probable visit by Guarini to Lisbon before 1660 gives us reason to anticipate the date given. The church was destroyed by an earthquake in 1755.

[75]This distinction goes back to H. Sedlmayr, op. cit., p. 108, who characterizes the *Raumverschmelzung* as "eine gesteigerte Form der Raumdurchdringung. Beispiel: S. Maria della divina providenza. Diese grossen Ovalzellen würden, wenn man sie vervollkommt denkt, sich gegenseitig anschneiden. Aber anders als in dem Beispiel der Raumdurchdringung treffen die einzelnen Raumeinheiten nicht in einem klaren Schnitt aufeinander, sondern dort, wo die Zellen einander treffen, fiessen sowohl die Gewölbe wie auch die senkrechten Hüllen der einen Raumeinheit in die der anderen in weicher Kurve über."

[76]Guidoni, op. cit., p. 7.

[77]Typologically, however, the building is quite conventional.

[78]We have found an analogous "openness" in some of the churches of Borromini, hardly, however, a similar separation of structure and "skin."

[79]See D. De Bernardi Ferrero, "I Disegni d'Architettura Civile e Ecclesiastica" di Guarino Guarini e l'Arte del Maestro, Turin, 1966.

[80]R. Wittkower, *Art and Architecture in Italy 1600-1750*, p. 274.

[81]See M. Passanti, "La Cappella della SS. Sindone in Torino di Guarino Guarini," *L'architettura*, VI, 1961.

[82]For an interpretation of its symbolism see M. Fagiolo dell'Arco, *La Geosofia del Guarini*, Accademia delle Scienze di Torino, 1970.

[83]The building was completed in 1680, except for the façade. See G. Brotto, V. Todesco, "S. Lorenzo a Torino," *L'architettura*, VII, 1961. Also G. Torretta, *Un'analisi della cappella di S. Lorenzo*, Turin, 1968.

[84]The term has been introduced by Heinrich Gerhard Franz.

[85]Only today the full implications are understood and exploited, particularly in the architectural works of Paolo Portoghesi.

[86]Unfortunately the project was never carried out. The existing Theatine church in Prague was built in 1691-1717 on a more conventional plan. The façade was added by Johann Santini Aichel.

[87]G. Guarini, *Architettura Civile*, I, iii.

[88]Forssman, op. cit., p. 91.

[89]Borromini and Guarini often preferred the perhaps still more comprehensive Composite order.

[90]Argan, *L'Europa delle Capitali 1600-1700*, p. 106.

CHAPTER FOUR

[1]Colbert spoke thus of Bernini's project for the Louvre: "The Cavaliere has planned banqueting halls and filled the rest with immense rooms. But for the personal well-being of the King he has not done anything." Chantelou, op. cit. (Colbert's answer to Chantelou's petition of 15 June 1668).

[2]In a few cases the courtyard was made circular to stress this basic character: Bramante's project for S. Pietro in Montorio, Vignola's palace at Caprarola and Machuca's palace for Charles V in Granada.

[3]In later literature the solution was called *appartement-semi-double*.

[4]The first important example is the Palazzo Medici-Riccardi by Michelozzo (c. 1444-64).

[5]Alberti had already introduced the superposition of orders in the Palazzo Rucellai (c. 1450). The most interesting experiments of the Cinquecento are found in the works of Raphael, Peruzzi, Giulio Romano, Sanmicheli, Sansovino and Palladio.

[6]The first important example is the Palazzo Baldassini (1512). The solution was given a fine interpretation in Raphael's unfinished Palazzo Pandolfini in Florence (1520).

[7]The treatment of the top floor was changed by Michelangelo.

[8]On the ground-floor, however, a slight echo of the engirdling horizontal continuity from the Palazzo Caetani is still present.

[9]For the complex history of this palace see H. Hibbard, *The Architecture of the Palazzo Borghese*, Rome, 1962.

[10]In some of his projects, however, Sangallo attempted a more regular distribution, such as the grandiose scheme for the Palazzo de' Medici in Rome (1513), which prefigures certain concepts of the Late Baroque. See G. Giovannoni, *Antonio da Sangallo il Giovane*, Rome, 1959, fig. 239. The Roman disregard for correspondence between interior and exterior is still found in Borromini's final solution for the Casa dei Filippini and his S. Maria dei Sette Dolori. The latter, however, shows a new kind of correspondence which we have called "complementary."

[11]The back of the palace has been closed after it was taken over by the *comune* in 1850. See L. Vagnetti and others, *Genova, Strada Nuova*, Genoa, 1967, p. 215.

[12]See A. Blunt, "The Palazzo Barberini," *Journal of the Warburg and Courtauld Institutes*, XXI, 1958.

[13]In general a similar disposition is used in most of the villas of Palladio. For the Farnesina see C.L. Frommel, *Die Farnesina und Peruzzis Architektonisches Frühwerk*, Berlin, 1961.

[14]The breaking through of the main axis was done in 1670, perhaps by the same Bernini. Maderno probably planned a small *giardino segreto* behind the oval room, while the original structure by Bernini did not have any opening from the portico to the garden. See E. Hempel, *Francesco Borromini*, Vienna, 1924, p. 26.

[15]Argan, *L'Europa delle Capitali 1600-1700*, p. 18.

[16]See F. Borsi, *Il Palazzo di Montecitorio*, Rome, 1967.

[17]The literature on the Louvre project is vast. The most important source is M. de Chantelou, *Journal du voyage du cav. Bernin en France* (1665), Paris, 1885.

[18]The researches of A. Laprade have shown that Claude Perrault can be given little credit for the design, which was commissioned from Le Vau but mainly executed by D'Orbay. See A. Laprade, *François d'Orbay*, Paris, 1960.

[19]The design may possibly have been influenced by A. Le Pautre's project for an ideal château published in his *Dessins de plusieurs palais* (1652). The attic was interpreted by Colbert as in incorrect rendering of the French crown. See R. W. Berger, "Antoine Le Pautre and the Motif of the Drum-Without-Dome," in *Journal of the Society of Architectural Historians*, XXV, 1966/3.

[20]Notice how the arcades end with pillars, joining them visually to the "massive" lateral wings.

[21]Wittkower, *Art and Architecture in Italy 1600-1750*, p. 125.

[22]The ground-plan of Cortona's project is not preserved.

[23]P. Portoghesi, "Gli Architetti Italiani per il Louvre," *Saggi di Storia dell'Architettura in onore del professor Vincenzo Fasolo*, Rome, 1961, p. 246.

[24]In fact, preliminary designs by Le Vau and F. Mansart also have a "drum-without-dome" crowning oval vestibules. For a discussion of the problem, see Berger, op. cit.

[25]See Portoghesi, op. cit., p. 254.

[26]The project discussed here probably goes back to c. 1644. See Portoghesi, *Borromini*, p. 172.

[27]The final project for the Propaganda Fide palace was probably made after 1654, and the construction took place between 1660 and 1664. See Portoghesi, op. cit., pp. 277 ff.

[28]The open side, giving on to a garden, was later closed.

[29]The solution is clearly inspired by Bernini's first project for the Louvre; Guarini's treatment of the spatial relationships, however, is more free and he arrives at a more advanced interrelation between the elements.

[30]The most extensive use is to be found in K.I. Dientzenhofer's project for the Customs-house in Prague (c. 1726). See C. Norberg-Schulz, *Kilian Ignaz Dientzenhofer e il Barocco Boemo*, Rome, 1968, p. 92.

[31]Lavedan, *French Architecture*, p. 194.

[32]In fact, it became very popular to hang covered wooden balconies on the outside of the Roman palaces, especially on the corners, to allow for a good view of the street scene.

[33]The castle in Chambord was probably designed by the Italian, Domenico da Cortona. The building-type, however, is entirely French, with only the prudent articulation by means of superposed classical orders betraying an Italian hand. The example is characteristic: travelling Italian architects usually brought with them means of articulation rather than fixed building-types.

[34]See A. Blunt, *Philibert de l'Orme*, London, 1958, pp. 28 ff.

[35]See A. Blunt, op. cit., pp. 80 ff.

[36]Only small fragments of the château remain standing. The project of De Brosse is shown in J. Marot, *Recueil des Plans, Profils et Elevations* (after 1654), reprint 1969. The extensive use of rustication obviously goes back to Italian models, such as the courtyard of the Palazzo Pitti in Florence.

[37]See A. Roussy, *Le Palais du Luxembourg*, Paris, 1962. After the Revolution the palace became the seat of the *Sénat conservateur*, and in 1837, A. De Gisors started the construction of a large

assembly hall on the main axis. It was covered with a new garden façade, which in general is a copy of the original façade of De Brosse.

[38]The idea, however, had precedents. Already in Chambord we find separate corner apartments.

[39]Quoted from Lavedan, op. cit., p. 198.

[40]The Orléans Wing is only a fragment of a much larger plan which would have made Blois a grander and more monumental version of the Palais du Luxembourg. See A. Blunt, *François Mansart*, London, 1941.

[41]It is highly probable that the works of Mansart might have been one of the sources of inspiration for the vertically organized spaces of Guarini.

[42]See J. Stern, *Le Château de Maisons*, Paris, 1934.

[43]The palace was destroyed during the Revolution. See J. Marot, op. cit.

[44]In 1645 Bernini had not yet, however, reached his mature style.

[45]The history of Vaux-le-Vicomte is well known. "On 17 August 1661, Fouquet entertained there the King, the Queen, Mlle de la Vallière, and the whole court. After a supper prepared by Vatel, they were offered a new comedy-ballet, *Les Fâcheux*, composed for the occasion by Molière, with décor by Lebrun and music by Lully. La Fontaine, Fouquet's poet, was in the audience, and wrote a description of the evening, which ended with a splendid firework display. Three weeks later Fouquet was arrested for embezzlement: all his property was confiscated; and his enemy and destroyer, Colbert, took over his artists to work for the King." A. Blunt, *Art and Architecture in France 1500-1700*, p. 137.

[46]A double corps de logis had already been introduced by François Mansart in the Hôtel du Jars in Paris (1648).

[47]In general, see J.F. Blondel, *L'architecture française*, VI, Paris, 1725-56.

[48]Quoted from H. Rose, op. cit., p. 175.

[49]Lavedan, op. cit., p. 197.

[50]For a detailed description of the uses see A.C. Daviler, *Cours d'Architecture*, Paris, 1691, new edition 1720.

[51]H. Rose, op. cit., p. 178 ff.

[52]In his *Cours d'Architecture* Daviler therefore integrates the stables in the main courtyard, saying ..."j'ay preferé la symétrie et la magnificence à une distribution plus ménagée comme par exemple, s'il y avoit sur la même étendue de place une Basse-cour séparée pour les Ecuries & Remises..." (p. 172).

[53]It seems reasonable to assume that the system of the courtyard stems from the original Hôtel de Bouillon (1613) by De Brosse, whereas the garden façade must have been designed by Lemercier when he enlarged the building in 1623.

[54]The hôtel was pulled down in the nineteenth century.

[55]It was adopted by Daviler in his "standard" hôtel in the *Cours d'Architecture*.

[56]The hôtel has been extensively rebuilt. It is also known under the name Hôtel de Toulouse and today forms part of the Banque de France.

[57]Nothing remains of the house.

[58]The hôtel was demolished in 1844. The Hôtel Bautru, probably built by Le Vau after 1634, still shows a decorative old-fashioned approach (see G. Pillement, *Paris disparu*, Paris, 1966, p. 122). Le Vau may have designed the Hôtel d'Aumont during the thirties; the house was finished in 1649. Stylistically it represents a step towards the grand simplicity of the Hôtel Tambonneau.

[59]We find the broken roof at Hôtel d'Aumont, Raincy and Vaux-le-Vicomte. The corner pavilions of Vaux-le-Vicomte, however, have steep roofs, which (together with the giant order) defi-

ne them as "towers" that surround the voluminous corps de logis. Le Vau, thus, used the orders with much understanding, although he broke the traditional rules.

[60]J.F. Blondel confirms that small orders should be used on walls that are seen from nearby, while façades seen from a distance were to have a giant order. See *Cours d'Architecture*, III, Paris, 1772.

[61]Blunt characterizes Le Vau's use of the orders as "incorrect" and "showing a lack of feeling for the plastic unity of the whole"... (*Art and Architecture in France*, p. 134). A structural analysis of Le Vau's works demonstrates that his articulation is determined by the whole and that he was one of the great innovators among the architects of the seventeenth century.

[62]The building was demolished in 1827. See Pillemont, op. cit., p. 136.

[63]The project for the *enveloppe* stems from 1667 and was integrated in a larger scheme in 1669. Le Vau died in 1670, and François d'Orbay probably played an important part in the development of the project, particularly in the design of the garden façade. See A. Laprade, *François d'Orbay*, Paris, 1960.

[64]Le Vau used straight windows, but Hardouin-Mansart evidently wanted to increase the glazed area still more. He also obtained a rhythm of repeated units rather than one continuous horizontal line.

[65]The palace was destroyed during the Revolution.

[66]The palace was destroyed during the Revolution.

[67]In his few city-palaces, Hardouin-Mansart obviously could not realize the same ideal of extension. The basic intentions, however, are clearly present, as he tries to transform the building into a "transparent" skeleton (*Hôtel de Lorge*, 1670). A late project for a "Maison à bâtir" (see Bourget/Cattaui: op. cit., p. 152) shows a well-disposed plan with a double corps de logis and a displaced main axis.

[68]Thus Daviler says that the orders are so praiseworthy because they are based "sur les raisons les plus vraysemblables de la nature, sur la doctrine de Vitruve, & sur les exemples des plus excellens Edifices de l'Antiquité." A.C. Daviler, *Les cinq ordres d'Architecture de Vincent Scamozzi*, Paris, 1685, Préface.

CHAPTER FIVE

[1]For a general theory of "environments," see T. Parsons, *Societies*, New York, 1966. Also A. Rapoport, *House Form and Culture*, New York, 1969.

[2]A monograph on Della Porta is still lacking. Already in 1912 Giovannoni wrote: "...egli può in questo campo dirsi la figura centrale del periodo di transizione che va dall'architettura del '500 a quella del '600... nella sua fecondità straordinaria traduce i nuovi concetti e le nuove forme in così molteplici applicazioni pratiche da rendere poi agevole il lavoro di continuazione" (G. Giovannoni, "Chiese della seconda metà del '500 in Roma," *L'Arte*, XV-XVI, 1912-13).

[3]R. Wittkower, *Art and Architecture in Italy 1600-1750*, p. 73.

[4]To our knowledge the motif of the triple columns was never repeated again. In the abbey church of Zwiefalten by Johann Michael Fischer (1740-65), the entrance is flanked by triplets consisting of one pilaster and two columns.

[5]Wittkower, op. cit., p. 115.

[6]Portoghesi, *Roma Barocca*, p. 86.

[7]See E. Panofsky, "Die Scala Regia im Vatikan und die Kunstanschauungen Bernini's," *Jahrbuch der preussischen Kunstsammlungen*, 1919.

[8]The general motif was repeated by Kilian Ignaz Dientzenhofer in St. Nicholas/Malà Strana in Prague (1739).

[9]A convincing simplification and integration is found in his late church Gesù e Maria al Corso (1670-80).

[10]The villa was in ruins already at the end of the seventeenth century, but is known from several prints.

[11]A monograph on Cortona with a satisfactory analysis of his architecture is still lacking.

[12]Similar intentions are found behind the art of the Roman and Byzantine empires. In fact, Louis XIV imitates ancient Roman symbolism.

[13]A similar process had already taken place during the Middle Ages, when the "classical" Mediterranean basilica fused with local "nordic" types of structure. See W. Horn, "The Origins of the Medieval Bay System," in *Journal of the Society of Architectural Historians*, XVII/2.

[14]The façade was built by Clément Métézeau, probably on the design of De Brosse.

[15]The motif is already indicated by Lescot in the courtyard of the Louvre (1546) and fully developed by De l'Orme in Anet (1550).

[16]See A. Braham and P. Smith, "Mansart-Studies V: The Church of the Minimes," *Burlington Magazine*, 1965, pp. 123 ff. Only a small fragment of the façade remains.

[17]The building was executed by François d'Orbay who made essential contributions to the detailing of the church. See A. Laprade, op. cit.

[18]Blunt, *Art and Architecture in France 1500-1700*, p. 130.

[19]It is generally attributed to the amateur Claude Perrault, because of his "archeological knowledge." A. Laprade (op. cit.) has reduced his contribution to its real dimension, that is, nothing. François d'Orbay studied in Rome in 1659-60, and obviously played a decisive role during the years of transition from the "High Baroque" of F. Mansart and Le Vau to the new approach of Hardouin Mansart. D'Orbay is probably also the author of the Observatoire in Paris (1668) which is usually attributed to Perrault.

[20]See R.W. Berger, *Antoine Le Pautre*, New York, 1969.

[21]A Blunt, op. cit., p. 216.

[22]Even the Dôme of the Invalides represents the State rather than the Church.

[23]A general survey is given in G. Kubler and M. Soria, *Art and Architecture in Spain and Portugal 1500-1800*, Harmondsworth, 1959.

[24]The idea is typical for Spain and culminated with the *Transparente* in Toledo Cathedral by Narciso Tomé (1721-32).

[25]J. Summerson, *Inigo Jones*, Harmondsworth, 1966, p. 139. To compare this approach with the principles of Palladio's architecture, see R. Wittkower, *Architectural Principles in the Age of Humanism*, London, 1949.

[26]Thus the building could become a natural part of the later, grandiose scheme of Wren.

[27]J. Summerson, op. cit., p. 89.

[28]J. Summerson, op. cit., p. 134.

[29]Quoted after P. Murray, *A History of English Architecture*, Part II, Harmondsworth, 1962, pp. 188 ff.

[30]Quoted after Murray, op. cit., p. 193 ff.

[31]P. Murray, op. cit., p. 197.

[32]Praising the "rich and brilliant detailing," John Summerson (op. cit., p. 132) says: "The entire conception of the St. Paul's elevations is, in fact, a "working up" of the Banqueting House to a new plane of monumentality." Actually, Wren, made the same error Antonio da Sangallo had made more than a hundred years earlier in his project for St. Peter's in Rome, when he tried to articulate an immense building by adding up members borrowed from buildings of a much smaller size. The weakness of St. Paul's, thus, is not one of detailing, but one of scale.

[33]J. Summerson, op. cit., p. 133.

[34]The mansion was burned down in 1952.

[35]See G.L. Burke, *The Making of Dutch Towns*, London, 1956.

[36]The churches were destroyed already in 1567.

[37]For a general introduction to the subject, see T. Paulsson, *Scandinavian Architecture*, London, 1958.

[38]For the original appearance of the Bonde palace and other Swedish buildings of the period, see E. Dahlberg, *Svecia Antiqua et Hodierna*, new edition Stockholm, 1924.

[39]Tessin visited Italy, France, and Holland in 1651-3. His ecclesiastical architecture mainly reflects Italian infuence, while the secular works are based on French and Dutch models. In the Bäät Palace in Stockholm (1662) thus, he introduced the cour d'honneur and a giant order of Le Vau extraction. The palace for the Royal Bank (1668), however, is Roman in character.

[40]For Tessin the Younger, see the magnificent monograph by R. Josephson, *Tessin*, 2 vol., Stockholm, 1930-31.

[41]Josephson, op. cit., I, fig. 148.

[42]In 1704 Tessin designed a grandiose project for the Louvre, transforming the courtyard into a circular space, and making a cour d'honneur by adding wings to D'Orbay's façade.

[43]These walls do not exist any more.

[44]The works of Fischer von Erlach, Hildebrandt, the Dientzenhofers, and the Vorarlberg builders, therefore, will be treated in the next volume of this history.

[45]See D. Kessler, *Der Dillinger Baumeister Hans Alberthal*, Dillingen, 1949. The church in Eichstätt was rebuilt according to the original plan after a fire in 1634, when the town was sacked by Swedish troops.

[46]The Counter-Reformation also brought about an importation of more conventional types of churches from Italy. As an example, we may mention the Cathedral of Salzburg by Santino Solari (1614-28).

[47]Mathey studied in Rome with Carlo Fontana and arrived in Prague in 1675, where he remained until shortly before his death in 1695.

[48]Martinelli is by far the most qualified of the Italian architects working in Central Europe towards the end of the seventeenth century. He studied with Carlo Fontana in Rome (1678) and taught at the Accademia di S. Luca.

[49]The wings were later extended by Josef Emanuel Fischer von Erlach. A U-shaped disposition is already present in the palace at Roudnice in Bohemia (1652-84), possibly by Francesco Caratti.

[50]The towers, as well as the dome, were completed by Enrico Zuccalli, whereas the façade was finished by François de Cuvilliés in 1765-68.

[51]The palace was continued by Zuccalli after 1674, and later by Viscardi and Effner.

[52]Towards the end of his career, Schlüter built a more sensitive, Borrominian garden palace in Berlin for Von Kamecke (1711-12).

[53]Thus Werner Hager says: "Das Leben in Europa erscheint uns zu jener Zeit von einem künstlerischen Impuls so durchdrungen und durchwirkt, dass das historische Gesamtbild davon bestimmt wird." (*Barockarchitektur*, Baden-Baden, 1968, p. 5).

[54]Descartes, Spinoza, and Leibniz all created centralized (i.e., dogmatic), integrated and extended ("open") systems; the one of Descartes being the more rational, the one of Spinoza the more static, and the one of Leibniz the more dynamic.

[55]A. Hauser, *The Social History of Art*, Vol. II, London, 1962, p. 167.

[56]This structure is also found on the "lower" levels. The development of the diagonal axes in François Mansart's churches, thus, may be compared to the urban *rond-point*.

[57]In Dutch art, therefore, infinity is expressed in painting rather than architecture.

[58]The recognition of Baroque architecture being one of the "constituent facts" of modern architecture is due to Siegfried Giedion, *Space, Time and Architecture*, Cambridge, Mass., 1941.

SELECTED BIBLIOGRAPHY

SOURCES

BLONDEL A., *Cours d'architecture*, Paris, 1675.

BORROMEO C., *Instructiones Fabricae et Suppellectilis Ecclesiasticae*, Milan, 1577.

BORROMINI F., *Opera et Opus Architectonicum*, Rome, 1722-25.

CAMPBELL C., *Vitruvius Britannicus*, London, 1715-25.

CHANTELOU P.F. de, *Journal du voyage du Cav. Bernin en France (1655)*, Paris, 1885.

DAHLBERG E., *Suecia antiqua et hodierna*, Stockholm, 1716.

DAVILER A.C., *Cours d'architecture*, Paris, 1691.

DE ROSSI D., *Studio d'architettura civile*, Rome, 1702-21.

DE ROSSI G., *Insignium Romae Templorum*, Rome, 1684.

GUARINI G., *Architettura civile*, Turin, 1737.

LE PAUTRE A., *Les Oeuvres d'Architecture*, Paris, 1652.

MARIETTE J., *L'architecture française*, Paris, 1727.

MAROT J., *L'architecture française*, Paris, c. 1660.

MAROT J., *Recueil des plans, profils et élévations*, Paris, c. 1654.

Theatrum Statum Regiae Celsitudinis Sabaudiae Ducis, Amsterdam, 1682.

MODERN WORKS

ARGAN G.C., *Borromini*, Verona, 1952.

ARGAN G.C., *L'architettura barocca in Italia*, Milan, 1957.

ARGAN G.C., *The Europe of the Capitals 1600-1700*, New York, 1964.

BATTISTI E., *Rinascimento e Barocco*, Turin, 1960.

BERGER R., *Antoine Le Pautre*, New York, 1970.

BLUNT A., *Art and Architecture in France 1500-1700*, Harmondsworth, 1957.

BLUNT A., *Artistic Theory in Italy 1450-1600*, Oxford, 1956.

BLUNT A., *François Mansart*, London, 1941.

BORSI F., *Il palazzo di Montecitorio*, Rome, 1967.

BORSI F., *La chiesa di S. Andrea al Quirinale*, Rome, 1966.

BOURGET P., and CATTAUI G., *Jules Hardouin-Mansart*, Paris, 1956.

BRAHAM A., and SMITH P., "Mansart Studies I-V" in *Burlington Magazine*, 1963-65.

BRAUER H., and WITTKOWER R., *Die Zeichnungen des Gianlorenzo Bernini*, Vienna, 1931.

BRAUN J., *Die belgischen Jesuitenkirchen*, Freiburg, 1907.

BRINCKMANN A.E., *Die Baukunst des 17. und 18. Jahrhunderts in den romanischen Ländern*, Berlin, 1919.

BUSCH H., and LOHSE B., *Baroque Europe*, New York, 1962.

CAFLISCH N., *Carlo Maderno*, Munich, 1934.

CARBONERI N., *Ascanio Vitozzi*, Rome, 1964.

CAVALLARI-MURAT A., *Forma urbana ed architettura nella Torino barocca*, Turin, 1968.

COUDENHOVE-ERTHAL E., *Carlo Fontana und die Architektur des Römischen Spätbarocks*, Vienna, 1930.

DE BERNARDI FERRERO D., *I 'Disegni d'architettura civile ed ecclesiastica' di Guarino Guarini e l'arte del maestro*, Turin, 1966.

DE LOGU, *Architettura italiana del Seicento e del Settecento*, Florence, 1935.

Dizionario Enciclopedico di architettura e urbanistica, ed. by P. PORTOGHESI, Rome, 1968-69.

DONATI U., *Artisti ticinesi a Roma*, Bellinzona, 1942.

DONATI U., *Carlo Maderno*, Lugano, 1957.

D'ONOFRIO C., *Le Fontane di Roma*, Rome, 1957.

DOWNES K., *English Baroque Architecture*, London, 1966.

ELLING C., *Form and Function of the Roman Belvedere*, Copenhagen, 1950.

FAGIOLO DELL'ARCO M., *Bernini*, Rome, 1967.

FAGIOLO DELL'ARCO M., "Villa Aldobrandina Tuscolana," *Quaderni dell'Istituto di Storia dell'Architettura*, Rome, 1960.

FOKKER T.H., *Roman Baroque Art*, Oxford, 1938.

FORSSMAN E., *Dorisch, Ionisch, Korintisch*, Stockholm, 1961.

FOX H.M., *André Le Nôtre*, London, 1962.

FRANCK C., *Die Barockvillen in Frascati*, Munich, 1956.

FÜRST V., *The Architecture of Sir Christopher Wren*, London, 1956.

GALASSI-PALUZZI C., *Storia segreta dello stile dei Gesuiti*, Rome, 1951.

GANAY E. DE, *André Le Nôtre*, Paris, 1962.

GERSON H., and TER KUILE E.H., *Art and Architecture in Belgium 1600-1800*, London, 1960.

GIEDION S., *Space, Time and Architecture*, 5th edition, Cambridge, Mass., 1967.

GRIMSCHITZ B., *Johann Lukas von Hildebrandt*, Vienna, 1959.

GRISERI A., *Le metamorfosi del barocco*, Turin, 1967.

Guarino Guarini e l'internazionalità del barocco, ed. by V. VIALE, Turin, 1970.

HAGER W., *Barockarchitektur*, Baden-Baden, 1968.

HAUSER A., *The Social History of Art*, London, 1962.

HAUTECOEUR L., *Histoire de l'architecture classique en France*, 4 vols., Paris, 1943-57.

HEMPEL E., *Baroque Art and Architecture in Central Europe*, Harmondsworth, 1965.

HEMPER E., *Carlo Rainaldi*, Munich, 1919.

HEMPEL E., *Francesco Borromini*, Vienna, 1924.

HIBBARD H., *Bernini*, Harmondsworth, 1965.

HIBBARD H., *The Architecture of the Palazzo Borghese*, Rome, 1962.

HITCHCOCK H.-R., *Rococo Architecture in Southern Germany*, London, 1969.

HOFFMANN H., *Hochrenaissance, Manierismus, Frühbarock*, Zurich, 1938.

JOSEPHSON R., *Tessin*, 2 vols., Stockholm, 1930-31.

KESSLER D., *Der Dillinger Baumeister Hans Alberthal*, Dillingen, 1949.

KUBLER G., and SORIA M., *Art and Architecture in Spain and Portugal 1500-1800*, Harmondsworth, 1966.

LAPRADE A., *François d'Orbay*, Paris, 1960.

LAVEDAN P., *French Architecture*, Harmondsworth, 1956.

LAVEDAN P., *Les Villes Françaises*, Paris, 1960.

MAHON D., *Studies in Seicento Art and Theory*, London, 1947.

Manierismo, Barocco, Rococò. Concetti e termini, Accademia Nazionale dei Lincei, Rome, 1962.

MARCONI P., "La Roma del Borromini," in *Capitolium*, Rome, 1967.

MILLON H., *Baroque and Rococo Architecture*, New York, 1961.

MORTON H.V., *Fountains of Rome*, New York, 1966.

Mostra del barocco piemontese, catalogo, ed. by V. VIALE, Turin, 1963.

MÜLLER L.P., *Bartolomeo Bianco,* Rome, 1968.

MUÑOZ A., *Roma barocca,* Milan, 1928.

NOEHLES K., "Die Louvre-Projekte von Pietro da Cortona und Carlo Rainaldi," in *Zeitschrift für Kunstgeschichte,* 1961.

NOEHLES K., *La Chiesa dei Santi Luca e Martina nell'opera di Pietro da Cortona,* Rome, 1970.

NORBERG-SCHULZ C., *Kilian Ignaz Dientzenhofer e il barocco boemo,* Rome, 1968.

L'opera di Carlo e Amedeo di Castellamonte, ed. by G. BRINO, A. DE BERNARDI, G. GARDANO..., Turin, 1966.

PANE R., *Architettura dell'età barocca in Napoli,* Naples, 1939.

PASSANTI M., *Nel mondo magico di Guarino Guarini,* Turin, 1963.

PAULSSON T., *Scandinavian Architecture,* London, 1958.

PILLEMENT G., *Les Hôtels de Paris,* Paris, 1945.

PILLEMENT G., *Paris disparu,* Paris, 1966.

POMMER R., *Eighteenth-Century Architecture in Piedmont,* New York, 1967.

PORTOGHESI P., *Borromini nella cultura europea,* Rome, 1964.

PORTOGHESI P., *Roma barocca,* Cambridge, Mass., 1971.

PORTOGHESI P., *The Rome of Borromini,* New York, 1968.

PORTOGHESI P., "Gli architetti italiani per il Louvre," in *Saggi di storia dell'architettura,* Rome, 1961.

RIEGL A., *Die Entstehung der Barockkunst in Rom,* Vienna, 1923.

ROSE H., *Spätbarock,* Munich, 1922.

ROSENBERG J., SLIVE S., and TER KUILE E.H., *Dutch Art and Architecture 1600-1800,* Harmondsworth, 1966.

SEDLMAYR H., *Die Architektur Borrominis,* Munich, 1930.

SEDLMAYR H., *Johann Bernhard Fischer von Erlach,* Vienna, 1956.

SEKLER E.F., *Wren and His Place in European Architecture,* New York, 1956.

SEMENZATO C., *L'architettura di Baldassare Longhena,* Padua, 1954.

SPAGNESI G., *Giovanni Antonio De Rossi,* Rome, 1964.

STERN J., *Le Château de Maisons,* Paris, 1934.

Studi sul Borromini, Accademia di San Luca, Rome, 1967.

SUMMERSON J., *Architecture in Britain 1530-1830,* Harmondsworth, 1953.

SUMMERSON J., *Inigo Jones,* Harmondsworth, 1966.

SUMMERSON J., *Sir Christopher Wren,* London, 1953.

TAPIÉ V., *The Age of Grandeur: Baroque Art and Architecture,* New York, 1966.

TEYSSÈDRE B., *L'art du siècle de Louis XIV,* Paris, 1967.

VAGNETTI L., *Genova. Strada Nuova,* Genoa, 1967.

WACKERNAGEL M., *Die Baukunst des 17. und 18. Jahrhunderts in den germanischen Ländern,* Berlin, 1915.

WITTKOWER R., *Art and Architecture in Italy 1600-1750,* Harmondsworth, 1958.

WITTKOWER R., "Carlo Rainaldi and the Roman Architecture of the Full Baroque," in *Art Bulletin,* 1937.

WÖLFFLIN H., *Renaissance and Baroque,* Ithaca, 1966.

LIST OF PHOTOGRAPHIC CREDITS

NOTE: *Photographs by Pepi Merisio and Bruno Balestrini.*
All those supplied by other sources are gratefully acknowledged below.
The numbers listed refer to the plates.

Alinari, Florence: 80, 195, 203, 266, 275

Anelli, S., Electa Editrice, Milan: 13, 14, 17, 27, 57, 59, 65, 66, 82, 83, 194, 196, 202, 204, 215, 237

Archivio fotografico Gallerie e Musei Vaticani, Rome: 12

Biblioteca Ambrosiana, Milan: 223, 224, 250

Biblioteca Apostolica Vaticana, Rome: 15, 159, 160, 213, 214

Biblioteca Reale, Turin: 51

Bighini, Otello, Madrid: 287, 289

Birelli, D., Mestre: 97, 274

Bruno, G., Mestre: 52, 53, 54, 55, 56, 58, 88, 180, 184, 186, 187, 189, 219, 220, 221

Bulloz, Paris: 11

Cassa di Risparmio delle Province Lombarde, Archivio fotografico: 94

Connaissance des Arts, J. Guillot, Paris: 90, 278

Editions Vincent-Fréal, Paris: 102

Foto Mas, Barcelona: 288

Keetman, J., Bavaria Verlag, Gauting (West Germany): 307

Keetman, P., Bavaria Verlag, Gauting (West Germany): 312

Lennart af Petersens, Stockholm: 306

Mairani, G., Milan: IV

Musée du Louvre, Cabinet des Dessins, Paris, Musées Nationaux: 205, 211

Nationalmuseum, Stockholm: 305

Norberg-Schulz, Ch., Oslo: 18, 33, 74, 81, 300, 304, 313, I, III, V, VI, VII, VIII, IX, XI, XII, XIV, XV, XVI, XVII, XVIII, XX, XXII, XXIII, XXIV

Photographie Giraudon, Paris: 229, 276, 280

Photo Meyer, Vienna: 311

Richard, J., Paris: 3

Rijksdienst v.d. Monumentenzorg, The Hague: 301, 303

Savio, O., Rome: 127, 147, 163, 270, 271

Schmidt-Glassner, H., Stuttgart: 231

Sheridan, R., London: 292, 293, 297, 299

Staatliche Museen, Kunstbibliothek, Berlin: 315

Staatliche Schlösser und Gärten, Berlin: 314

University Press, Oxford: 296

Verroust, J., Neuilly: 281

Windstosser, L., Bavaria Verlag, Gauting (West Germany): 309